For the Life of Me

ROBERT BRISCOE

From the original Portrait by Rev. Father Aengus Buckley, O.P.

For the Life of Me

by
ROBERT BRISCOE
with
ALDEN HATCH

Little, Brown and Company

Boston   Toronto

Published simultaneously in Canada
by Little, Brown & Company (Canada) Limited

PRINTED IN THE UNITED STATES OF AMERICA

Contents

For the Life of Me

CHAPTER I
Against the Odds

Dɪᴄᴋ ᴡʜɪᴛᴛɪɴɢᴛᴏɴ, the poor country street urchin who rose to prominence and fortune, was the most famous Lord Mayor ever. I do not expect to rival him; though I have achieved a certain notoriety by the accidental fact that I became the first Jewish Lord Mayor of Dublin. But this I can say for certain. Dick's chances of achieving the great position he held were in the beginning no dimmer than mine; and I believe the road he traveled was less perilous.

For however difficult the conditions of Dick's rise, at no time were the British Army, and the Royal Navy chasing him. Nor did his own countrymen turn against him as mine did when the Free State Government ordered that I be taken, not as is customary "dead or alive"; they only wanted me dead.

Of all the narrow escapes I had, the closest was the day the Staters had me in their hands and let me slip through their fingers. It was near the beginning of our civil war, which, in the way of such things was even more lacking in civility than our fight for freedom against England. The war against the British had ended with the shameful treaty, signed under coercion in London, by which Ireland's plenipotentiaries gave up the things we Republicans held most dear, our individuality as a nation and six of the nine countries of the North known as Ulster. We decided to fight for them even against our own countrymen.

That the Free State Government singled me out as such a dangerous character was a tribute I valued, for it showed they knew I had served Ireland well; but it was an uncomfortable sort of honor. The fact that they knew me so well, we having fought together

3

these four years, made it impossible for me effectively to disguise my tall, lean body and long, broken-nosed face. For this reason, our Army Council decided that I was no further use to this underground fight for freedom. But since I knew America well, having been in business there before the Troubled Times, they decided that I could best serve Ireland there.

So I went on the run with orders to report to Republican headquarters in Cork, and then try to slip aboard a ship. I reached Cobh safely; but there I found that a Free State regiment held the road to Cork. In the Irish Republican Army you obeyed orders no matter what stood in the way. I decided to attempt to reach Cork by rowing the six or seven miles up the River Lee.

I stole a rowing boat and began pulling up the estuary with the long, slow fisherman's stroke I had learned as a boy. The luck went against me. It was unbelievably bad. First thing, coming around a bend, I saw lying at anchor a little old rusty tramp steamer called the *City of Dortmund*. I recognized her — and should I not! I had owned her myself and used her to run arms through the British blockade. As I came closer I saw a familiar-looking man standing on her stern whom I soon knew to be John Dowling, who had been with me in the gun-running but was now turned Stater. He recognized me, and waved and shouted amiably. Then he did a double take as he remembered that I was now his enemy. I saw him scuttle into the pilothouse and knew that my presence in the Cork area would soon be reported to Free State General Emmet Dalton, commanding there.

Around the next curve of the Lee at a place called Passage were *two* unpleasant surprises. A platoon of Staters were on the left bank. I slowed up my stroke and tried to act nonchalant, but they decided they wanted to talk to me. Their way of inviting me over for a chat was to start firing just over my head.

Now came the second surprise. A squad of the Irish Republican Army showed up on the right bank. I found out later that they were commanded by my good friend Martin Corry, but it did not help me then. They, too, invited me ashore by shooting in front of me. Then both sides began shooting at each other, with me underneath a bee swarm of singing bullets. I shipped my oars and lay flat in the boat with my nose pressed on her dirty bottom. While those fellows were busy with each other my boat drifted back around the bend.

Sensibly, I decided that the water route to Cork was impracticable, and rowed back to Cobh. There I hid out in Carroll's Hotel, an obscure little place. I managed to contact a girl working in a chemist's shop who belonged to Cumann na mBan — the women's auxiliary of the I.R.A. — and sent a message by her to the MacSwineys in Cork.

During the night the Free State troops took Cobh. In the morning I got word that General Dalton had ordered a search for me, and I knew I had better move fast.

I was just coming out of my room when two troopers closed in on me. They poked pistols in my belly, and I thought it was all up with Bob Briscoe. Once General Dalton saw me, there would be no such amenities as a court-martial or even waiting for sunrise. He would follow his orders to shoot me on sight.

Of course, I tried one last desperate bluff. "What do you want of me, a peaceable wool merchant of Dublin?" I asked.

"We're after Briscoe," one of them said. "You fit his description."

"That doesn't make me him," I argued. "I'm just quietly doing me business."

"Come along and tell it to the general!"

Now I knew I was dead.

While they marched me down the stairs one of them looked at me very curiously. As we got to the main landing, he asked, "Are you a Jewman?"

"Yes," I said quickly. In a great flash of hope I realized that those former friends of mine were so used to me that they had forgotten to put "Jewish" in my description.

The trooper said to his pal. "Hold on! He's only a Jewman. We'd be wasting our bloody time with him."

He swung back his foot, and gave me a great kick in the pants that sent me flying down the stairs and out the door.

I kept on flying into the chemist's shop where the Cumann na mBan girl sheltered me at the risk of her life. And then secretly onto a ship, and to freedom.

It seems that I have never stopped flying since then. All I have become stems from the impetus of a well-applied boot.

On September 25, 1894, I was born; not that it mattered to anyone but my parents. The place was a small, little one-story house on Lower Beechwood Avenue, Ranelagh, a suburb of Dublin. This house still stands in a solid row of others like it; but it has no particular meaning for me, because my father moved out of it when I was only a few months old.

We then went to live in an apartment above the shop and warehouse of my father's place of business, Lawlor Briscoe on Lower Ormond Quay down by the Liffey River in the heart of Dublin. That is a place I like to remember.

It is true that before we moved again, we were a little crowded in it. There were my older sister and brother, Rachel and Arthur; then myself, Robert; followed like stair steps by my brothers Herbert David, and Wolfe Tone, the latter named after the Irish hero of the rising of 1798. Then came another sister, Judith. Finally Henrietta, the youngest of the seven Briscoes, was born after we moved away. That made seven children; and with my parents and our two maids there were eleven people living in six rooms.

There were two large rooms to each floor. On the first, right over the premises, was the boys' dormitory-bedroom, with a place partitioned off for Rachel; and my parents' bedroom where the current baby also slept. Above that was a dining room-kitchen and a proper drawing room. On the top floor was the maids' room, and also a back room with a bathtub and toilet; and a place screened off where members of the family could sleep if they felt in need of a change. It sounds miserably congested, but the fact is it was a wonderful place to grow up.

You see, Lawlor Briscoe was a workshop where furniture was made by hand, and also an import-export business and a storage company. In the carpenter shop men were working all day with the fine, sweet-smelling wood. There I learned early how to use a plane and chisel, saw and bandsaw, to upholster and to French polish; also how to turn a fine leg — of a table, of course. But it was the long, musty spicy storage warehouse that was our playground. It had a tented skylight running the whole length of its peaked roof and in it were stored the most exciting things a boy ever had to play with. We would gather our friends for a treasure hunt and roam through the place; opening up the old trunks to see what was in them. The greatest find we ever made was a whole set of ancient cap-and-ball revolvers just the thing for playing Indians and the U. S. Cavalry, who had in fact used just such weapons.

British officers used to store their trophies at Lawlor Briscoe. Old hunting rifles, tiger skins and big game heads. One lot consisted of African spears and long oval shields. Picture us, then a bunch of howling Zulus, brandishing spears; fending them off with our great shields taller than we were; fighting from behind wardrobes and bureaus, beautiful Chippendale buffets or Queen Anne chairs, until we debouched into the carpet room, where we rolled the fine orientals up into breastworks.

It is a marvel none of us was killed either in the battle; or by Pappa later. That, by the way, was what we called my father. Indeed, all Dublin called him Pappa.

In the warehouse, too, I learned how to ride a bicycle someone had incautiously left there, tooling over the dark dusty floor, missing crates and furniture by inches until I became a real expert.

One final joyous recollection was the time a large consignment of candy came to Lawlor Briscoe. For the next several days all the little Briscoes were busy as squirrels in Autumn, prying open the cases and carrying boxes of chocolates, toffees, bulls-eyes, aniseed balls, and other sweets upstairs and storing them in secret places, because we could not eat all our eyes could see.

Now you must not get the idea that we spent all our time inside. On fine days we walked along the quays with the dank exciting smell of the river in our noses, watching the Guinness boats which looked huge in the little Liffey, and imagining ourselves seamen sailing to far-off, spice-smelling ports. We took out our spirit of adventure by sailing paper boats among the ducks and swans in the little lake in St. Stephen's Green.

One time we had a spell of very cold weather, a regular American winter. The lakes in the parks froze solid. Of course we had no skates, nor was Pappa thinking of buying us any. Instead he told us how to make them. Following his advice we went to the butcher's and each bought two shinbones of an ox. These we tied to our boots with the razor-sharp edge downwards, and were able to skate as merrily as the rich young chaps with fancy British racers.

In summer we had holidays in the country. My mother's sister, Martha, had married a nephew of my father's named David Cherrick. They lived in Arklow in County Wicklow, which is a beautiful place with green hills curving out into the sea. Though his house was small, Uncle David always had room for some nephews and nieces. We used to go down in relays for our holidays by the sea.

It was there I got my first, almost my only, hint of racial prejudice. Uncle David was buying a bag of feathers from a countryman. He weighed it and looked surprised. Then he plunged his hand to the bottom and brought up a handful of gray sand. "I'm buying feathers, not sand," he said angrily.

The huge farmer glared down at him and roared, "You damn Jewman!"

And it was in Arklow that I saw the divil. One night my uncle had occasion to call on a farmer back in the country. He asked me to walk along with him. When we got to the farmer's house he told me I must wait outside. It was a beautiful soft night with a milky sky and a three-quarter moon shining over a high hedge on the far side of the road. I walked peacefully up and down beside the hedge until suddenly I froze stiff with horror. On the roadway in front of me, black as tar against the white shine of it, was the shadow of the divil. There were his horns and sometimes the long tail of him silhouetted on the ground at my very feet. How long I stood there petrified I cannot tell, but it was years, maybe aeons, while that awesome shadow moved back and forth, coming at me, then retreating. I knew the divil was playing cat-and-mouse with me and would take me the moment he felt like it.

At last the door of the farmhouse opened, letting out warm yellow light, and my uncle walked down the path. At the same moment the divil disappeared.

I ran to Uncle David and clutched his leg. Daring to look back, I saw that my divil was a cow looking over the hedge, and the moon had thrown the shadow of her horns and switching tail to give me the fright of my life.

By now it must be plain that the Briscoes were a close-knit family who had a tremendous amount of fun for very little money. But there were serious things, too. The most important of these were our religion and our love for Ireland. To understand the deep meaning they had for me, and why they never clashed at all, you should first learn something about my father and mother. For it was they who taught me the eternal values which I have held to all my life.

CHAPTER II

Dublin Quays

MY FATHER, Abraham William Briscoe, was born in the village of
Zagar, province of Kovno in Lithuania. In a way he was fortunately placed for a subject of the Czar, because Zagar was too
small to have a ghetto. Besides, Jews were generally better off in
Lithuania than in most other parts of Russia. There were never
any pogroms there, and living by the Baltic Sea, they traveled a
good deal in the course of business to Russian ports and even to
other countries. They were considered the intellectuals of Russian
Jewry.

But make no mistake about it, a Russian Jew was always a sec-
ond- or third-class citizen. There were many professions which
he was forbidden to follow. He could not own land, but must rent
it at exorbitant prices from the great landlords; and he was not allowed to live in either Moscow or St. Petersburg. One of the few
exceptions to this last rule was made in the case of Jewish prostitutes, but they always had to carry a yellow ticket.

Of course our people were subject to conscription like all Russians, and in the army they were liable to all sorts of indignities.
They were given the dirtiest jobs; and never could they hope to
become regular officers. In short, there was no freedom and no
future for a Russian Jew.

When Father was about fourteen years old, my grandfather,
who had a small mill in Zagar, scraped up enough money to send
him to Dublin, where some relatives already held a beachhead, so
to speak. This made him that rare bird, an immigrant *to* Ireland,
whose best young people are always leaving her. To Father the
soft green hills of Dublin Harbour were the sheltering arms of

justice, and Ireland seemed the very land of liberty — though he soon learned to think differently.

Nevertheless, compared to Lithuania, it was indeed a land of freedom, where a man could worship and work and rise unfettered by the stigma of race; where a Jew could freely associate with his fellow citizens; which was, I think, the freedom Father valued most of all. He took the country as his own and never once looked back. At least, from my earliest memory he thought of himself as an Irishman.

When he landed in Dublin he had only a few shillings in the pocket of his only decent suit — of course his cousins gave him shelter. He had no knowledge of English at all. In this connection, people wonder how we came to have such an English-sounding name as Briscoe. I have wondered myself; but I never thought to ask Pappa. I know he did not change his name, but I think it may have been spelled differently in Lithuania. Since at this time Father could only write Yiddish and Russian, which use quite different alphabets from ours, the immigration officer most likely asked his name and spelled it phonetically, Briscoe. In any event it is a good name.

The first thing my father had to do was to learn the language as quickly as possible. With the last of his money, or more likely some he borrowed, he engaged, of all things, a Protestant minister to tutor him. This amiable gentleman also taught him to play the violin. All his life my father loved to play that instrument. But he was very shy about it. Nobody, not even my mother, ever *saw* him play. He would lock himself in his room and through the door would come the faint strains of his fiddle.

As soon as he could speak English at all, Father got a job as a traveler in brushes — a sort of Irish Fuller Brush man. He was a very hard worker and had an engaging personality. Medium tall he was, with sandy hair, a big straight nose and bright blue eyes. To this was soon added a neatly trimmed beard. Charm and hard work must have sold a lot of brushes, for by the time he was twenty-one he was able to start a little brush factory of his own.

Each year after that he traveled to the great fair at Leipzig in

Germany to buy bristles for his brushes. On the way he fell into the habit of staying in Frankfurt with a Jewish family named Yoedicke, who became my grandparents. The Yoedickes had emigrated from Russia for a very different reason than my father.

My grandmother's family, the Klonskis, were great swells in Russian Jewry. Some of them were doctors in the Russian Navy with the status of officers, an almost unheard of thing; and they were allowed to live in St. Petersburg *without* a yellow ticket. When their daughter married my grandfather, it was a terrible misalliance, and the young couple left the country to avoid embarrassing the stylish Klonskis.

There were five Yoedicke daughters. Father fell in love with Ida, the third. His once-a-year courtship prospered despite a noticeable lack of enthusiasm on the part of Grandfather Yoedicke. But in accordance with our custom Father first had to help the old man get the two older daughters married off before he could claim his bride.

Having served, not as long as Isaac, but long enough, the time finally came. Stylishly clothed in a Prince Albert coat and a shining new topper, Father was married to Ida Yoedicke. They went straight back to Ireland, and when the Irish mail boat left them on Kingstown pier, my father was obliged to confess to his bride that his business had gone bad. In addition to his wedding garments he had exactly one shilling.

Self-confidence is an ineradicable attribute of the Briscoes. However his bride may have felt, Pappa was not at all worried. He went back to traveling again; but he kept his eyes and ears open for opportunity's knock. It came in the shape of a cargo of tea, which had been damaged by a fire at sea, and was advertised to be sold at auction "as was." Pappa examined the tea in Becker's warehouse and found many of the chests to be in good condition. At the auction he was the highest bidder, and the cargo was knocked down to him.

The following day he went to the Royal Insurance Company, which had sold the tea, and told them he had no money to pay for it. The officials raised a tremendous row, to which he meekly listened. When their anger had cooled a little, he said, "Gentlemen, all this excitement is unnecessary; I have a plan, and you don't have to trust me at all. Put all the tea in a warehouse, and I will take delivery, either chest by chest, or lorry by lorry. I will pay cash for each delivery as I take it. In this way you will get the highest bid for your tea and still be protected."

Abraham Briscoe was indeed a salesman, for he persuaded the indignant insurance men to accept his proposition. He then rented a small shop near Terenure Bridge, and installed his bride behind the counter to sell tea, measuring it out into pound and half-pound packets. Meanwhile he took to the road to sell it wholesale.

That deal was the foundation of his little fortune. He cleared enough profit to buy an interest in the Lawlor furniture business. The firm became Lawlor Briscoe. When Mr. Lawlor died, Pappa bought his share and became sole owner of the greatly expanded business. If you walk on Lower Ormond Quay today, you will still see the sign of Lawlor Briscoe, though we no longer have an interest in the firm.

My mother was a great help to her young husband. She was a beautiful and charming lady who wrote poetry and taught in the Jewish Hebrew school, and was an even better salesman than he. She knew quality when she saw it, in furniture, rugs and pictures. In Lawlor Briscoe, as in the little shop by the bridge, she often sold behind the counter. Many of our customers refused to be served by anyone else. She was a shrewd judge of people's reactions. One thing she told me was, "If a customer praises something he is sure not to buy it; but if he runs it down, he is really interested."

The one treasure that my father brought to Ireland and kept inviolate was his religion. He was an orthodox Jew who implicitly followed the Law as given to our people by their great prophets and the priests of our church. The dietary rules, so complicated and difficult to follow in a non-Hebraic country, were the absolute rule of our house. You may realize how strictly they were observed when I tell you that such great orthodox rabbis as Doctor Isaac Herzog who is now Chief Rabbi in Israel, his father who was Chief Rabbi of Paris, and his father-in-law Rabbi Hillman who succeeded Herzog senior in Paris, often sat down to eat at my father's table.

To us of the younger generation, who tended to become impatient with such minutia as special dishes for Passover, the ritual of purification and the ordinance against using dairy products and meat at the same meal, Pappa said, "Our Jewish laws and customs have been preserved by our ancestors for two thousand years or more, at the cost of great hardship, suffering and extreme peril. They are a precious heritage. Are we in our comparative comfort and ease lightly to abandon these things they strove so hard to hand down to us merely because they are inconvenient?"

And again he said, "We are the people chosen by God to suffer and strive and serve him; let us do so thankfully."

Of course Pappa taught us Hebrew so that we could read our prayers and study the Torah, which is the Old Testament. We learned many of the Psalms by heart. The poetry of David, which is so beautiful even in the King James translation, is even lovelier in the liquid syllables of its original tongue. We also learned many of the solemn, resonant verses of the different rituals, which we offer in the temple on our holy days.

When I was in America in 1923, on the eve of the anniversary of Pappa's death, I went to a synagogue and asked the beadle if I might come the next day to say the memorial prayers. He assented, and then asked, "Where are you from?"

I answered, "I am an Irishman."

"Then I will keep close to you," he said, "so that I can prompt you."

When the time came I put on the praying shawl and intoned the full service of morning prayer. In the evening, I again was able to complete the prayers without once faltering.

After the service the beadle came smiling to me. "You said you came from Ireland," he remarked, "but I've never known a man from that country with such a knowledge of Hebrew and so great a capacity for prayer. I think you're a phony!"

Indeed, Pappa loved all great literature in any language. He read and reread the plays of Shakespeare and these he taught us, as well as many of the other English classics.

However, this gives too solemn a picture of him, for he had an irrepressible sense of fun. He liked to have people around him. After service on the Sabbath he stayed home all day, and people kept dropping in. The house would be full of laughter. Often in the evening his great friend Joseph Isaacs would come by, and the two of them would sit talking and drinking far more than Mother thought was good for them. It must be admitted that Pappa was very fond of drink, though he never let it interfere with business. Often people tried to get him tipsy to soften up his judgment. On these occasions Pappa used to sit with an umbrella over his arm taking glass for glass. But when they were not looking he poured the drinks into his slightly open umbrella.

Nor was our religion always as somber as you might think. I remember several occasions when Pappa's sense of humor considerably irritated his co-religionists. One was at our festival celebrating the saving of the Jews by Esther. It is always a gay, even raucous ceremony. When the name of our oppressor, Haman, who was something of an early Hitler, is mentioned, we express our opinion of him with very rude noises. It is a time when you can have a bit of fun in church.

Pappa particularly disliked one rather pompous member of our synagogue, and on this Queen Esther festival he incited us boys and our cousins to come with our pockets full of chestnuts. We sat at some distance from him. At the right moment he gave us the signal. We all stood up and began throwing chestnuts at the pompous gentleman's high silk hat. Pappa rose in a righteous indignation and called upon the beadle to throw those rowdy boys out. As he finished, he gave us the high sign again, and another cascade of chestnuts rattled off that silken topper.

Just as he did not leave his love of practical jokes outside the synagogue, he did not leave his morals in church. His integrity in his business was absolute; his word was, in truth, his bond. Shady practices filled him with rage.

15

It may seem odd to those whose ideas of the business methods of our race are formed by the unfortunate Merchant of Venice; but the people my father abhorred most of all were unscrupulous moneylenders. The first time I came back from America, cutting a rather dashing figure in my New York clothes, I began going out with a certain very beautiful Jewish girl. When my father learned of it he called me to his room, and said, "I hear you are keeping company with Esther. You know her father is a moneylender, and I am sure you know how much I love you. Now I solemnly tell you this, rather than see you married to a moneylender's daughter, I would prefer to see your right arm cut off at the shoulder."

Mother shared this feeling of his. One time a moneylender died who had never paid his subscription to the Jewish cemetery of which Pappa was a trustee. His relatives, who were forced to pay a large capital sum to get him buried there, came to Pappa to complain. Mother hearing the argument, said to them, "Those good Jews who lie in the cemetery will rise when the Messiah comes. But your uncle will be there forever. He's getting a bargain."

I was so impressed by Pappa's abhorrence of moneylenders that when I first went into the Dáil, I joined with Patrick J. Little to introduce a bill which would put an end to their worst abuses. They often juggled loans so that they received as much as a thousand per cent interest, and once in their clutches a man had as little chance of escaping as a rabbit in a boa constrictor's jaws. My bill regulated the interest that could be charged, and also made it illegal for a married woman to borrow money without the knowledge and consent of her husband, for these foolish ones are always the easiest prey of the moneylenders. The act was passed and is today the law of Ireland.

As my father got better off, he played a leading part in the community. He was instrumental in raising funds to build the synagogue in Adelaide Road, where we still worship. Before that we went to an old ramshackle converted dwelling on a narrow slit of a street, oddly known as Mary's Abbey. You could say that the new synagogue was the beginning of the modern history of Dublin Jewry.

Father also helped to get the land for our cemetery, and established the Board of Shechita, the controlling body of Kosher butchering, so that our people could live according to the dietary laws.

But all these things that he did for the community were simply expressions of his religious faith, not his race. His nationality was Irish, and all the time I was growing up I was also learning from my father — I was being steeped in — the dark, storm-wracked, light-shot history of my country — of Eire. I learned about the mysterious druids, and the prehistoric Firbolgs, and of the great days of the Irish kings, though I confess there was also terrible fighting among them and seldom peace for long; of Saint Patrick, and the time that followed when Ireland was the only center of learning and culture in these northern lands and the spear point of the Christian faith.

It is remarkable to think what she has survived since then until now. I learned how one marauding race after another crossed the narrow northern seas to plunder and tyrannize, until at last came the English, who were the worst of all. The reason I say that is because, of them all, only England made a systematic effort to destroy the Irish people or assimilate them into the Anglo-Saxon race.

At first they were content only to rule and exploit us. But when they found us stubbornly resisting, they passed the Penal Laws — that was after the Battle of the Boyne in 1690, when King William's Orangemen beat Prince Charles Stuart. These laws were aimed at the very souls of the Irish. Any kind of teaching, whether religious or secular was denied to all who would not foreswear the Catholic Church. We survived even that; for the children gathered to be taught behind the tall hedges or in the hay barns in what were called the hedge schools, in which the great scholars taught, unpaid and hunted.

Finally came the effort to destroy the Irish language, and that came near to succeeding. It was forbidden to write it. Shopkeepers who put up their signs in it were prosecuted and imprisoned, and children were beaten in the schools for speaking it.

On top of that there was the great potato famine of 1847, in which nearly a million Irish died of starvation, and more millions emigrated, so the population fell from eight million to four, while the British landlords, who held all the best land, shipped boatloads of wheat and cattle out of the country and began driving the people out of their miserable, thatched-roof, single-room cottages, because they wanted to enclose their lands, and turn them from tillage to grazing cattle, which was more profitable.

My father told me tales of the great Irish leaders who had resisted these things; of Wolfe Tone leading his scythe-swinging peasants in 1798, and poetic Robert Emmet, dangling from the gibbet at Dublin Castle. He spoke of the moral force of Daniel O'Connell, a member of the British Parliament, who secured the repeal of the penal laws and Catholic Emancipation Act in 1832; and of the leaders of the Young Ireland movement of 1841, from whom the Irish learned to hope again. He ardently supported the new Gaelic League, founded the year before I was born, which provided centers where those who loved the best things of the old days could gather and spread Irish ideals; and relearn our lovely language that was being lost. Our native tongue became, and still is, the symbol of Irish freedom.

Most of all, I learned about the great patriot, Charles Stewart Parnell, who had been untimely dead only a little while when I was born.

My father was foremost a man of peace, who loved deeply. He loved his wife and his children; and I believe he truly loved humanity. And he hated the killing of men. So Parnell was his chosen leader; because he did not preach revolution and war against England; but the achievement of freedom for Ireland by constitutional means. He asked only dominion status like Canada; and he nearly succeeded in getting it. I think that if England had granted it then, we would have been her faithful ally in the great wars. But by the time she was willing to give it, the toll of spilt

18

blood was too great, the tide of bitterness too high for us to accept less than complete freedom.

When I said Parnell nearly won dominion status, I mean that Britain's great Prime Minister, William Gladstone, twice staked his government on Home Rule. Once the House of Lords beat him. The second time it was the scandal of Parnell and Kitty O'Shea, whose husband sued the Irish statesman for adultery.

Father always thought, as many Irish did, that the O'Shea scandal was a Tory British plot. And when Parnell died by his own hand, or so they said, Father would not think that he was dead; but implicitly believed the legend that the body of a black man had been buried in Parnell's coffin, and that the great Irish leader had been spirited away to Australia; from whence he would some day return to lead the Irish people peacefully to freedom.

Peacefully is the key word here; for after Parnell there was no man who had a chance to set us free without war, and, as I said, my father was a man of peace. In his last days this caused a breach between us; for by then I knew that only by bloodshed could the Irish break loose from British domination. I was already enlisted in the fight.

This, I think, was the one big thing in which I went against his wishes. In most of the things which I have done in my lifetime, the major decisions I have made, I have acted as I believed he would have done, and decided in the way he would have wished.

CHAPTER III

A Little Learning

My EDUCATION was distinctly catholic, using that word in the sense of widely inclusive. First off I went to the Strand Street School on a narrow alley directly back of our warehouse. That was a Catholic school where we were taught by the Christian Brothers, who were not priests but devout laymen who volunteered for this work. It was a small, humble sort of place that hardly went beyond the kindergarten stage of learning.

Next I was sent to the Kildare Street National School, run by the State — a public school Americans would call it. Our teachers were Church of Ireland Protestants, who were properly trained for their profession. There I learned the fundamentals of reading and writing and simple arithmetic. We sat on long benches in a cold, dimly lit room, and did our work on slates with squeaky pencils. It was a very humdrum sort of teaching, but our games were as exciting as our lessons were dull. I loved the games they taught me.

We played football with a rag ball; and cricket, of course. There was rounders, out of which baseball evolved in America, and a piggy-back game in which one boy mounted the shoulders of another and we charged each other like knights in a tournament, each fighting to unhorse the other.

However, Pappa was not pleased with my intellectual progress; nor should he have been! So he sent me to St. Andrew's College, which was a Presbyterian preparatory school that took boys all the way up from the fourth grade until they were ready for a university. The masters were great nonconformists, their Presbyterian rigidity alleviated by personal eccentricity. For example, the chemistry and science master was a Yorkshireman named William Normington, who still wore eighteenth century knee breeches and was known affectionately as "Bagsey." We had a wide range of subjects, mathematics and Euclid — which some people call geometry — Latin, French, German, science, and English grammar.

I cannot say that I won any scholastic honors at St. Andrews, but I made my mark at Rugby football; and football left its mark on me. I was tall and strong and full of fight, and in my final year I made the cup team. But I did not play in the classic match against our arch-rivals, Blackrock College. The Saturday before it, I was playing against Terenure College, when I stuck my long nose in the way of a flying boot which plastered it flat on my face. The doctor molded it back into place the best way he knew, but it was left with a permanent list to port. This was a most unfortunate circumstance, not only from an esthetic point of view, but because in the dangerous days to come it was almost impossible to disguise my lopsided proboscis.

Pappa's business was prospering and we began to live quite luxuriously. He rented a beautiful Regency house at 58 Upper Leeson Street — though he owned at least a dozen houses in Dublin, he always lived in a rented one. Our life there was decidedly different from the overcrowded flat above the warehouse. There was serenity about that house, guarded as it was from the street by a high wall with a wrought-iron gate from which a gravel path ran between bright flowerbeds and close-mown lawns to its classic front door. Behind the house was another big lawn where we could play our games.

From the windows of that house I watched the grand procession when Queen Victoria came to Dublin on her last visit. It moved up the road from Kingstown where she landed from the royal yacht, right past our front gate. First a British general and his staff in plumed helmets and flashing uniforms mounted on beautiful prancing chargers; then the bands, and the Queen's Irish Guards, Irish pipers in swinging saffron kilts; the Lord Lieutenant looking very stern and noble, followed by eight white horses pulling an open carriage with turbaned, dark Indians standing at the back, and on the cushioned seat a little old lady all in black, with a crepe veil and a black lace parasol. The head of the procession had trouble at the bridge over the Grand Canal, and the royal carriage stopped directly in front of our house. For five minutes it stayed there, while I stared, never taking my eyes off the Queen. She was so small to be so great; and so very old. During those endless minutes she sat as still as her own image in wax at Madame Tussaud's. Even a child felt death so close that only the shell of the Queen was sitting there.

In that house in 1910 my oldest sister, Rachel, married the younger brother of Father's crony, Joseph Isaacs, which eventually made her my aunt by marriage.

Pappa also rented a small fisherman's cottage on the exquisite little harbor of Dalkey. Some of the old fishermen there still remember the man with the beard who used to come down to the wall of the quay and talk to them. They loved to tell him tremendous yarns of hairbreadth escapes from sea monsters or of crossing the Irish Sea in a rowboat; and it amused him to pretend to believe every word they said.

Prosperity also added variety to my schooling. For two years I was taken out of St. Andrew's and sent to the Townley Castle School at Ramsgate in England. This was a very stylish Jewish school designed in the likeness of those incubators of English gentlemen, Eton and Harrow. The headmaster was Jewish, but almost all of our other teachers were Oxford or Cambridge men. The school was housed in a genuine castle, all crenelations and gray battlemented towers, in which Queen Victoria had once lived as a girl.

There were six boys from Ireland in the school, including my oldest brother, Arthur, and our childhood friends Maurice and Jack Isaacs. We used to go back and forth to Ireland together for our holidays. One time we decided not to return to school, and left the train at Chester. For a few hours we had a jolly time wandering around that lovely walled city which had begun as a Roman camp. Since we knew far more about English and Roman history than we did about our own country's, we were pleased to be walking on the battlements of a real Roman wall, and charmed by the sagging old Elizabethan buildings with their diamond-paned windows and the complicated patterns of black beams on white stucco. The most beautiful thing of all to our eyes was an extraordinary clock erected in honor of Queen Victoria's Diamond Jubilee. It was a gaudy object in bright green paint with the royal arms crowning it, supported on top of the wall by the most intricate ironwork grill I have ever seen.

However, our finances were hardly equal to our imaginations, and within a few hours six very hungry boys surrendered to the authorities at discretion. After that they always locked us in a compartment of the train.

At Townley, I first learned to know people from beyond our limited island sphere. The only things the boys there had in common was their Jewish faith, for they came from all parts of the world. One of the few English boys in the school was Leslie Hore-Belisha, who long afterward became Secretary of State for War in the British Cabinet of Prime Minister Neville Chamberlain.

While Hore-Belisha held the post I made a special trip to England to try to induce him to grant a reprieve to the first Jewish boy sentenced to death for anti-British activities in Palestine. My old schoolmate refused to see me, probably feeling that such a great patriotic Englishman could not discuss this matter with an Irish rebel.

But I did see Hore-Belisha on my way home from South Africa in 1940. I was having tea on the terrace of the House of Commons, when Belisha came over to talk with me. After an exchange of greetings, I decided to tease him a little. "By the way," I said, "I have just been reading your life story in the *South African Picture Post*. It was very complete, but I couldn't find a word about Townley Castle in it."

"You should know why," Belisha grinned. "Don't you remember that I ran away on the eve of the day I was to be publicly expelled? You wouldn't want me to put that in my autobiography!"

After that we became very friendly, and Belisha took me to tea

23

with Lloyd George's daughter, Miss Megan Lloyd George. She told me that her father wanted to meet the man who had fooled him so neatly in running guns from the Continent through the British blockade during the Irish revolution.

I refused. It was easy for Lloyd George to forgive and forget circumstances which meant so little to him, but I still felt too great a bitterness against the man who had loosed the Black and Tans on my countrymen and imposed partition on Ireland to trust myself in his presence. Having tea with his daughter was tolerance enough.

Incidentally, I became involved in my first rebellion at Townley. One of the boys broke a window while we were playing football indoors, which we should not have been doing. Unable to discover the cuplrit our headmaster decreed that everyone's allowance would be stopped until he gave himself up. The injustice of it was not to be born. Our council printed placards of protest. Then twenty of us went up on the castle roof, and barricaded the trapdoors so no one could get at us. When we were secure, we began marching around the battlements shouting out our woes and waving our placards in full view of the townsfolk, who soon gathered a cheering crowd beneath us.

Poor Rabbi Harris was distraught. He stood below alternately shouting threats and wringing his hands — oh, the disgrace of it! Of course we would soon have been starved out, but Harris had no iron in his soul. He surrendered completely, agreeing to restore our allowances if we would only please stop making a spectacle of his beloved school.

At Townley the friends I made who best stood the stringent test by which true friendship is assayed were Reuben and Joseph Arbib from America, whence their family had immigrated from Tripoli. Reuben eventually returned to America, and Joseph established a business in England. In time I was to call on each in turn when I was beyond the law; and each responded with all his heart, risking ruin and prison in a cause not their own, simply because I asked their help.

There was a Jewish boy from Arabia at Townley named

Hamui who was the hungriest human being I have ever seen. He was as thin as a tent pole, and he would eat all day long if he could. My brother Bert, who also attended Townley Castle, discovered that the cook was Irish, and made up to her; so we were well supplied with delicious porridge and drippings that dampened our appetites for our regular meals. At table Hamui would absorb his portion like a vacuum cleaner and watch the rest of us wolfishly. "How much am I bid for the rest of this stew?" one of us would ask him.

He'd usually start the bidding at a ha'penny, but we never sold for less than a penny, and if he looked especially hungry we could get him up higher.

Another source of income was a slot machine at Ramsgate, which was a race between two bicycle riders. Two boys each put two pennies in and the winner got three pennies back. We discovered that if you cut pieces of heavy cardboard the size of pennies the machine would work, returning coppers for cardboard. We had quite a nice thing there until one day the police arrived at the Castle. The way they discovered that the culprit was from Townley was that one boy had used a piece of cardboard with some Hebrew prayers written on it.

Another time, though, we were on the side of law and order. About a dozen of us slept in a great dormitory room at the Castle. For our own naughty purposes we had our silent signals to give the alarm of the approach of a master or prefect. One night I was alerted by a twitch on my bedclothes. All around the room the signal traveled until every boy was tensely waiting, though apparently asleep. Looking at the open window I saw the dark form of a cat burglar slip through it.

We waited until he was well inside; then at another signal we leaped for him all at once. The poor man went down with a crash under half a ton of howling savages.

The first thing was to tie him up. We bound him rigid and straight like a mummy with the cords of our dressing gowns — such little gentlemen we were that we had both pajamas and robes. Then we sat on him and held a council.

No band of Indian braves ever cooked up more fiendish tortures. Each blood-curdling suggestion was greeted by us with giggles of approval, and drew groans from our wretched captive. We began his punishment by taking off his boots and tickling his feet. His agonized laughter was stifled with a pillow. After that we stood him up straight with his arms and legs pinioned and let him fall over. Next we sloshed icy water over him from our pitchers.

By this time the uproar had brought the senior boys and the masters in. Somebody sent for the police. Before they arrived, we loosed our victim's legs so he could stand, and crowned him king of the dormitory with a chamber pot.

The heavy tread of the constabulary crunching down the corridor must have sounded like the United States Marines to the unhappy burglar. He flung himself into their astonished arms shouting, "Save me! Save me!"

The next day we all appeared as witnesses at his trial. The judge was a humane man. Addressing the prisoner he said, "you have suffered punishment enough for half a dozen crimes. I'm going to let you off, and sure I am that never again will you try to enter Townley Castle."

When my two years at Ramsgate were over, I returned to St. Andrew's College, from which I was graduated in 1912. Then came the question of my future. I wanted to go to the Royal College of Science to become an engineer, but my father felt I would do better to go to Germany and study business methods, and electrical engineering. His word was still law to me, so to Germany I went. And that was the beginning of my troubles.

CHAPTER IV

Prisoner of War

My brother Bert and I went to Berlin in the summer of 1912. Father apprenticed us to the import-export house of Hecht Pfeiffer and Company. They were one of the best-known commercial firms in Germany, with connections all over the world. The exporting side of the business was much the larger since Germany was at its pinnacle of production, and "Made in Germany" a familiar phrase to Hottentot and heathen Chinee. The management was set up in different departments, each named after the country it served — the Spanish Department, Chinese, Japanese, American, Australian, and so forth.

Though I was only a bottom-rung apprentice, my knowledge of English made me very valuable to the firm. I was set to writing business letters to English-speaking countries, and in time I was permitted to sign many of those letters on behalf of the firm. The connections I thus made in America and South Africa were soon to be of great value to Ireland's fight for freedom, and, in an unthinkable future, to Israel.

In addition to working, Bert and I enrolled in the Salaman Handel Akademie, a commercial school in the Spittelmarkt. At Father's wish I also studied Hebrew religion and history at the famous Hildesheimer School, which was a seminary for training rabbis.

All this kept us pretty busy, but we were young and very strong, so we had a good deal of fun as well. The firm paid us twenty marks a month, which Pappa supplemented by an allowance of twenty-five marks a week. Out of this we had to pay for our board and lodging in a pension. It was hardly affluence, but we made out. We knew the cheapest restaurants where the largest portions were served, and the shops that did not count the little pieces of bread very carefully. So we had quite a lot left over for amusement.

Berlin was a city of gaiety in 1912; not the frenetic, die-tomorrow gaiety I knew there in the twenties, nor the terrible, solemn strength-through-joy of Hitler's capital, but genuine lightness of heart. There were wonderful concerts and operas to which one could go very cheaply since they were subsidized by the Kaiser's paternalistic state. We brought our sandwiches with us, and munched while we listened to Greig or Brahms played by the best musicians in Europe. Or you could spend half the night in a beer hall, drinking the dark foaming brew at five pfennigs the glass and roaring out German drinking songs in an atmosphere of *gemütlich* good fellowship. There was also boating on the lakes, or long walks in the storybook German countryside; and hospitable cottagers who invited you in for milk and coffee cake when you got tired. It was all so serene and happy that one felt it would go on forever. I am sure the Germans did.

Of course there were many soldiers in the streets in their smart, bright uniforms and *Pickelhaube* helmets. The finest of all were the Emperor's Guards in silver breastplates and crested helms. Kaiser Wilhelm often swept by in a long open car with a horn that rang a bugle call, *Ta te ta ta, ta-te ta ta,* to which the irreverent Germans chanted, "With our money, with our money."

Once I went to a great review at Tempelhof. The Kaiser was there on a white Arabian horse dressed in imperial splendor, with his withered left arm resting on the hilt of a long curved saber. I can still see his gray face with its black needle-pointed mustache under a great plumed helmet.

His son, the Crown Prince, led his famous Death's Head Hussars by at a gallop, every line as straight as a bayonet's edge; every saber flashing in salute. Their high gray shakos were adorned with the skull-and-cross-bones badge of the regiment.

There was nothing very menacing in this martial display. The bright flags and fancy uniforms, the superb bands blaring out gay

28

marches; the crowd of spectators around the field — men in top-
pers and morning coats and highborn ladies in their great cart-
wheel hats and elaborate, lacy dresses, like Ascot on a summer
day — made it seem more like a splendid fete than preparation
for war.

Nobody thought there would be a war until the day when, between two strikes of a clock, these kindly, hospitable German folk
were changed by the alchemy of hate and fear into blood-hungry
mobs.

I never took much interest in international politics until they
forced themselves upon me. In Germany I did not even read the
papers carefully. When Archduke Franz Ferdinand and his wife
were assassinated at Sarajevo in June, 1914, it meant nothing to
me, nor to most of my German friends. Nor did we notice the
building up of tensions during that long, beautiful July. While the
statesmen of Europe exchanged angry notes and ultimatums, we
went on picnics and listened to the band concerts in the public
parks quite ignorantly, sure that it did not concern us.

So war burst upon us suddenly, like a thunderstorm leaping
over the Dublin mountains to spoil a summer outing. One day
was just as it had always been. The next, the angry black headlines shouted WAR! and all the hoardings blossomed placards calling the conscripts to arms, while cheering crowds threw roses at
the long columns of field-gray troops marching through the
streets to the waiting trains.

Even then it did not seem my concern; I watched it as an exciting spectacle. Though the German people were exalted by
false visions of glory, they were not yet angry.

I remember the night, almost the minute, that everything
changed. It was just after midnight on August 5, 1914, when England declared war on Germany. Why this was the torch that lit
the fury of the Berlin mobs is hard to say. They had not believed
the British would fight, so perhaps they felt it was some sort of
betrayal; or perhaps it was fear of England's naval might Suddenly the streets were filled with crowds of crazy, angry men

bent on wrecking everything British and attacking everyone who looked English.

That night I stayed in my pension, looking incredulously out of the window at the roaring mobs. The next morning, moved by a kind of natural instinct, I made my way fearfully to the United States Embassy. Hundreds of other British subjects had done the same thing. The great rooms and the gardens behind the high iron fence were crowded with them. American Ambassador James W. Gerard was a humane man with strong pro-Ally sentiments. He sheltered us all there overnight. The next day he devised a plan, probably illegal, which enabled us to move safely about the streets. He issued us American passports — I have mine still. At the top left-hand corner in very small handwriting were the words: "This passport has been issued to a British subject at the request of His Britannic Majesty's Government."

Now when the mobs surrounded me all I had to do was to flash this document with the guardian American eagle stamped in gold on its cover. Nobody bothered to read the small print.

Thus I had a respite to plan what to do next. My parents were in Carlsbad, Austria; and Austria was not yet technically at war with England. I decided to try to join them. I packed my bag, paid my landlady, and went to the station to get a train for Dresden, where I would change for Carlsbad.

Even the pressure of mobilizing several million men had not quite clogged the efficient German railway system. Trains still ran. Civilians could take them by simply buying a ticket; but, of course, there was a great deal of confusion. The manpower of a nation was on the move. Every train was packed with reservists going to join their regiments, while cars filled with singing, shouting troops were hitched to the regular trains. I crammed myself into a compartment and nobody bothered me, except to ask, "Are you joining up?"

In my excellent German I replied, "Yes, I'm joining up."

At Dresden, I had to wait until morning, so I lay down with hundreds of young German men on the station floor and slept.

The first newspaper I saw the next morning struck a chill into my empty stomach with the news that Austria had declared war on England. There was nothing to do but go on, so I took a train for Carlsbad. We passed the German border safely, but just as I started to relax, the train stopped at the Austrian town of Komotau. Police and soldiers began a minute examination of every passenger. Now my heart was really in my boots. When my turn came, I handed in my phony American passport. It did not fool the Austrian guards for a minute. I was promptly arrested.

A scared bedraggled group of us were bundled onto another train and taken to a place called Eger, famous for its excellent Pilsener beer which I had been happily guzzling a few nights before. We were marched in a woeful column to a military barracks which had been hastily prepared as an internment camp, though that hateful word had hardly been invented. My fellow prisoners were Frenchmen, Serbs and Russians, with a sprinkling of German deserters. I only saw one other British subject.

It was rough and frightening, but not deliberately brutal. We slept on loose straw on the stone floors, eight of us crowded into a barracks room. Our food was a sloppy stew handed out in tin bowls. There were no amenities. However, the Austrian soldiers were hardly any better off. In the rush and confusion everything had to be improvised.

One thing, though, was efficiently done. Each day we took our exercise for two hours in the yard, and when we returned to our room, the population of it was always different. They were not going to give us a chance to conspire for a break-out.

Many of my German friends, who had been called up, had sent me post cards from their regiments. When these were found on me I became a suspicious character. I was brought up for interrogation before three big, Austrian officers.

"Why have you got all these post cards? Aren't they military intelligence?" they demanded fiercely.

I tried not to show how frightened I was, and answered truthfully. I explained my position and asked them to get in touch with Mr. Hecht of Hecht, Pfeiffer and Company.

I was sent back to my cell to wait anxiously for their verdict.

While there I pondered my unhappy position. I was a prisoner simply because I was a British subject. It did seem rather tough to be jailed for that reason, when, if I was not quite as Irish as Paddy's pig, I was heart and soul an Irishman who detested British rule.

Mr. Hecht must have sponsored me nobly, for in a few days I was released and told that I might join my parents in Carlsbad. But I was forbidden to leave Austria.

It was hardly a happy reunion. My father, who had retired from business in 1912 after a severe heart attack, was ill and anxious. He was in Carlsbad to take the waters. Mother maintained her usual courageous gaiety by sheer will power. They were far more worried about me than about themselves, for I was of military age.

There were a large group of elderly civilians trapped in Carlsbad waiting unhappily to be exchanged for German civilians caught in England. Sir Henecker Heaton was the leader of the group, among whom was the aged opera singer Adelina Patti and her husband Baron Cederström, the sewing machine millionaire. There were also three Irish clerics, Doctor Patrick Finnegan, Bishop of Kilmore, and his assistants Father Brady and Father Flynn, who were friends of my parents and customers of Lawlor Briscoe. True friends they were. The bishop used every ounce of his influence with the Papal Nuncio in Vienna to work for my release.

For several weeks nothing happened. The kindly priests arranged to give me a temporary job in a convent. Twice each day I had to report to the chief of police. One morning he told me that I was to be taken back to Eger for further questioning.

A little before noon an officer and eight soldiers with fixed bayonets came to get me. I can still see the expression of horror and sorrow on my sick father's face as he said good-by. He was, as always, impeccably dressed in a morning coat, with a stiff white collar, an ascot tie and a heavy gold watch chain looped across his waistcoat. Somehow the formality of his dress added poignancy to the despair which disintegrated his once handsome

32

face. He plunged his hands into his pockets and brought them out dripping with gold and paper money which he thrust at me; and stood weeping as I marched away between the bayonets.

However, this incident had a happy ending. My examination was a preliminary to my permission to return to Ireland. The only condition was that I sign a parole not to fight against the Central Powers. This I gladly did, since I had no desire whatever to take part in England's wars. It was the first of the many ironies of my life that I owed my release to the powerful persuasions which the Pope's Nuncio exercised on behalf of a Jewish boy he had never seen.

The long train to freedom was finally assembled; we were carefully ticketed with a brassard on our arms, and placed on board. At the Swiss border, high in the snow-covered Austrian Alps, we were formally handed over to the Swiss. As each of us crossed the dividing line our Austrian guards tore a perforated slip from our brassards which was a receipt for our safe delivery.

After a few days' wait in Geneva, another train was assembled to take us to Le Havre. It took a couple of days to make the journey across France, inching along and sitting down on every siding, while troop trains went hurtling by with blurred white faces looking out of the cattle cars; or gleaming white ambulance trains swept past leaving a fetid smell of putrefaction in their wake.

One of those long, exhausting nights was made memorable when Madame Patti was persuaded to sing in the swaying corridor of the car the song for which she was famous. The thin, quavering voice, which once had shaken the chandeliers of the great opera houses of the world, singing *Home, Sweet Home* was more moving in those circumstances than the greatest music ever written.

We finally reached Le Havre, and crossed the Channel to England. Thence we hurried to Holyhead, and boarded the Irish Mail.

33

On a lovely rainy October morning our ship rounded Howth Head and steamed over the slate gray water of Dublin Bay toward the worn gray houses of Kingstown climbing up mist-green hills. I suddenly knew how dear Ireland was to me.

CHAPTER V

I Make a Very Small Fortune

MY FATHER, I have said, was a man of peace. He was badly shaken by his first-hand glimpse of nations at war; sickened by the reports of the mass slaughter in France. When we consulted together about my future, he wanted to get me as far away as possible from this upside-down-world. He wanted to send me to America.

It was a sensible thing to do. John Redmond, the Irish leader in the British Parliament, relying on Prime Minister Herbert Asquith's promise of Home Rule for Ireland when peace came, was urging young Irishmen to enlist in the British Army. Thousands of them were doing so. But even had I wanted to, which I did not, my parole would prevent me. Thus my position was a touch queer in the midst of Dublin's sudden patriotic fervor. In addition, trade was brought to a standstill, its future unforeseeable. For a young man of twenty, the only opportunity seemed to be across the sea.

So in December, 1914, I sailed for America in the steerage of the White Star Liner *Baltic*. In those old ships, built to carry emigrants packed like cattle, the steerage on a winter crossing was no bed of roses. But I enjoyed myself. This was mainly due to an Irish girl — with whom I fell in love for the voyage. Her name was Norah Connolly, daughter of the Irish patriot who was later killed in the Easter Rising of 1916, which was the beginning of our fight for freedom. Norah's spirits were as high as the color of her cheeks; she acted as carefree as a cricket. And she seemed to like me.

One night when we were standing near the stern, shivering in the icy wind, but not wanting to leave a lovely moon, she gave me a sealed envelope saying with simple trust, "Please take care of this for me. I'm so scatter-brained I'm fearful of losing it."

Highly flattered by her confidence I put it in my breast pocket and thought of it no more. On the windy dock in New York, when we had passed the immigration officials, she was met by James Larkin, whom I recognized as one of the great leaders of the Irish workers seething beneath the crust of British rule. She asked me, then, for the envelope, and handed it to him. I realized that I had been her courier, but did not mind the risk she had put on me. Much later I learned that the papers I had carried into America were dispatches from James Connolly to German Ambassador Count von Bernstorff. They were the beginning of what was known as the "German Plot," the attempt of Irish patriots to enlist German aid and German arms in Ireland's fight for liberation.

I claim no credit for the service rendered. It was done in all innocence, out of what I thought any young man should do for a lady. But had I known what it was, I would still have done it gladly.

As things worked out, I escaped Ellis Island. You had to have fifty dollars in those days to get into America. I had my fifty when I boarded the *Baltic*, but a young fellow gets thirsty on a ship. I peeled a bill off my roll and another to buy a few beers. So I had only forty-seven dollars when I landed. I shoved the packet of bills at the immigration officer guessing he would not count it. Nor did he.

When Norah and Mr. Larkin had gone I was left alone on that wide, windy street, with great drays rumbling and banging over the cobblestones, taxis tooting and everybody in an awful hurry.

The people seemed to me rough and ruthless and I was afraid to ask my way.

I was in fact in a rather confused state of mind. I had left Ireland in all the uncertainty of the most terrible war ever seen until then. I had left my father with the sickness that might suddenly be the end of him. And I was frankly frightened of this cold new world.

But with all that, I was excited, too; intensely curious, and blazing with ambition to make my fortune, as so often happened in the tales of Irish immigrants. I could hardly wait to get started. At the same time I hardly dared to cross the street.

In my pocket was the address of my Aunt Bertha who had married a man named Brodie and lived on Bath Avenue in Brooklyn. I finally got up courage to show the writing to a policeman — Irish, praise be! — who gave me directions. Picking up my only piece of luggage, I started off.

I remember climbing the steep, high steps to the elevated railroad train, and crossing the Brooklyn Bridge, looking backward through its spider web cables at the terrible tall towers of Manhattan. Then I came down into the dismal ugly streets of Brooklyn, and began to walk, asking my way at every corner. By the time I reached Aunt Bertha's house I was very tired, very cold and terrifically hungry.

Food, warmth and sleep worked their usual healing. By next morning I was full of ambition and ready to go. I had a very high opinion of my own capability and wasn't afraid of showing my measure.

I paid my first call on the Import Sales Company on East 21st Street, a connection of Hecht, Pfeiffer and Company, to whom I had written on business. Robert A. Kahn and a Mr. Goldberg were the partners. They said they had no proper work for me; the only job open was for a packer.

"Why could I not be that?" I asked.

"It's rough work," Mr. Kahn told me. "You have to saw up the boards, make packing cases to fit the goods in so they won't break, and nail them up. Of course, you have to shift the heavy cases around, too."

"I may look thin, but feel me muscle," I said, showing him my arm, with it bulging under my coat sleeve.

"It's your job if you want it," he told me.

So I started work that very first day. If I say so I was a very good packer. Carpentry I had learned in Lawlor Briscoe's work-room — so the crates I made were the best. My knowledge of electrical gadgets also came in handy, as these were the firm's principal business and I knew just how to protect them.

I found a lodging house on the same street as my work and for a little while I never went off it. I remember watching the beautiful buses going up Fifth Avenue, and trying to get up courage to ride them. Finally I did, and looked with wonder at the mansions of the rich, like the palaces of the dukes of France. Broadway was dazzling and dizzying, with its blare of shifting lights.

Gradually I became acclimatized. New York became my city, a familiar place where I swaggered casually. I found it was a friendly city, despite my first impression of harsh buildings and soulless people. I made a few friends. All you had to remember was that the individual you met was just as simple a human being as yourself, and if not himself an immigrant, then his parents or grandparents were.

One friend I made was not lucky for me. He taught me about the Stock Exchange, not the great building where the big people traded in thousands and millions, but the Curb, where the brokers stood in a crowd on Wall Street and signaled their bids up to their partners leaning out of the windows of the tall buildings. My friend told me to buy a copper stock. It was only ten cents a share and I'd make my fortune. So I bought one hundred shares for ten dollars. I don't know what the company was, or what has ever become of it; or where my friend disappeared to. But I know I had not a copper left.

Then I found Reuben and Joe Arbib again. That really established me, for they were true friends on whom I could always count in trouble, though for a wonder I did not get into trouble.

Instead, I got promoted to shipping clerk after only three months. My career seemed to be going smooth, like glass, but I would not have been a true Irishman if I had not got into a row. It was a real brawl. The manager of the company came angrily in one day, and threw on my desk a complaint from somebody in a western state about a shortage in a case of goods. He accused me of neglect or worse.

Whether from environment or what, I have a sudden Irish temper. It went off like black powder all smoke and noise. There were the two of us roaring with rage when Mr. Kahn came dashing in to see if he needed the riot squad. He got us calmed down enough to look up the facts, which were that this had been a special order which the manager himself had handled. Result: Mr. Kahn fired him, and gave me his job.

Now I could feel that I was really on my way. The firm did business with Sears, Roebuck and Company, and I wrote the directions for the use of our goods which went in their catalogue. As a result I was offered a job with this great mail-order house checking instructions attached to imported goods and rewriting them so simple people could understand. This was a compliment indeed. I suppose I was able to do it well, because I was accustomed to talking to our farmers and other country folk and knew the sort of wording they could grasp. I refused the job, but I wonder now what would have happened had I accepted it. I might be an American millionaire with a great house at Lake Forest, and three Cadillacs in the garage. This I do not regret.

One reason for refusing was that my brother Bert was coming to America. He was reaching military age, and there was talk of conscription in Ireland. Father could not bear the thought of him in a war, especially in the British Army; and sent him to me to look after. I got Bert a job with my employers as an outside salesman. He was an immediate success. He had a pleasant affable manner and liked meeting people so well that he was a natural salesman. Soon he had such big connections that he was earning more than I was.

This put the spur to my ambition. I left my job to join with a

Hungarian named Joseph Kelbersberger, who had a small plant for making Christmas tree lights in Weehawken, New Jersey. He was a glass blower by trade. His wife was a glass blower, and even his young children were glass blowers. Of course, I had very little capital saved up, but I put this into his business and we became partners. I was works manager, bookkeeper and chief and only salesman. He attended to production. We had hardly any machinery. The bulbs were all blown by hand and Kelbersberger oversaw the coloring of them and inserting the carbon filament which was used in those days. Our production was very small, five thousand bulbs a week at top; but they were well made and very sturdy. It was something to be proud of. I'd take the day's production in a small satchel and deliver them to the customers I rounded up.

Now a very strange and interesting thing happened, as it only could in America. In my bombastic optimism I called at the head office of F. W. Woolworth and Company. There I met a Mr. Reynolds to whom I showed my wares. Woolworth's sold such lamps at ten cents apiece in their two hundred and twenty stores, we could deliver them for seven cents. Mr. Reynolds called in his experts, who tested my samples. They *were* good bulbs. The price was right. In a few days he sent for me and gave me an order for a million bulbs.

I rushed back to Kelbersberger highly elated. The poor man nearly fainted. "Did you figure how long it would take us to make a million bulbs?" he asked. "It would take *four years!*"

"Can't we expand?" I asked.

"Without capital! Go back to your Mr. Reynolds and ask him please to reduce the order, otherwise we will disappoint him."

I went back, considerably deflated, but sure that somehow it would come out right. I realize now how foolish I was; but in business, like life, believing is halfway to achieving. When I explained our situation to Mr. Reynolds, he asked, "Who are your bankers?"

"The Hudson Trust Company."

It was true. We had had a savings account there, but no regular account, not even a checkbook.

I Make a Very Small Fortune

"All right," Reynolds said. "I'll write you a letter to take to them. You request a loan to enable you to buy what machinery and raw material you need, and to pay the extra wages. We pay fourteen days from the date of delivery of each lot, and will undertake to send all checks to the bank against your invoices. I'm sure they'll take care of you."

"Do you really think so?" I asked naïvely.

Reynolds smiled at me in a fatherly way. "Yes," he said. "You are a young fellow who I think will go far, and I want to be one of the first to help you on your way."

It worked like magic. The bank manager read the letter and told me to calculate just what capital we would need, and some to spare. "We'll take care of you."

Kelbersberger and I worked it out carefully — up to now our bookkeeping had been haphazard to say the least. We put in a forty-dollar-a-week drawing account for each of us, and since we were now big businessmen, a Model T Ford apiece. When we showed it to the banker, he said, "Start right away."

Off I went to the great Corning Glass Company, with my chest out as a potential customer. I made my deal with them, and felt terribly important when they showed me around the factory with all the people busy at work making glass for me. Then I went to Libbey Glass and put in an order with them. At this time Corning made glass with a lead base and Libbey with lime. We needed both kinds.

Within six weeks our company went into large-scale production. When Christmas came around nine months later and we totaled up the take, we found ourselves with a handsome profit. It was a little over a year since I had landed at the pier at West 19th Street.

We did not have much time to enjoy our success. By now there were about fifty of these small companies like ours in New Jersey, making little light bulbs for Christmas trees, automobile headlights and so forth. We were cutting into the sales of General Electric, and they decided to crack down on one of us and prove we were infringing their patents, which we were. All fifty companies formed an association of which I was named secretary. We did not know which company would be attacked, but we agreed to join forces to support whichever company was the victim as if it were in full production. We did not call ourselves an association of independent lamp makers, for fear of trouble with the anti-trust laws, but took the name of a kegel (bowling) club.

Apparently General Electric got the word. They sent for me. I still believe that my good friend Mr. Reynolds had a hand in this pie, too. Instead of trying to lick us, they let us join them. We were all offered a license to operate under G.E. patents. In return we admitted that we had been infringing their patents and made agreements as to our production. This made us respectable businessmen with an assured future. Indeed, some of the companies are still in business.

At this time my third brother, Wolfe Tone, came over to join me. I was so prosperous that I had a room in a real hotel, and this I shared with him.

Despite my being so well settled in America, my mind was turning toward Ireland. It was a time when all Irishmen, wherever they lived, were deeply concerned for their homeland. On Easter Monday, 1916, the armed revolt against British tyranny, inspired and led by the secret Irish Republican Brotherhood, began with what came to be called the Easter Rising. On that holiday morning the Provisional Government of the Irish Republic was proclaimed by the leaders of the I.R.B. At the same time the Dublin Brigades of the Irish Volunteers, who had been openly arming and training themselves for years, seized buildings in the heart of Dublin, including the Four Courts, which with its massive stone walls and its ten-foot spiked iron fence is a natural fortress. Other buildings they seized along the Liffey River and on wide O'Connell Street, including the General post office, which became Republican Headquarters of the commander-in-chief, Padraic Pearse. One brigade held Boland's Mills on the Kingstown Road. Barricades were thrown across main streets.

There were too few volunteers — no more than a thousand — to expect to keep control of Dublin, but they hoped to be reinforced by a great rising in the country of volunteers armed with guns which Germany was supposed to send them.

Of course no German guns ever came, nor did the reinforcements. The British Army blocked off the country roads, and then set to work to reduce the strong points the Republicans held in Dublin. Two brigades of infantry, a battery of artillery and a gunboat were sent to strengthen the British garrison.

It was a bitter week. Street by street the British drove the Irish back. Their eighteen pounders firing down O'Connell Street wrecked half of that beautiful avenue, and turned the post office into a shambles. Against the cannon the Volunteers had only a few machine guns and modern rifles. The rest were armed with every odd weapon from converted flint locks to double barrel shotguns. But they held out for nearly a week before they gave up and were marched off to English prisons. The last Republican strongpoint to surrender was Boland's Mills. It was commanded by a young schoolteacher whose name I had never heard before. Eamon de Valera became the hero of the new nation and of Irishmen throughout the world.

Of course I did not learn all these things at the time. The accounts of them in the American papers were inaccurate and slanted toward the British. But even from such stories I could picture the black smoke and flame and ruin of my beautiful city. Some of the fighting was right in front of Lawlor Briscoe on the familiar quays where I had played as a boy.

Then came the news of the executions by the British of the leaders of the Rising. All seven men who had signed the Republican manifesto, including Padraic Pearse, Joseph Plunkett and James Connolly — Norah's father — were shot. All the brigade commanders except Thomas Ashe and de Valera were also executed. This was the worst mistake England ever made, for it aroused a fire-storm of resentment in Irishmen throughout the world.

My own heart was torn for these men, who were the latest of the thousands who had died throughout the centuries for Irish independence. For seven hundred years the British had tried to subdue us; and in all that time we had risen against them two or three times each century, every time to be beaten down in bloody subjection. But we had never given up. And we never would!

However great my sympathy, I could not at first see what I could do to help. Then some of the leaders of the Rising who had escaped, came to America. Clan na Gael, the organization of Irish-Americans who were working for our freedom, arranged meetings for them to address. To many of these I went. The man who had the most influence on my final decision was Liam Mellows, who later became my friend and then my trusted leader throughout the Troubled Times.

Mellows was a most charming man, stocky and blond, with a power of oratory that made you see the things he had experienced, and dream the same great dreams. He held his audiences enthralled as he told of the long, sorrowful history of Ireland's struggle for independence; and fairly lifted you out of yourself as he described the bloody, desperate, glorious days of that Easter Week. He said that though the movement had been temporarily crushed and forced underground, rebellion was seething beneath the still surface of Irish life. He told us that Ireland was being secretly organized for a far greater effort than she had ever made before.

The greatest adventure of a lifetime, he said, would be to go home to take part in the coming struggle. He offered those who went only danger and sacrifice; but from that sacrifice, he prophesied, the dream of seven centuries would come true; Ireland's freedom would be won.

His appeal struck deep into my soul, bludgeoning my common sense. At this very time my business was prospering, and I was offered an opportunity to go to Japan to start a factory for making electric light bulbs with ample financing. I have no doubt it would have made me rich; but such was the persuasive power of this man; and the force of my own conscience, that I turned the offer down and decided like a romantic fool to go home to tilt against the British windmills.

It was by now the spring of 1917. America had entered the war, and every citizen, as well as those of the Allies, had to register for the draft. I registered and went to the British consul to whom I showed the parole I had given in Germany. He agreed that I could not fight in this war, and gave me permission to return to Ireland — poor man he knew not what he was doing!

My brothers also registered. Bert was turned down for physical reasons, and Wolfe enlisted in the American Merchant Marine, in which he served throughout the war.

When he learned that I was returning to Ireland, Kelbersberger decided to accept a good offer he had for the business. We sold it for forty thousand dollars, of which my share was about six thousand dollars.

In August, 1917, I succeeded in getting passage home on the S.S. *St. Paul.* Lying alongside the dock in her coat of zigzagged camouflage she looked like an abstract painter's idea of a liner. I went straight to my room and there met my cabin mate. He was a short, stocky man with the fair freckled Irish skin that went with his red hair. Later, much later, I found he was that unusual and valuable contradiction; a man of great personal courage, who also had the common sense which heroes usually lack. His name was Eamon Martin.

CHAPTER VI

Bombs and Bloomers

W<small>HEN</small> I boarded the *St. Paul* I was in a contrary state of mind. Though I had determined to enlist in the movement for Irish independence, I had not the least idea of how to go about it. This uncertainty made my decision to cut my profitable business ties in America look downright foolish. The escort of American destroyers plunging along beside the sixteen ships of our convoy made evident the danger of torpedo attack. When they turned for home and left us on the hostile sea it made me feel even more of a damn fool. It was Eamon Martin who set me straight on the course I followed the rest of my life. One thing I never knew was whether our sharing a cabin was a happy chance, or whether Liam Mellows had planned it.

First off, Martin showed me the horrible great scar on his back from a bullet that hit his shoulder in front and went right on out through his lung, which was his souvenir of the Easter Rising. He had been taken to a hospital, and his life saved by the great British surgeon, Sir John Myles. From the hospital he had escaped to America. Now he was going back, to hide and plan and fight again.

During our long talks together, Martin briefed me on the state of the Irish politics, if you could describe such a violent situation by that mild term. There were at least four principal parties or organizations working in different ways for Ireland's liberation. One was John Redmond's Parliamentary Party, whose leaders sat in Westminster as members of the British Parliament. The Redmondites were the political successors of Parnell and wanted only Home Rule.

The three others were all committed to absolute independence, and they were closely woven and interwoven by what in business is described as interlocking directorates. First came Sinn Fein — "Ourselves Alone." This was a recognized political party founded in 1905 by, among others, Arthur Griffith and Sean T. O'Kelly, who is now President of the Irish Republic. It openly proclaimed its objectives as complete separation from England and a republican government. De Valera was elected President of Sinn Fein, succeeding Griffith, at a great convention in the Mansion House just after I returned home.

Co-operating with Sinn Fein, but determined on armed revolution, was the Irish Republican Brotherhood. Founded in America in 1858, the I.R.B. had been transplanted to Ireland, and had gone underground in 1886. This secret society was the hard core of rebellion. But the fighting men were the Irish Volunteers, who shortly changed their name to the Irish Republican Army. Michael Collins, Austin Stack, Cathal Brugha and Diarmuid Lynch were among its great leaders.

In November, 1917, the Volunteers elected de Valera their President. He thus headed both the civil and military sides of the Irish Republican Movement.

Two most useful auxiliaries of the Volunteers were the Cumann na mBan (pronounced Coman na Mahn), composed of women and young girls, who nursed our wounded, carried dispatches, transported ammunition; in fact, did everything but actually shoot; and Fianna Eireann. Fianna had been founded in 1909 by Countess Markievicz, Bulmer Hobson and Liam Mellows. On the surface it seemed to be the Irish equivalent of Sir Baden Powell's cherubic Boy Scouts. But it was a far, far different thing.

Fianna was, in fact, the organization which trained the boys of Ireland to fight when they became men. Instead of learning how to tie knots, the Fianna boys were taught how to shoot to kill; how to use hand grenades and land mines. Instead of woodcraft, they were taught the techniques of ambush and sabotage. Long before they were old enough to fight they were the secret messenger boys of the Irish Republican Army.

And do not think that because they were trained fighters, they were juvenile delinquents. The Fianna boys were a picked lot, chosen for courage and idealism. They were taught the history of their country and imbued with such a passion for liberty as made them not only fearless of death, but, what is harder, willing to subject themselves to a stricter discipline than the King of England's Guards. For they who fight in a secret war, as these children did, must often act alone; and keep the faith with none to lead them and no comrade at their side.

Eamon Martin confided in me that he was going back to Ireland to take Liam Mellow's place as "Chief Scout" of Fianna Eireann. He asked me to become associated with its headquarters staff. The maximum age of Fianna boys was sixteen, after which they became full-fledged members of the I.R.A.; but, of course, headquarters was manned by older men. I accepted, provided we ever got back to Ireland, which at the moment seemed a little doubtful.

Our voyage was as slow as the snailiest ship in the convoy. The U. S. Navy gun crews on every ship enlivened things by shooting their three-inch guns at barrels floating astern. Twice a day we had boat drills. Eamon Martin, with typical Irish contrariness, refused to take part in them or put on a life belt because, "they give you a slow death rather than a quick, but no less certain, one."

The captain sent for him and threatened to put him in irons for insubordination. Martin said, "Go ahead!"

Then they sent a Protestant minister to plead with him. Martin remarked, "If I were as sure of the next world as you are, I'd not be as worried about going there as you seem to be."

Three days out from Liverpool, knife-thin, little British destroyers with big white ensigns at their sterns came to escort us. Those were the tense days; false alarms every few hours. Then came the real thing.

It was at dusk, when the gongs sounded, and we tumbled out and took our boat stations — Martin stayed in bed. We thought it was another false alarm until there came a vivid flash of light ahead, and the great crack of an explosion. The destroyers began racing around us like whippets at fault, their depth charges raising pillars of water; and all the gun crews started shooting. More great flashes showed that other ships were hit.

Then we sailed through the wreckage of a lost ship. It was heartbreaking to see the survivors in the lifeboats, sending up rockets for help, and we steaming on at full speed. The passengers led by Martin and me protested to the captain, who told us to go to hell. We were too ignorant to realize that if the ship stopped she would be like a fish in a barrel. That was before I learned that in war only the ruthless survive.

We got to Liverpool all right. Martin was wanted, of course, but he had a forged passport. We could only hope he would get by. I stood in the queue immediately in front of him determined to create a diversion if I could. When the immigration official asked my religion, I answered, "Mosaic."

He said loftily, "I am not asking you about buildings, I'm asking what is your religion."

To irritate him, I said, "I can't help your ignorance, I am Mosaic."

The officer went into a red rage and roared that he would lock me up if I didn't answer properly. Seeing I had pushed him as far as was safe, I said, "Well, if it will make it easier for you, I am a follower of Moses, you must have heard of him. Would it help if I said I was of the Jewish faith?"

He was so mad at me that he paid scarcely any attention to Martin beyond asking him, "If you stay in England, will you report for National Service?"

Martin replied, "If I stay here I'll have to." And that was that.

We had no trouble slipping aboard the Irish mail at Holyhead; and the next morning landed at Kingstown. I went straight to my father's house.

When I saw him I knew we would not be together long. His illness had made him very irritable, so different from the joke-loving Pappa I remembered. The Easter Rising had been a dreadful shock to him. He told me that from the back bedroom window of his house in Ranelagh Road, he had seen the Irish sharpshooters on the elevated railroad only a hundred feet away firing toward Dartmouth Square; had seen them killed by the return fire. He begged me not to join the revolutionary movement, foreseeing more blood being spilled and the hopeless situation of a small nation pitting itself against the mighty British Empire.

His sympathy was for Irish Home Rule, and he believed that after the war Britain would honor her word to give Ireland dominion status. He bemoaned the weakness of the Parliamentarians and the rise of Sinn Fein, whose members he considered fanatics.

I told him that I knew many of them, and found them to be dreamers and poets and great idealists. To counter me he spoke of his friend Arthur Griffith, with whom he often played chess at the Dublin Bread Company Tea Room. Griffith, he said, was a loyal Irishman who did not advocate violence, but believed that Irish freedom could be secured by peaceful means.

Those first weeks at home were the hardest I ever spent. Not only because of my sorrow at Pappa's illness, but because my conscience made me go against him. Although I tried to keep it from him, he soon learned that I was up to my neck in the revolutionary movement. His distress was harder to bear than any personal peril.

I remember how, when people came knocking on the door to see me, he would glower and angrily protest. One night a man came with an urgent message while we were at dinner celebrating the Jewish New Year. Pappa cried out loudly, "Can we not even eat this sacred meal in dignity and peace?"

I tried to soothe him, for I knew that the excitement was bad for him. But I stubbornly kept to my course; for I was convinced that only by physical force would Ireland ever gain her freedom. So was I forced to break our commandment to honor my father. In the torment of my conscience, I sometimes wondered if I loved Ireland more than I did my God.

When Pappa died in late November, 1917, it was a great sorrow. At the same time, there was a guilty sense of relief. Now I could devote myself completely to the cause to which I was so utterly committed with no clashing loyalties to distract me. Or so I thought.

I had begun my association with the Irish Independence movement the day after I landed at Kingstown. Eamon Martin's first step was to introduce me to some of the leaders of Fianna Eireann. These included Garry Houlihan, Liam Langley and several others, among them a man from Belfast named Padraig Ryan, and Hugo McNeil, later consul general in San Francisco. But the most important to me was Barney Mellows, Liam's brother.

Barney looked enough like his older brother to be his twin, and it was he who had engineered Liam's escape from England by a very simple ruse. He got permission to visit Liam, and for a brief moment had been alone with him. The brothers had quickly changed clothes. Liam walked out a free man leaving Barney in his place. Since there was no charge against Barney, except helping his brother to escape, he was in no danger of execution — the British were too just to do a thing like that.

Barney was, in fact, released not too much later. The first thing he did was to buy a new pipe. Settling back in the railway carriage, he carefully filled it, savoring in anticipation this longed-for smoke. Then he lit the pipe. The heavenly aroma of that first long drag so bemused him, that instead of the match, he hurled his pipe out of the open window of the train.

At first it was a question of whether these men of Fianna were prepared to give me their trust and confidence. They were just beginning what was known as the second phase of the revolution — the re-arming and reorganizing of the Volunteers. They had to be exquisitely careful. But I was with them a great deal, and from this constant association came friendship and then, formal acceptance.

I remember the day when they asked me if I would become associated with them. Very earnestly, I said, "Yes." Then they asked me to take the oath of allegiance to the Irish Republic. It was a very simple ceremony. Anyone in a responsible position could administer it. Raising my hand I said, "I, Robert Briscoe, do solemnly swear that I do not and shall not yield any voluntary support to any pretended government, authority or power within Ireland, hostile or inimical thereto; and I do further swear that to the best of my knowledge and ability I will support the Irish Republic, which is the Dáil Eireann, against all enemies, foreign or domestic; that I will bear true faith and allegiance to the same; and that I take this obligation freely without any mental reservation or purpose of evasion, so help me God!"

For all the lack of ceremony these words were to me the most solemn obligation I have ever undertaken. To uphold them I have been prepared to kill or be killed; to risk the lives of those dearest to me, and to sacrifice their happiness and security. I have even broken most of the Ten Commandments. But this I can say, I never broke my oath.

Now that I was a full-fledged member of Fianna Eireann, the question was how I could best serve. Since I had taken no part in the Easter Rising or any previous activities, I was unknown to the authorities. I could be very valuable to the movement because I could go about freely and unsuspected. It was decided that the best thing I could do was to provide an unofficial headquarters for Fianna's secret activities — of course there was a public headquarters which had to be kept free of suspicion.

Eamon Martin was a tailor by trade, so using my American capital we opened a small shop for manufacturing men's and boys' clothing at 9 Aston Quay, almost directly across the narrow Liffey from Lawlor Briscoe. We bought cloth in wholesale lots and engaged a crew of cutters and sewers. It will not surprise anyone that every member of our staff was in sympathy with the movement. Nevertheless, the girls at the sewing machines, the man at the cutting machine and the tailors working the presses or hand-stitching the garments on the upper floor had no idea of what was going on in the offices below.

Naturally most of the illicit activity took place at night when the premises were closed and empty. At first these consisted largely of planning meetings of the leaders, in which I took little part. It was the policy of all the revolutionary organizations to have their members know next to nothing about each other's activities. Except for the famous leaders we did not even know each other's real names.

I took the greatest care to learn as little as possible of my associates and their doings. For I did not know how resolute I could be under torture; but I could be sure that I would not blab what I did not know.

Eventually someone recognized Eamon Martin, and overnight he disappeared. I did not know whether he had been taken, or was just on the run. Shortly after the Terror started some months later, I was sitting alone in a pub when a Protestant minister sat down beside me. His hair was long and shiny black, as were his eyebrows and even the hair in his ears. The skin of him had a curious greenish pallor and he wore thick myopic glasses.

This weird man of God introduced himself to me as the Reverend Cardiff. When he spoke I knew Eamon by the wheeze and flutter of his collapsed lung. To my horror, I saw three Black and Tans at the bar turn towards us. Between set teeth, lips not moving, I said, "We're watched. For God's sake, clear."

Unctuously my parson observed, "It is a pity to see a good-looking young fellow like you drinking all afternoon. If you won't take my advice, all I can do is to leave you with my blessing."

He stood up and paced slowly out, pausing at the door to bow benignly.

Such were the tensions of the times and the excitement of laying down the foundations for future military activities that my memory of those days is like a badly cut cinema film made up of disconnected, sudden pictures of secret meetings in small smoky rooms; hurried dashes through familiar Dublin alleys made strange by danger; of quick trips to the country villages by train or rickety car to deliver arms to military commanders, who were lying hidden in small thatched-roof cottages, to satisfy the needs

53

of their brigades; and, with it all, the ridiculous episodes which set us roaring with laughter that eased the strain better than any pill.

The main thing we were trying to do was to accumulate a store of arms and ammunition for the next phase. Before the fighting started our best means of doing this was either to steal them or buy them from the enemy. The British garrison was lavishly equipped with everything from machine guns to the World War I hand-grenades known as Mills bombs. These were the shape of corrugated turkeys' eggs and about twice as big. Machine guns were very hard to come by, for obvious reasons, but the Tommies were willing to sell anything that might not be missed. They did a thriving trade in small caliber ammunition and Mills bombs.

Another source of supply were the Dublin Metropolitan Police. They were armed with revolvers and issued ammunition for target practice. Many of these upholders of law and order were on our side; and we did not even have to pay for the cartridges they slipped us.

Transporting the ammunition was the next problem. You could not go around with your pockets bulging with bullets, for all of us were stopped and searched many times. For some time I acted as a carrier, and well do I remember the cold sweat on my palms every time a soldier looked queerly at me.

In my capacity as delivery boy to the I.R.A. I established myself as an eccentric character with a passion for feeding the animals in the zoo. Each day at a certain hour I went there carrying a little workman's lunch box full of scraps — bananas, potatoes, lettuce, oranges and nuts — an assortment to please everything from a monkey to an elephant. Soon all the keepers knew me by sight. The British soldiers, and later the Black and Tans, on their days off, got used to the dim-witted Irishman who had nothing better to do than feed monkeys. They often smiled and chaffed me. But on certain days my little box had only a top layer of food and a heavy ballast of bullets contributed by my friends on the police force. On my way out I'd leave my box with a zoo employee who was a member of the I.R.A. The next day I'd pick it up empty.

Mrs. Andrew Woods had me beat as a carrier. She was a fresh-faced, energetic, very buxom woman about forty years old, who used to waddle down O'Connell Street at high noon, innocent as you please, with her bloomers full of Mills bombs. Heaven help any lad who made naughty advances to her!

The Woods family lived in a little house at 131 Morehampton Road in the Dublin suburb of Donnybrook. This was one of our arsenals. I remember one time Mary Woods had just come in with a fresh consignment of cartridges when the doorbell rang. Quick like a wink she popped them in the oven and answered the door. It was one of those gossipy old women who like to stand on the doorstep and chatter for hours. Mrs. Woods was making herself as agreeable as possible when she heard a sort of snap-crack in the kitchen. In a flash she knew somebody must have lighted that oven. Her luck was that the gossip was a little hard of hearing. *Pop, bang, crash* and a rattle of ironmongery! *Thunk, ratatatat.* The caller paused. "Is Mr. Woods beating carpets?" she asked.

"The good Lord knows what he's doing. I'd better see. If you'll excuse me . . ."

"Certainly," said the gossip graciously. "I well know how worrying it is when a man gets thumping around in your kitchen."

Mary Woods was quite a talker herself, but she never let slip a single secret or confidence. I never knew what Michael Collins had said to her, nor did he know what I had confided. She was a woman of great courage who believed ardently in our fight for freedom, as did her whole family. Tony, her eldest son, was imprisoned in Kilmainham Jail when he was only sixteen. The younger boys, Andy and Enda, and the two girls were all part of what you might call the Woods Brigade of the Irish Republican Army.

It was an extraordinary household. Everybody seemed to be happy no matter what the strain and stress. Mrs. Woods could deal efficiently with any situation. I remember the time some young fellows had been ordered to burn a railway cabin used by the military. They burned it all right, but one of them got covered with flaming petrol. He was carried to Mrs. Woods's home in the most dreadful condition. She comforted him like a mother; nursed him like an R.N.; and conveyed him secretly to a safe hiding place with never a sign that she knew he might have been followed by the Black and Tans to bring disaster on her house.

When Liam Mellows finally came back from America early in 1920 he stayed at the Woods's. His *nom de revolution* was Mr. Nolan, for by that time the Terror was on full force and he would have lasted about five minutes undisguised. Mrs. Woods fixed him up in a nice room with a double bed, which he hardly ever left by daylight. Many times I slept in it with him when circumstances made it unwise for me to go home.

The first time I did this I sleepily saw Mellows sneak out of bed early in the morning. Presently he came back carrying two plates. Then he suddenly got a funny, horrified expression on his face, and whirling on one foot like a ballet dancer, dashed out. I could not imagine what awful thing had happened.

When he came back he laughingly said, "I'd fixed you *bacon* and eggs for breakfast, and it suddenly hit me that you don't eat bacon. Here's a plain boiled egg."

One close call the Woodses had when the house was raided while Liam was there. The Black and Tans thundering on the door caught them all in the parlor. Upstairs in a space between the ceiling and the roof was a whole cache of guns, bombs and ammunition. Things were very tight.

Mellows was introduced as Mr. Nolan, a nephew of the proprietor of Nolan and Company, an old established firm in the wholesale butter business. The enemy took him at his face value; but were questioning the Woodses sharply, when there was a knock on the back door. A private opened it to a fair-haired, poetic-looking man named Sean Keating. Being a bit of a dreamer, Keating did not notice the danger signals.

"Come in. What do you want?" said the private.

"I want to see Mr. Woods."

"Just a minute."

Instead of Woods, the officer went to interview Keating. "What do you want with Mr. Woods?" he asked.

Keating finally caught on. Grasping at a straw, so to speak, he said, "I want to sell him a load of hay."

This was about as foolish as you could get, for Woods was a mechanic with a motor repair shop back of the house and a petrol pump in front of it.

Very suspicious, the officer returned to the parlor. "Do you know a Mr. Keating?"

"Never heard of him," said Woods.

"He told me he had business with you."

"What business?"

"To sell you hay."

Woods thought fast. He saw that unless he denied everything and threw Keating to the wolves, they would all be lost and the guns as well — at this point guns were more valuable than people.

"He's a bloody liar!" Woods roared. "What would I be wanting with hay?"

The logic was incontrovertible. Forgetting to search the house, the Black and Tans marched Keating off to Kilmainham Jail, where he stayed until the Truce. The guns were saved; but Sean Keating never lived it down. To this day we all call him, "Hay" Keating.

The beginning of the Terror came in April, 1918. Field Marshall Lord French, who had bungled in France, was sent over as Lord Lieutenant, and the garrison was beefed up. It was proposed to enforce conscription and "Johnny" French boasted, "If they leave me alone I can do what is necessary. If [the recruits] do not come in, we will fetch them."

In May, a whole bagful of Republican leaders were arrested and sent to jail in England, including Countess Markievicz, William Cosgrave, Arthur Griffith and de Valera. Michael Collins got away, and went on the run.

Meetings of any sort were forbidden. The police and military even broke up football games, hurling matches, boat races, and concerts by baton and bayonet charges. John Dillon of the moderate Parliamentary Party declared, "Ireland is lying under the unfettered tyranny of military government."

We struck back with a counter Terror. *An T-Oglach*, the secretly printed paper of the Volunteers declared: ". . . Anyone, civilian or soldier who assists . . . in this crime against us, merits no more consideration than wild beasts, and should be killed without mercy or hesitation as the opportunity offers."

There were now over a hundred thousand Volunteers. Of course, most of them were only armed with broomsticks, but those who had guns of any sort could do a lot of damage.

The ending of World War I in November, 1918, eased the situation a little. There was no more talk of conscription. Over forty-nine thousand Irishmen, who had voluntarily joined the British Army, had been killed. In the general election that followed the Armistice Sinn Fein won seventy-three out of one hundred five Irish seats in the British Parliament. These men had announced that they would refuse to take their seats at Westminster. Instead they proclaimed the Republic of Ireland. On January 21, 1919, the first Dáil Eireann met in the Mansion House. Only thirty-seven Republican deputies were present. The other thirty-six were in English jails, as was Sinn Fein's president, Eamon de Valera.

The first act of the Dáil was to vote Ireland's Declaration of Independence beginning: "Whereas the Irish people is by right a free people . . ."

On February 3, 1919, Harry Boland and Michael Collins engineered de Valera's escape from Lincoln Jail. After hiding out in England for a few weeks, de Valera returned to Ireland and was elected President of the Republic at a secret meeting of the Dáil.

During that year the power of the Republic steadily increased. The British held only the big cities where they maintained garrisons, and even in these they were subject to constant harassment — the bombing of installations and ambushes by flying columns. But despite the fact that we were waging guerrilla war, the Irish Republican Army, as the Volunteers now became known, held to the strictest discipline. No damage was done wantonly; no man was robbed or killed without reason and justice.

A fair-minded enemy, English Lieutenant General Sir Henry Lawson paid them this tribute, "The captains of Volunteers . . . must be considered to have a good deal of education (and) as a class were transparently sincere, single-minded idealists . . . (who) represented the best in the countryside. . . .

"They and their Volunteers were trained to discipline, they imbibed the military spirit, the sense of military honor . . . members of the I.R.A. acting under military orders — young men imbued with no personal feelings against their victims, with no crimes to their record, probably shedding blood for the first time in their lives . . . Behind their organization is the spirit of a nation . . . [which] believes that the I.R.A. are fighting for the cause of the Irish people."

The Republican Government even set up courts of law throughout the land. They had no legal means of enforcing their judgments, but the people obeyed them because they represented the laws of free Ireland. Even English litigants sought justice in our courts — and got it — because the British courts were powerless in the face of the revolt.

This wonderful discipline of the I.R.A. and the Irish people in a time of violence and near-anarchy was largely due to one man — Eamon de Valera. He had the indomitable determination of a Washington; the militant faith of St. Paul and the moral grandeur of the Prophet Elijah. It is remarkable that he also had a sense of humor which was noticeably lacking in the great men to whom I have truthfully compared him.

It was de Valera's leadership that kept the movement on a high plane. His firm insistence on justice and restraint; his determination that the Irish Revolution should not fall into the barbaric abuses to which uprisings are so prone, welded the whole loose structure of civil and military organizations into a single instrument pursuing a high purpose with utter dedication; meeting terror with violence and ruthlessness with equal ferocity, but never disintegrating into mere savagery.

For the Life of Me

Well do I remember my first meeting with the "Chief." It was shortly after de Valera escaped from Lincoln Jail that Eamon Martin asked me if I would like to meet him. This was the greatest honor that could be bestowed by the I.R.A., for Dev was the most wanted man in Ireland; his whereabouts the topmost of top secrets. To be allowed to meet him was the sign that I had won their complete confidence.

On a drizzly afternoon Martin took me to Brown and Nolan's Bookstore on Nassau Street, which had a fine library. We were browsing among the books when I noticed that a very tall man dressed all in black had come in. At first I took him for a priest, then recognized those strong somber features and brilliant gray eyes. Martin took me by the arm and we drifted over to where de Valera was examining a pile of books. In a whisper, he said, "Chief, this is Bob Briscoe of whom you have heard."

De Valera turned and looked down on me. Though I am not short, I felt small before him. He took my hand in a firm grip, and shook it silently. I was too awed to speak at all. Nor did I have to. Our eyes meeting for those few seconds said all that was needed; his the warm friendly look of a leader toward a trusted subordinate, mine a pledge of utter devotion to him and to the cause he served.

In the great events I have spoken of I only played a subordinate role. It was my part to accept the discipline, obey orders and never reason why. Despite my preoccupation with the revolution, my business managed to prosper. I was able to hire another workshop in Coppinger's Row, a narrow alley close by Dublin's main shopping center of Grafton Street. This second floor workroom, which was always deserted at night, became what was called "an unknown destination."

There was many a time when I received word that a certain person was suspected of activities against the Republic. Darkness comes early in the Irish winter. Between the fall of night and the British curfew, I took a car and driver, or a safe cab, and went to the place where the suspect lived. Sometimes I went alone; at others I had a companion. There I confronted him and ordered him to come with me. Occasionally I was armed, but more often my only weapon was my thumb stuck in the pocket of my coat like a concealed gun. People seldom tried to call my bluff.

I had the car with the shades down driven around a maze of streets and even out into the country to confuse him. Then my customer was unloaded, blindfolded, at Coppinger's Row, and taken upstairs to my tiny office to be questioned by my superiors. Very often he might turn out to be associating with our enemies in all innocence, in which case, since we did not hold with "guilt by association," he was let go. If he proved to be really guilty, he was subsequently dealt with as our enemies dealt with us.

There were other occasions on which I blindly followed orders not ever knowing why, though I might suspect. Such was the case of Richard Barton. Barton was a very brilliant detective sergeant of the Dublin Metropolitan Police, who knew a great deal about our activities, which were not the concern of the ordinary police. He received a very tempting offer to join the British Central Intelligence Division. In the C.I.D. he would be very dangerous to the Republican movement. He was warned not to accept, but did so anyway.

The next day I was ordered to give an impromptu party at Mother's house in Monkstown. I was told to invite people who were completely unconnected with the movement. The peculiar phase of the instructions was that the clock was to be set half an hour slow. I got up a gay party of girls and young men I knew, some of them student doctors. One of the innocents was an American, Doctor Kantorowitz. They came about four-thirty in the afternoon! At six, *by my clock*, when the party was going full blast with the Gramophone playing, friends unexpectedly appeared and said they hoped they were not late, and I pointed to the clock and remarked that it was only six. About seven o'clock people began to leave.

The next morning I read that Barton had been killed near College Green in the middle of Dublin at about six o'clock. *Verbum sap*. If anyone at my party had shot him, there were thirty innocent people who could swear that at six o'clock he was in Rathgar, three miles from College Green.

Quite often Coppinger's Row became a front-line dressing station. It was, of course, illegal for physicians to treat our wounded without reporting them to the authorities, but this law never stopped the Dublin doctors. I remember one night when a young fellow was carried groaning up the narrow stairs and laid out with a bullet through his leg. I jumped into a cab, and stopped at the first house with a doctor's sign. The brass plate read *Arthur Brooks, M.D.* Young Doctor Brooks did not seem in the least surprised when I said, "I'd like you to come with me to attend an injured man. I can't give you his name or address, but I'll take you there."

Brooks said, "Righty-o!" and picked up his kit.

I drove him around for a few moments with the shades of the cab drawn. Then I took him up to my office, where he went skillfully to work. When the wound was properly bandaged, I took Brooks home again by a roundabout route. He is now one of the leading physicians of Dublin, and charges proportionately high fees. He took no money for that night's work.

As the Republic grew stronger, the British increased their forces and their ruthlessness. Two special bands of irregulars were recruited in England and sent over to fight a counter-guerrilla war against us. One of these was the Auxiliary Police, largely made up of former British officers retired from England's great armies of World War I. The other was the notorious Black and Tans — so called because their uniform consisted of tan breeches and a black tunic and beret. They were recruited from the gangsters and gutter sweepings of England. The principal qualification for membership was ferocity.

The Black and Tans cared not whom they killed. Great lorries full of them roared through the narrow streets swaying with speed while pedestrians jumped into doorways or flattened themselves against the houses. The lorries would stop at some pub or hall suspected of harboring Republican sympathizers. The troopers would pour out of them and dash through the door arresting everybody inside. At the slightest excuse their Thompson submarine guns would open up, leaving the floor strewn with wounded and dead, and drenched with blood and beer.

Naturally we fought back. One way was ambushing the lorries on country roads or blowing them up with mines. Another was tossing Mills bombs into them from the windows under which they passed. This was so effective that tents of wire netting were put over the open lorries, which we then derisively called chicken coops.

Even in Dublin, British military installations were raided. In 1920, we pulled off one very amusing coup. A single officer used to ride on horseback from Dublin Castle to the general post office every morning for the official mail. One day we surrounded him and tied him up. One of us, who resembled him, was dressed in a replica of his uniform. He mounted the officer's charger and rode to the post office, where he collected the mail without question. After examining it, we dutifully forwarded it to the Lord Lieutenant. I would like to have seen Johnny French's face when he opened his letters stamped, "Passed by the I.R.A. Censor."

Fianna Headquarters were linked up with the Intelligence Department of the I.R.A., and since I was still unsuspected of being connected with them, I was able to do a certain amount of intelligence work. This consisted mainly of frequenting hotels and bars where the British Intelligence people or the Black and Tans congregated, and picking up stray bits of gossip. Sometimes I was merely a link in the chain of information, receiving a message while I was having my hair cut in a barbershop, and relaying it on to the proper quarters.

This was not particularly dangerous, but you had to be constantly on the alert. If you found that the enemy was getting suspicious of you or one of your friends, you had to be quick off the mark to change your habits and associates.

However, my main preoccupation was still acquiring arms and ammunition and distributing them to the I.R.A. brigades. It was very nervous work because of the constant searches of your person. Often when I had a stock of pistols or cartridges I would not be able to deliver them promptly. How I sweated until I finally got them to their proper destination! What troubled me most was not so much the fear of being caught with this contraband, as the danger of losing matériel that was so urgently needed.

I must have been particularly successful in these activities, for one day I received a message that Michael Collins himself wanted to see me. At this time Collins was theoretically finance minister of the Irish Republican Government, and was, in fact, the leading spirit of the Irish Republican Army. I was told that the interview was in regard to my being transferred from Fianna Eireann to G.H.Q. of the Irish Republican Army.

In the records of our Defense Department my service with Fianna Eireann is not listed as "active service," though there were times when it seemed downright frenetic; and, what with business, war and love, it was certainly schizophrenic. Now, I was to be the real thing. As a result of my meeting with Collins my personality parted like you'd part your hair. One of me remained Robert Briscoe, a small Jewish merchant of Dublin. The other became the notorious Captain Swift.

CHAPTER VII

Companion in Adventure

Now I must go back a little, for during these years I had acquired a partner in crime or, better still, a comrade in adventure — in short, a wife.

When first I came home from America I went frequently to the house of Pappa's old friend and drinking companion, Joseph Isaacs. When Mr. Isaacs had come from Edinburgh, Scotland, to take charge of the Dublin branch of B. Hyam, Clothiers, which he and his brothers had just then inherited from their father, the friendship between our families had begun. Though Mr. Isaacs, being bred in Scotland, was a Unionist and my father for Home Rule, they managed to differ on politics without becoming estranged, and they worked together as a team for the betterment of the Jewish Community. Soon they were as close as twins. These ties became even stronger when Mr. Isaacs's younger brother, Benjamin, married my sister Rachel.

I don't think I have mentioned that one of Mr. Isaacs's eight children was a daughter named Lillian. This is because I had not thought much about her. When I used to go to the Isaacs's fine house to play cricket with Maurice and Jack, she was a small, string bean of a girl with a flying banner of gold hair, who liked to play with us boys. Lily was a most gracious young girl, and her obedience to her brothers and to us was something to be astonished at. We included her in our team as a fielder, for she was a very useful adjunct. Occasionally she would demand her turn at bat, but this caused us very little annoyance as one good bowl usually settled Lily's innings, and she was back again fielding like nobody's business.

We also utilized Lily, who could run like a hare, to skin over the garden wall and pinch the neighbors' apples. Of course, we watched carefully from the safe side of the wall and told her when to run. I can still see her flying for her life with her skinny legs in black cotton stockings flashing like pistons.

The first faintly romantic passage between Lily and me came when Rachel and Ben invited us to visit them in their new home. Lily's recollection of the incident is more vivid than mine. She says, "I remember feeling quite bored one rainy day, wondering what we were to do, because always playing with boys made me anxious for something exciting. We decided to explore Uncle Ben's attic, which had nothing much in it but rolls of linoleum. However, I found a mouse in one of them, and leaped from one end of the roll to the other trying to catch it. Bob joined me in the hunt, and we had great fun until the mouse came dashing out of the roll and Bob stamped on it. He killed the mouse and nearly killed me as well, for his great boot came down on my foot.

"I think it was on that occasion, I began to take notice of Bob. Of course he was only sixteen — I was thirteen — but I thought he was a rather nice-looking boy."

For my part, I did not then take notice of Lily. Soon afterward, I went to Germany for two years; and then to America. It was when I came back in 1917 that I really saw Lily for the first time. She had grown tall and willowy, as we said then. Her ash-blond hair was piled up on her head, and with her straight nose, fair, rosy skin and bright blue eyes she looked like a heroine out of Sir Walter Scott's romantic novels. I annoyed her quite successfully by telling her she had the makings of a fine young woman.

From then on I saw a good deal of Lily — and of several other young ladies as well. My courtship, if you could call it that, since I had not made up my mind about her, took place in the intervals of my violent life as a member of the Fianna Eireann. Her wit and gaiety made her great fun to be with, but she seemed to me somewhat flighty. Being a very practical person, I wanted to be sure that when I took a companion for life, she would be a real companion; one who would be loyal, who would understand the difficulties of my position, and who would not run home to mother when the going was sticky.

I remember well the first serious talk I had with Lily. It was in the summer of 1918. We were going somewhere on top of one of our double-decked buses and looking down on the little rain-bright suburban gardens outside of Dublin. Lily told me that she was secretly troubled. Her two brothers were serving in the British Army in France, and she felt that she had not been doing her bit. She had taken a first-aid nursing course, and was on the verge of signing up to go overseas.

That set me back more than a little. Indeed, I could scarcely bear the thought of Lily over in the rough, muddy, shell-torn world of war. Even harder for me to accept was the idea of her in a British uniform; though I knew that all her family's loyalties were with England. I told her that she should not do it, and we got into a serious argument. She spoke of her brothers and of her sense of obligation of being actively on their side; of participating with them in England's greatest battle. I argued about her responsibility to the country of her birth. Without telling her how deeply I was committed to the cause of Ireland's freedom, I tried to show her that England's cause was not ours, and that to join with them was, in a sense, a betrayal of her natural loyalty. Speaking of these things which I believed in so passionately, I became eloquent with a violence of emotion which I attributed to patriotism, though looking back, I think that it was love. Certainly it was not my impassioned dialectic of Ireland's wrongs that won the argument. It was Lily's love for me which made her promise not to join up.

It was soon after this that I proposed to her. I did it in a cruelly casual way, for while I can express my love for Eire with true Gaelic flamboyance, I suddenly went tongue-tied and shy when I spoke of love to Lily.

We had been to the house of my Uncle Henry, whose daughter Annie was her close friend; and I was walking her home through a soft evening drizzle, when it came to my mind to speak. I said, "You know, Lily, there are two other girls I have been seeing, and people are beginning to talk about me and one of them. Don't you think it would be a good idea if we proved them wrong by getting engaged?"

Instead of slapping my lantern jaw as she had the right to do, Lily said, "Oh yes, Bob!" The darling had made up her mind long before, and nothing ever swerved her love thereafter.

She had plenty to test it, for the path of true love immediately got as rocky as a sheep trail in the Wicklow Hills. I left her at her front door, and she went in, all radiant, to find her father and mother waiting up. She told me they asked where she had been and she said, "I spent the evening with Annie. Bob Briscoe saw me home and proposed to me."

"What did you say?" they asked together like a well-rehearsed chorus.

"I agreed that I would like to marry him."

Mr. Isaacs's voice rasped with the Scot's burr which thickened when he was excited, as he said, "Well, he had better come and see me. *I* have something to say about this!"

Then as his choler took hold, he shot a series of furious questions at his daughter: "What sort of a position is that young man in? Does he think he'll be able to keep you as I have always kept you? Do you think you'll be happy if you haven't the ordinary comforts of life, let alone the luxuries you have here? Do you think this is what I planned for you?"

"Father," Lily said, "I haven't thought of anything at all but Bob. I want him, and I mean to marry him."

Considering the intimacy between our families it may seem surprising that Mr. Isaacs was so upset, but I could understand it. He was very rich, and somewhat socially ambitious. He had reason to hope that his lovely daughter would make a great match. I was surely no catch with my small uncertain business, and no family fortune to fall back on. But his reasons went deeper than that. For he was a red, white and blue Unionist and I a double-dyed green Sinn Feiner. Though he did not know how deeply I was involved in the movement, he had no doubts of where I stood.

Our meeting was highly unpleasant. He told me that he was deeply disappointed. That though I was the son of an old friend and he liked me personally, I had no money and no prospects; that Lily was a romantic fool, and I had no right to take advantage of her infatuation. My fast temper blazed out, and I made some ill-considered remarks. The upshot was that he told me he would do everything in his power to keep his daughter from marrying me. Which he did, and so did all his family.

Lily's Uncle Harry Isaacs in Edinburgh, who had no daughters of his own and loved her dearly, was perhaps even more upset. He offered Lily a trip around the world and ten thousand pounds outright if she would promise not to marry me. Lily gently but quickly turned this magnificent offer down. I had not thought I was worth so much to anyone.

Meanwhile the Isaacs imported a whole tribe of other suitors. I met one of these fellows one day, and I think I frightened him out of Ireland entirely, for he has not been back since.

Then Lily was taken on a nice tour of England and Wales. Quite by accident a young solicitor from Manchester whom the Isaacs knew happened to be staying at the same hotel. He proposed to Lily after three days. Apparently she made a fair comparison between this solicitor and myself, and had no hesitation in rejecting his offer.

There were others, including my own cousin Reuben, Uncle Henry's son. Reuben was really a nice kind of chap, somewhat simple if you like; and he was so fond of Lily, he used almost to be her lackey. Reuben had a notion that when he would say the word, Lily would succumb. I told him to keep off the grass; that I was going to marry her. He was very very agreeable and withdrew completely.

Soon he got engaged to a girl from Edinburgh. When she came to visit in Dublin, Reuben invited Lily and me to tea with them at Bewly's. "What do you think of my fiancée?" he asked Lily. "I selected her because she was so much like you."

His fiancée was not pleased.

Well may you imagine the stormy state I was in with all this going on at the same time I was carrying munitions around Dublin; taking people to "unknown destinations," and never knowing whether I'd have my head blown off or land in an English jail the next day. But Lily was staunch. There came a time, after nearly a year, when Lily told her father that if he would not consent to our marriage she would run off with me and get married in a registry office. Then Mr. Isaacs sent for me. I came into his office and found Reverend A. Goodansky there with him.

"Now as to this threat that you and my daughter will elope," Isaacs said. "I am a public man (he was a member of the Dublin Council), and I am a leading businessman. I cannot afford to be made a fool of. Now, since this situation is such that I cannot change it, I suppose I will have to be practical and agree to it. But I would like to settle with you what you expect in the form of a dowry."

"Well, what do you expect to give your daughter?" I asked.

"With you I would not give what I normally would expect to do with a suitable husband," he said. "But I am prepared to make the wedding, and I am prepared to give you a thousand pounds. This will enable you to furnish a house."

I took him up on that quickly. "I will accept on one condition," I said. "The condition being that on the morning of the wedding you will go to the bank and cash your check into one thousand one-pound notes."

"Yes," he said, "and then what?"

"You can stick them where the monkey stuck the nuts, one at a time!"

Like a flash Isaacs turned to the rabbi saying, "You are witness; you are a witness to this!"

Then for the first time in many months he cordially grasped my hand and said, "You're a boy after my own heart."

Lily told me later that he said to her, "I'll give you my blessing. Bob's an upright, fine type of young man. You'll have to make your lives the hard way, but perhaps that will be good for you. However, I've warned you so you will have no comeback."

Though things were better for a while, I seemed doomed to trouble with my father-in-law-elect. During the period of our engagement, the Dublin Corporation held its annual election. In those days both a Lord Mayor and a High Sheriff were elected by the councilors. Mr. Isaacs aspired to the latter office. If he should become High Sheriff, custom provided that he would give a large banquet for the Lord Lieutenant of Ireland — at that time Lord French. At the banquet it was usual for the Lord Lieutenant to knight the High Sheriff. My father-in-law-to-be pictured himself as Sir Joseph Isaacs.

However, he did not have quite enough votes in the Council. Sinn Fein had a few members including, William Cosgrave, who later became the first President of the Executive Council of the Irish Free State. Mr. Isaacs sent for me and asked if I would use my influence to swing the Sinn Fein votes to him.

Anxious to be helpful I got Eamon Martin, and together we canvassed the Sinn Fein councillors. Then I sent word to Mr. Isaacs that I had good news for him. He immediately invited Martin and myself to dinner, and a sumptuous meal he laid on. Over brandy and cigars we told him our news. Sinn Fein would support him on condition that he promise not to give a banquet for Lord French.

One minute and thirty seconds later we were out on the street, and the front door crashing shut behind us.

Despite all these flare-ups, the wedding finally took place on April 30, 1919, and a happy day it was, despite even Labor conspiring against us. Ordinarily it would have been held in the Shelbourne or some other large hotel, but on the chosen day there was a general shutdown by Labor. All the hotels were closed and there were no trains or boats leaving for anywhere. So it was held in the Isaacs's roomy house, and perhaps nicer that way. The leaders of the Jewish community were there, and, of course, all the members of both our families, who of themselves were a big crowd. There was an orchestra playing on a little balcony overhanging the hall, and a grand meal catered from Dublin.

Just for that day there was an unofficial truce in our war with England. Eamon Martin was my best man, and many "dangerous" rebels were among the guests. As for Lily, she was truly lovely in a white satin gown embroidered with seed pearls. She was so thin from worrying and working on the wedding that there seemed but a wisp of her enveloped in that gown, but her eyes were bright blue with the radiance of happiness.

This did not spoil her appetite. We Jews are supposed to fast until the marriage ceremony, and it was late in the afternoon before we sat down to our wedding breakfast. I have never seen a girl eat as hearty as Lily did. It made a man think.

Since no trains were running, or hotels open, my mother had found a place for us to spend the night at Kingstown. The next morning services were restored and we set off on our honeymoon. And who came down to the train to see us off? None other than my father-in-law! All the tensions between us forgotten, he was beaming and happy with a box of cigars for me and one hundred pounds in an envelope which he stuffed into Lily's hands saying, "Use it to enjoy yourselves."

Then, with a sense of humor like Pappa's, he went down the whole train telling the engine driver and all the passengers there was a bride and groom aboard, and they must take good care of us. As a result we had not a moment's peace with crowds of friendly Irish strangers coming to congratulate us.

I was much happier now that Lily had seen that her father had at last accepted me. From that day on he and I gradually became so great in friendship that I felt at times that I had taken the place in his affections which my own father had held.

We went to Glengariff near Ireland's southern tip, where we stayed at a country hotel overlooking Bantry Bay. It was a wonderful idyll in the very middle of the Troubled Times, like the still, sunny place in the eye of a hurricane. The countryside wore the exuberant brightness of an Irish spring than which nothing is ever so green and fresh. The calm, pale blue bay was dotted with so many small little islands that we could own an island for a day. Each morning we took a rowing boat with a luncheon basket packed by the hotel, and chose an island. There we would spend the whole day like Adam and Eve before the angel came to banish them from Eden. Indeed, Lily called it, "Paradise." I have never ceased to be thankful that she and I had those untroubled days.

For we were banished from our Eden, too. The "angel" was a boy from the post office with a telegram saying that Mother had been taken to a nursing home for a serious operation. So we packed up and left at once.

We had made no arrangements for a place to live. I confided that Mother, who was a director of Lawlor Briscoe and very capable, would have found us a place and furnished it before our return home. In fact, it was one of those things which in my family there was no need to discuss, we knew that something would be done to make us comfortable at the beginning of our married life.

However, this illness of my mother changed everything. We moved into her house at 181 Rathgar Road, and upon Lily was thrown the task of looking after everything — of me and my younger brothers and sisters, and of my mother when she came home. We lived there for over a year until shortly before our first child, Frances Joan, was born.

So Lily paid a heavy price for marrying me; nor did she guess how heavy it would be, for until we married I could not tell her of my part in the fight against England. I found I was a fool ever to have worried if Lily would be a good, loyal companion. She was staunch, and not sadly so, but gaily, taking the troubles as they came, and enjoying the good times and the laughter — for there was always laughter.

You see, the wives of the men who were fighting in this secret war had all the worries of soldiers' wives everywhere, and some that are not usual. For we could never tell them where we were going or what we were doing. Secrecy was necessary to protect both them and us, since, if they were taken and questioned rigorously by the soldiers they might break down and tell; but if they knew nothing and the British realized it, which they did, they would be left alone. So they could not have the solace of writing to us, or getting letters, except sometimes under cover; and sometimes a word spoken in the night, such as "Bob is well, and sends his love."

Often our house and my mother's too, were raided. I well remember the first time I was in a raid. It was on Bloody Sunday, the day in 1920 that the Black and Tans took their revenge for some spies we had executed, by firing on the crowd peacefully watching a football match in Croke Park in Dublin, and killing a dozen innocent people and wounding many more. The whole city was tense that day. I happened to be in my premises at 9 Ashton Quay, with my brothers Herbert and Wolfe, as the Tans came storming in. Knowing what I did, I was very humble and polite. But Herbert and Wolfe, who had no notion of what these premises were used for, were vociferously indignant. They complained bitterly while the soldiers searched the place, overturning everything. Finally Bert demanded their names and serial numbers. "I'm going to write to Lloyd George himself and tell him how you have behaved," he stormed.

One big trooper put his hand on top of Bert's bowler hat, and pushed it right down over his eyes and ears. "Write that to Lloyd George, too," he said.

Bert looked so comical I roared with laughter. Perhaps I was a bit hysterical with relief at the troopers going.

Most of the raids on my own home took place while I was away, the most rigorous during our civil war by fellow Irishmen. Lily took them as a matter of course, and did not allow them to frighten our small daughter.

Only if I was concerned did Lily become upset. One time, very early in the civil war, she was with me and our friends the Schulers from Germany, at my place of business on Ashton Quay,

74

when in came three detectives of the Free State force to raid the premises. They searched the place thoroughly and ended by arresting Schuler and me and marching us off to police headquarters. The two women were left in the wrecked offices with my faithful factotum Jamie, a pugnacious little fellow scarcely five feet tall. For once Lily's splendid nerve broke and she began crying hysterically, "I'll never see him again. What shall I do? What shall I do?"

By way of comforting her, little Jamie said fiercely, "Don't you worry, Mrs. Briscoe. I'll go down to the police station, and if I find Himself dead I'll have me revenge on them."

Sometimes, as I shall tell, Lily went on dangerous missions with me, nor did she ever lose her courage, no matter how great the peril. Occasionally her insouciance seemed downright feckless. There was a time when we were in England to carry dispatches to the I.R.A. underground there. These men were carrying the war into the enemy's country — blowing up railway bridges and docks, burning warehouses and rescuing Irishmen from British jails. The English took such happenings in Ireland as a matter of course, but not so in "this sceptered isle . . . this England." They hated the I.R.A. invaders with a special venom, and treated those who were caught with the utmost rigor.

Knowing that I might be searched, I gave the documents to Lily to put in her handbag, a large beaded affair that was then the style. We took the underground across London. Lily was carrying baby Joan and an umbrella. We were scarcely off the train when she gasped, "Good Lord, I left my handbag on the train!"

That scared me I can tell you. If ever the British read those dispatches, we would both be thrown in jail. In a blaze of fear and rage, I talked pretty roughly to her, I'm afraid. When I calmed down a little, I said, "There's only one thing to do — brazen it out! We'll have to go and claim it."

After a dreadful night of worry we went to the Lost and Found Department. Lily, with splendid nerve, calmly asked for the bag, and the official asked what train it was lost on. She told him and described it to him.

Then he asked the sixty-four million dollar question, "What were its contents?"

Lily prevaricated in that she did *not* say, "Dispatches for the Irish Republican Army." Instead she replied, "A compact, a change purse and a letter addressed to me at St. John's Wood."

The official produced the bag, glanced at the envelope of the letter, and handed it over without further examination. Thank God those English are so honest!

As you can see, from the day Lily married me she became as loyal to the cause I served as Dev himself. Sometimes I think I did wrong to subject a young girl to the precarious, anxious sort of life that my service in the Irish Republican Army entailed. But when I spoke of this to Lily not long ago, she answered, "With all its hardship and worry and danger, I would do it just the same again."

CHAPTER VIII

Dispatches and Diapers

THE winter of 1919-20 was the dead center of the Irish Revolution. The fighting was a stand-off, with British garrisons holding the large towns and British mercenaries like the Black and Tans roaring around the country in their great lorries killing indiscriminately. Frightfulness was their official policy. In Dublin itself the curfew imposed by the Castle emptied the streets at night. What happened thereafter has been well described by Erskine Childers:

> As the citizens go to bed, the barracks spring to life. Lorries, tanks and searchlight cars muster in fleets, lists of "objectives" are distributed . . . [and through] the pitch dark streets the weird cavalcades issue forth to the attack. Think of raiding a private house in the dead of night in a tank whose weird rumble and roar can be heard miles away . . . The "objectives" are held for the most part by women and children . . . thunder of knocks . . . [as the door is opened], in charge the soldiers — literally charge — with fixed bayonets and in full war kit. No warrant shown on entering; no apology on leaving, if, as in nine cases out of ten, suspicions prove groundless . . .

Meanwhile, we made things as unpleasant as possible for our enemies with sudden raids by our flying columns to surprise their country garrisons and capture arms; the burning of barracks; the blowing up of bridges, installations and supply trains; and the swift, secret executions of their spies.

However, it was a time of discouragement for the Irish people. Our envoy to the Versailles Peace Conference, Sean T. O'Kelly, had not only been unable to have the case for Irish independence brought before the Conference; but had even been refused a hearing by American President Woodrow Wilson, despite he was so concerned with the rights of small nations.

The Irish Republican Army was valiant but desperate. The little store of munitions they had built up during the phase of preparation was almost used up. They were in fact a shadow force, appearing and disappearing like the mists on magic Slievenamon Mountain. And they were frantic for arms to continue our fight for freedom.

I think it was in the depth of this winter that the tide began to turn. President Eamon de Valera of Dáil Eireann had sailed for the United States in May, 1919, hidden in a closet storeroom of the British liner *Lapland* and spirited ashore in New York by some of her Irish crewmen. He had a splendid reception there by great numbers of Americans of Irish descent, and in January, 1920, he launched the first external loan of the Irish Republic. Though these bonds were the obligations of a government-on-the-run whose officials were like hunted animals, our American sympathizers subscribed generously to these "securities." Their only guarantee was de Valera's word that, whenever and however a free Irish government came into being, the bonds would be redeemed. Eventually a total of five million eight hundred thousand dollars was subscribed by Americans.

Now leadership supplies the brains and morale of war, and brave men are its tempered instruments, but money is its lifeblood. This life-saving, economic transfusion revived the drooping tissues of the State; but it had to be transmuted into the means of action. The funds banked to the credit of the Irish Republic abroad would purchase arms; but these must still be brought through the British blockade.

It was at this time, in February, 1920, that I received word of my transfer from Fianna Eireann to the Headquarters of the Irish Republican Army; and the word that I was to meet Michael Collins. I learned later that my name was mentioned to Collins by Liam Mellows, and Collins must have made some inquiries about me, because out of the blue I was approached by a solicitor named Mr. J. Dixon, who told me that Collins wanted to see me.

This was a very tremendous thing to me, for in the absence of de Valera, Michael Collins was the most powerful man in Ireland. It is true that Arthur Griffith was Acting President of the Irish Republic, but he was a gentle, legalistic sort of man. Cathal Brugha was Minister of Defense, but he had not the power of Collins over the Army. Collins was Minister of Finance. He was also Director of Organization of the I.R.A., and Director of Intelligence. Beyond that he was President of the Irish Republican Brotherhood, which wielded an enormous, unseen influence. With the Chief in America, Michael Collins was the fighting leader of Ireland.

Our meeting was arranged in the cloak-and-dagger manner that was essential. On the chosen evening a messenger came to me who described himself as Collins's adjutant. Following his instructions, I went to the headquarters of the Gaelic League and asked for Mr. Sean O'Malley, who was its Secretary — I did not know that he also was a member of the I.R.A. Mr. O'Malley received me, and turned me over to another messenger. I followed this young lad, who brought me to a small hotel or lodging house in Gardiner Street. In its little, cold front sitting room I waited alone.

Suddenly the door flew open and there was Michael Collins. Though I had never met him, I would have known him anywhere; for he was the perfect picture of the mental image I had formed. Stocky, but swift moving, with a square, fighting Irish face, and a sort of jaunty swing to him; and that devil in his eyes. Though he was inconspicuously dressed as a bank clerk might be, there was no mistaking the quality of him.

He greeted me gruffly, with just one quick flash of his winning smile, and plumped down in a chair beside me. He wasted no time for there was none to spare; at any moment the premises might be raided. "You are now attached to G.H.Q." he said, "and you will take your orders from me and me only."

Then he told me I was to go to Germany to help secure arms for the I.R.A. He knew all about my knowledge of German and my commercial contacts in that country. He had the whole plan of operations worked out in his head, and his directions were clear, crisp and direct.

In Germany, I was to be the assistant and courier for John Dowling, who was already buying arms there. I was also to establish dumps of small arms at ports in Germany, Belgium and Holland. From these countries there were ships sailing for Irish ports, and also to Tilbury Docks in London and to Liverpool and Manchester. On all of these boats, or most of them, we had members of the I.R.A., who were willing to smuggle in small lots of revolvers and ammunition. They would call at my dumps and take whatever they thought they could handle.

"You must leave at once," Collins said. "The matter is most urgent. We've concocted a cover for you."

The cover was a firm to be called Kenny, Murray and Company, which would be established in Ballinasloe, County Galway. It would deal in imports and exports, the latter mainly Irish wool. Dixon, the solicitor, was to be a director, and I would be their foreign agent. I was to carry on a legitimate business for the firm, under my real name, which would give me an excuse to move around a lot. For the arms business I must take another name.

"You will be given five hundred pounds for your personal expenses," Collins told me. "That should be enough till we meet again. You must keep your personal accounts strictly separate from the large funds you'll be handling for the government. Now, how about your wife? Does she need support while you're away?"

"That she does," I said. "We have no outside income, and a new baby."

"Right," said Collins. "We'll allow her seven pounds a week."

I found out later that he had given me the maximum allowed to any member of the headquarters staff.

So it was all arranged in about forty minutes. Collins shook hands with that compelling warmth of his, and wished me luck. Then with a quick look around, he slipped through the door. I went home to tell Lily that I was going to be away for a long time.

In two weeks I was in Berlin, and different it was from the elegant, innocent, schmaltzy place I had known. For the gray sludge of defeat was spread over the land, and the eyes of the people were blank. But underneath this dreary monotone, the underworld seethed and churned and erupted through the crust in the horrible, frenetic night life of the post-war rich — the black-marketeers and the merchants of narcotics and sex. Thus, when defeat overturns society, the scum rises to the top; for national despair is the opportunity of the lawless.

It was my opportunity as well, for there were many willing tools to the hand that held a check book.

I must admit that our own people in Germany were also a weird lot. The representative of the I.R.A. was an American lawyer named John T. Ryan, who was known by the code name of Jetter. He had been mixed up in what the Americans called the German Plot, and fled to Mexico. The Irish Americans, who thought well of him, sent him fifty thousand dollars, to salve his hurts, and had him appointed our unofficial envoy to Berlin. It was in his office that I met my boss, John Dowling.

Dowling was an even odder fish. He had a forged American passport made out to James McGregor and we called him Mac. His idea of disguising his Irish nationality and appearing to be an American was to wear riding breeches and a five gallon hat. He would not have fooled a Bavarian shepherd.

My first job was to make connections — with merchants for my business cover; and with the German military underground. For the latter purpose, I assumed the swashbuckling name of Captain Swift.

The German military never quite give up hope — they are like the Irish in that. It was less than two years since Germany had been defeated. All her armed forces were disbanded and in accordance with the Treaty of Versailles, the Army and Navy had to destroy all military equipment under the supervision of the

Allied authorities. But the former army officers had a secret organization called the Orgesh, and the ex-naval officers had a similar thing. These people had secretly buried large stores of rifles, machine guns and ammunition, including captured British ammunition, against another *Tag*.

My business was to make contact with these ex-officers. It was not difficult, for they were in desperate straits, seeking any kind of jobs in order to exist. Through a business friend I found the ideal contact man — a gentleman named Major Hassenhauer, who was married to a titled lady of the Junkers class. I engaged Hassenhauer as my aide-de-camp, and agreed to pay him twenty pounds a week for the use of himself and his car. So great was his hatred of England, that I felt safe in confiding to him in detail the purpose of my mission. He was more than willing to help.

Now I had the means of meeting these bitter ex-officers. They were very anxious to deal with me, for they could use the money I paid for arms for the most needy in their organizations. Even the German Minister of Finance of those days, who had been a high-ranking officer, was a member of Orgesh, and I met him to discuss financial arrangements.

The arms were excellent. I bought large quantities of automatic pistols called Peter the Painters and also Parabellums. Both these guns could be had with detachable stocks which converted them into small rifles. I also bought considerable quantities of ammunition. Of course, I had to be sure it was not stale, so some of these officers took me to a secret place in a forest where we fired off lots picked at random. It was *not* stale.

Next I had to arrange to get these items into the hands of our merchant sailors. I had them shipped to warehouses in Hamburg, Bremen and Stettin. In these cities, Major Hassenhauer put me in touch with some sympathetic gentlemen who ran dockside saloons. For a fee and the chance to wipe an English eye they agreed to handle my wares and pass them on to the right people.

The problem now arose as to how the saloon keeper should know who his customers were. You could not have just anybody

walking in and asking for a load of lethal weapons. The Allied in-
spectors might get interested, and I was also alive to the fact that
the British Secret Service might be on my trail. I decided it was
time to go home, and co-ordinate the arrangements there, and also
to find out the needs of the different brigade commanders operating throughout Ireland so that the distribution of arms would
move as efficiently as possible.

I had one other reason for reporting to Collins. My long nose
quivered at the scent of something fishy about Dowling's operations.

A peaceful, rather humble, Jewish wool merchant had no difficulty in returning to Ireland via England. Whatever the British Secret Service knew about Captain Swift, they had no suspicion of Briscoe. Indeed, my race was a definite advantage in my
extracurricular career — a Jewish member of the I.R.A. was almost as improbable as a Jewish Lord Mayor of Dublin.

Lily and the baby, Joan, were well, and very happy when I
bolted in from the blue. Dublin was the same, only more so, for
the British were intensifying their campaign of terror.

Shortly after I arrived, I reported to Collins in that same dreary
little hotel on Gardiner Street. He questioned me keenly about my
work, impressing me with his extraordinary memory for detail. I
explained my difficulty about the delivery of arms.

Collins solved that quickly. "It is quite easy," he said. "You will
take some blank visiting cards and write anything on them you
please. Then tear them in half. I'll see to it, that our people who
make the pick-ups get half a card and you give the other halves
to your saloon keepers. They'll be fairly safe, since they only
need deliver arms to somebody who produces a torn visiting
card."

The simplicity of this was like genius; and it worked perfectly,
after I added the touch of numbering each half card.

Then, Collins asked about Dowling, and I gave him my impression of the man which was not flattering to his intelligence.

"We are looking into it," said Collins.

For the Life of Me

My immediate mission was to visit brigade commanders to ascertain their special needs. It was no use sending a brigadier a lot of 7.9 mm. ammunition if his men were mostly armed with .45 caliber revolvers. "We especially want information as to the arms situation in the Galway Brigade," Collins said. "It will be natural for you to go there since Kenny, Murray operates from Ballinasloe."

"Fine," I said. "How do I find the brigadier?"

"I'll give you a dispatch for him explaining your position, but for God's sake don't get caught with it. You go to Ballinasloe by train. There you hire a taxi and go through Ahasacragh to a place called Ballygar in County Roscommon. You needn't worry. You'll be contacted and given further instructions."

It was all very well for Collins to tell me not to worry, but British security was very tight, and I knew that I would be searched. I decided to take Lily and Joan along as cover, and consulted with my wife as to where to conceal Collins's dispatch.

"We'll hide it in Joan's diapers," Lily said. "No Englishman would undress a girl baby, whatever they may do to us."

So it was done. Sure enough, at a little country station the train ground to a stop between two lines of British soldiers. All the passengers were ordered out to be searched, while other soldiers searched the train. Of course, the train crew was on our side, and they hampered the soldiers as much as possible by starting a terrific row, howling and roaring about this terrible delay, and making insulting remarks. The soldiers were trying to do the job as best they could in the quickest possible time.

They finally came to us, and searched us thoroughly, while one young private politely held the baby. Lily was quite right about the gallantry of the British. Joan was not searched.

When we got to Ballinasloe, I called the offices of Kenny, Murray. Both Kenny and Murray came over to have tea with us at the country hotel, and while we stuffed ourselves with good strong tea and scones, they sent for a hackney car, as they call a taxi in those parts.

Dispatches and Diapers

As we all came out of the hotel together, I saw trouble. Our taxi was there all right, but in front of it was parked a big olive drab lorry full of constabulary and behind it another full of British Auxiliaries. This was more attention than I deserved or desired. But I said to myself, "Well, we must proceed."

A constable asked me where we were going, and I told him "To Ballygar on business." Then with Lily carrying Joan, we got into the taxi and started off. Most uncomfortable we were, with one lorry in front of us and one in back, as we churned slowly along the narrow country roads until we got to Ahasacragh. At the crossroads there, the front lorry stopped blocking us completely. Both the constabulary and auxiliaries tumbled out, and questioned me sharply. What was my business in a small place like Ballygar? Who was I going to see?

I had my answer ready. I was going to see a man named Nicholas Hughes who had a butcher shop in Ballygar. He was also a big buyer and seller of wool, and a director of Kenny, Murray. It was a good straight story, and they so took it. Both lorries went off down the crossroad.

I was rather jumpy and said to Lily, "Let's take our time starting off. They may come back."

At this point a countryman, who had been leaning on a pitchfork behind a hedge watching the proceedings, shambled across the road and said, like you'd pass the time of day, "The meeting will be in the bakery house at Ballygar at twelve o'clock tonight."

"Who are you?" I snapped, nervously.

He pulled out a picture of me. "I was told to expect this man," he said. "You are to be at the bakery at midnight."

Then he shuffled back to the hayfield.

In Ballygar we drove straight to Nicholas Hughes' butcher shop. He lived over the premises — and still does. When he heard the car, he came tearing down to greet me, and then pulled up in embarrassment. "If I'd known the missus was with you, Bob, I wouldn't have come down undressed."

Though fully clothed, he had come down without putting on

his stiff white collar, and in his sweet, simple country way feared that Lily might think it disrespectful. She still laughs affectionately about it.

We went up to Hughes' apartment and, after a bit, Kenney came over from Ballinasloe. Then we took a walk down the main street of Ballygar. As we strolled along I said to Hughes, "This looks like a thriving little town; how many shops are there?"

"Thirty-two, I think."

"And all of them pubs," I teased.

Hughes stoutly defended his village. "Not at all!" he said. "Only eighteen of them are pubs."

Then he added, "We've a fine chemist shop. Do you need any toothpaste or hair oil or anything from a chemist?"

"No, I don't," I replied.

"Sure you do," he said slyly. "You'd better buy some toothpaste."

In my circumstances you didn't argue about things like that. I went in to the chemist, who asked what I wanted.

"Toothpaste," I said.

"Yes, toothpaste. The brigadier and the flying column will be here at twelve o'clock. Did you get the message?"

"Yes," I said.

I took my little bit of toothpaste, had my tea, and waited then for the night to come.

The whole town was in this thing. After dark a young, round-faced priest came calling. He said he wanted to meet this distinguished traveler from Germany. He remained for quite a time, and finally told me that he feared the police might want to question me. "I'll raise a row to draw them off," he said.

The priest went down the street to the police station, which was, of course, in those days, barricaded, with iron shutters pulled down over the windows. He pounded on the door, and through the open window we could hear him complaining at the top of his voice that, "People are stealing my turf! And what are the police doing that ye are not protecting and minding people from thieves and rogues?"

We could hear the constables trying to pacify him, and the priest roaring out his woes.

He did not entirely succeed in taking their minds off me; for peeking out of the window I saw two policemen posted across the street. At eleven o'clock, we put out all the lights and sat in the dark. After a bit the constables went away.

At midnight, I poked my nose cautiously out of the door. The little street was pitch black and, as far as I could see, totally deserted. Trying to walk softly over the cobbles I stole along to the bakery and slid through the door.

I came into a big large room with the fine fragrance of new bread hanging in the air. It was dimly lighted, and around a white deal table sat ten or a dozen men, with pistols in holsters belted around their waists. Against the wall I saw a glint of stacked rifles. This was the headquarters of the Galway Flying Column — for tonight at least.

The brigadier and his staff told me what arms his men had, and their make; the number of machine guns and 303 rifles, the number and types of revolvers. Some of them were armed with guns like blunderbusses — muzzle-loading shotguns. They begged me to try to get them ammunition to suit each type of arm — a very difficult job.

After I had got the information and estimated the position, as I saw it, we talked and talked. Not about the fighting, but of all sorts of things. Somehow we got talking about the different races of mankind and the lad who had served me in the chemist shop brought up the question of what people had the greatest numbers. I told him I thought the Chinese, and he said it was the Jews.

"That's not true," I said.

"How do you know?"

"I happen to be a Jew."

A broad grin spread over his face. "Don't try to pull the leg of a poor country lad," he said. "You're no Jew."

I asked then, "Have you ever met any Jews?"

"That I haven't," he answered. "But I know what they're like, and you're not him."

There was no convincing him. He was the simple type of country fellow who was ready to do everything, even to giving up his life, in the struggle for Ireland's freedom. He told me to stop codding him. "I have no time for jokes," he said. "Only for to be serious."

Soon I sneaked back to Hughes's place, but not to sleep. During the night there was a good deal of noise, for the I.R.A. had been ordered to distract attention from Ballygar. They did so by blowing up houses in the country round about that might be occupied by enemy troops. In neighboring towns, business houses that sold tickets for emigration to America were destroyed on general principles. Sure it is that Ireland's trouble still is her best people leaving her; but our government no longer takes this means of discouraging emigration. Whatever, we were kept awake all night by the distant thud and shudder of explosions, and the circle of the horizon was red with flames.

In the morning the hackney car came to take us to the station at Ballinasloe. We cut it fine so as not to be left hanging around on the platform. In fact we calculated too close, and had to make a dash at full speed with the rickety old car bounding over the rocky roads seeming about to fall apart. It held up, but to Lily's horror we ran down a small young donkey, and had no time to see if it was badly hurt or even killed. At least it was our only casualty.

Another brigadier I talked with was Seamus Robinson. Seamus had come from Scotland to join us in 1916. He was arrested when the Easter Rising failed, and sent to an English jail. As soon as he was released, he came back to Ireland, and organized the Tipperary Division, which he commanded. He and I have been lifelong friends.

Robinson came to me unauthorized by G.H.Q., if you like. Because he was very disgusted at not receiving sufficient support from headquarters he decided to try to organize his own supply. He was so keen and anxious to get going at a faster rate that he repeatedly attempted to seduce me from my allegiance to G.H.Q., and get me to operate with his division alone. Later he actually sent two of his officers to Germany, who spent their time sitting around in cafés talking to waiters and using up what little money Seamus had been able to raise locally. I tried to help them, but they were never able to develop anything. At Seamus's request I finally sent these gentlemen home.

I went to many other parts of the country to talk to the local commanders, both on this and other trips home. Indeed, I had almost to commute between Germany, England and Ireland. I was always nervous about these expeditions to the country, but I must say the I.R.A. made special efforts for my security and would themselves take great risks to keep me safe. But it was not possible to plan ahead how you would meet danger if it developed. You had to think from incident to incident, from day to day, from meeting to meeting.

One time I was staying at St. Andrew's Hotel in Dublin. Lily and Joanie were with me. There were three Black and Tan officers at the hotel. One of them was a Major Lee, who had discovered a way to break our code. The others were his body guards. In the evening, during the curfew, when everyone had to stay inside, they were at me the whole time, trying to catch me up. One night Lee said to me, "We got Collins tonight. It was a terrific fight but we got him."

I kept my face blank, and said, "I don't know who you mean."

"Oh come, you must know Michael Collins. If not, you must know about him."

I just looked as stupid as I could, and hoped they were lying. Of course they were, with the intention of trapping me.

Nevertheless, Major Lee was not a bad fellow. Once I saw him object to the very rough treatment a civilian in the street had received from some auxiliaries. I heard one of these men mutter, "I don't care who Lee is, we'll do our business the way we want to, and if necessary, we'll take care of him!"

Later, when I got back to Germany, I heard that Lee had been shot dead in the streets of Dublin. I promptly wrote to the *Irish Independent* stating my belief that he had not been shot by the I.R.A., but by his own auxiliary comrades, because he had tried to curb their brutality.

Of course, sometimes Azrael hovered over you and you never even heard the wind in his wings. I learned of one such occasion only after I began to write this book, from the following letter:

To Mayor Bob Briscoe: 30th July, 1957

DEAR BOB,

Some time ago I read in the *Irish Times*, I think, you were contemplating writing your autobiography, so I thought I might be able to help. Doubtless you will recall your first visit to West Waterford on 9 June 1921 before the Truce. You came down to see Pax Whelan about the proposed landing of arms. When you arrived in Waterford, Pax was absent attending to some meeting near Mallow with Liam Lynch and other Southern Brigade O.C.'s. The O.C. Second Battalion, the late Thomas Reeckin, or it could have been his adjutant, sent me a dispatch that he had contacts with you in or around Kilmacthomas. The letter was to the effect that he had contacts with a foreign-looking gentleman most likely a super-spy, who was desperately anxious to contact Brigade H.Q. I sent back word to the Second Battalion that you should be brought along so that we might find out what was in the wind.

That was how you eventually presented yourself at Brigade H.Q., then located in the woods at Cappagh between Dungarvan and Cappoquin. I was brigade adjutant at the time, and, under interrogation, you informed me that you were acting on a secret and important mission for G.H.Q., the nature of which could be disclosed to the Brigade O.C. only — no other officer. I questioned you closely and indeed aggressively because I believed you to be temporising and stalling.

In the early part of our talk I remember I excused myself while I slipped out to the guards and informed them to be ready for the execution of a spy. I was certain you had come to find out all about our lines of communication and that to cover up you were being artful to asking for the absent O.C. Pax Whelan. I felt sure that had Pax been present you would have worked another line in the form of some other plausible story.

Yes, Bob, you came as close as makes no difference that day to being shot out of hand, because once I had seen you after what I had heard about you from the Second Battalion, I felt you were only acting when you stated that your business could be disclosed to Pax and to no other. I decided then and there to waste no more time questioning you. That is why I slipped out to fix your execution.

The guards were sent off to pick a suitable and handy place to dump your body, and your luck lay in the fact that it took them half an hour in place of minutes to make the choice. By the time they returned to give me the O.K. you had then, *and only then,* convinced me that after all you might be bona fide. Had the guards been less leisurely it was my idea on their return to entice you out on some pretext just a short distance and to shoot you through the back of the neck as we walked along.

I have been in Kilkenny for the past fifteen years, the Dispensary M.O. here; married, very happy. Pax Whelan's son Donald is on the Waterford team, playing right wing forward full and you can see him in action in the All Ireland Hurling Final.

That is about all. I hope you and yours are fit and well.

Yours very sincerely,
BEN McCARTHY

CHAPTER IX

Saving the Soul of Charley McGuiness

WHAT with one thing and another it was quite a relief to get back to Germany. Lily begged hard to go with me and on my next trip I brought her and Joanie over. I had two reasons for this. First because I wanted them with me so much and knew that they were really safer there than in Ireland; and secondly, because they made such a good cover. There is something so dull, solid and respectable about a man settled down with a wife and child that people are not at all apt to think he is up to terrible subversive activities.

We took a room in a pleasant pension where I had the facilities of the telephone, and a sitting-room where I could receive people quietly. It was a very central location just off the Kurferstendam. I also had arranged so I could always get a room at the Crown Prince Hotel in Hamburg, close by the railway station. It was convenient and very pleasant, for as a result of my frequent trips all the staff knew me. Lily and Joanie often went with me to Hamburg. On these occasions I went in the ordinary way by train, and openly conducted the affairs of Kenny, Murray.

However, when on the business of Captain Swift I took certain precautions. I'd go to the station, book my ticket through and take the train. I'd slip off it at Spandau, just outside of Berlin, where Hassenhauer would meet me with the car, and take me wherever I wanted to go. Thus, if I had a shadow, I would lose him. Even if he saw me leave the train, he could not likely find transport in a hurry at Spandau.

Shortly after my return to Germany, Dick Kenny arrived as a courier from Collins ordering me to take over from Dowling and investigate him. Collins had already told me that Dowling was paying out large sums of money with no results whatever. If I decided that he had been dishonest, he was to be returned to Ireland for trial and execution.

Dowling made no resistance to the order. In fact, he seemed downright relieved to be rid of the responsibility. He told me quite frankly about his transactions. He had been negotiating with a man named Jergens, who, he said, dealt in wholesale groceries, mainly butter and margarine — a German butter-and-egg man. But Jergens was also an ex-naval officer who claimed to be able to supply a large quantity of munitions and a ship to transport them to the west coast of Ireland.

Dowling had made inquiries which substantiated this story. He had then posted a deposit of twenty thousand pounds of I.R.A. money to get the deal started. That was some time before. Now Jergens had become evasive, and complained that Dowling was being "tiresome."

I decided that Dowling was probably not dishonest — just a sucker who had been taken in by a new sort of confidence game. So I said to him, "I'll not take action against you yet, but I will have to check your story. Will you agree to remain as my prisoner in Hassenhauer's apartment while I look into this?"

"Gladly," said Dowling.

We locked him up in the bathroom of Hassenhauer's flat for several days while I made inquiries. I learned that Jergens was in Hamburg, and decided that we would go down there to confront him. My squad consisted of Kenny, Dowling and a remarkably rugged individual who had just joined us from Ireland named Charley McGuiness, of whom much more later.

In Hamburg we conferred with Doctor Schuler, a lawyer who had been highly recommended to us. He listened attentively while I told him the whole story. Then he gave us his opinion, "You have no chance of recovering this money at law. It is illegal in Germany to deal in arms, as you well know, particularly for the purpose for which you want them. If you start a suit it will be thrown out of court. You will have to adopt extra-legal methods. First let me find out about this Jergens."

The next day Schuler reported that Jergens was a black-marketeer. He lived an openly opulent life with a magnificent motor car and a splendid villa. He was, in fact, extremely ostentatious in a country ruined by war and defeat. Schuler called him a *shieber* — a fellow who promotes all sorts of transactions, legal or otherwise, and is willing to take fantastic risks to make a fast mark.

"I advise you to use strong methods," Schuler concluded.

It was advice right after my own heart.

Schuler asked Jergens to come to his office one Friday afternoon, "to meet a client from abroad." The *shieber* fell into the trap. After a few moments Schuler made an excuse to leave him alone. The next thing he knew my four-man commando burst through the door. Jergens was sitting beside the desk; a magnificently built man, over six feet tall and beautifully dressed. When he saw us, his handsome face turned olive-green.

Though I knew he spoke English, I addressed him in German. Speaking in a guttural growl, I said, "We are members of the I.R.A. Dowling here is under arrest and will be sent home and probably executed. As for you, we want our money back!"

Jergens pulled himself together and tried to reason with us, but he kept nervously watching Charley McGuiness, who had the build of a gorilla.

"Gentlemen, gentlemen," said Jergens, "this deal is absolutely above-board. Will you let me prove it by taking you to see where the arms are stored!"

"We'll do no such thing," I answered. "Are you going to pay us the money?"

Jergens hesitated, switching his eyes from Charley to me and back.

"All right, gentlemen, get ready!" I said.

Kenny and McGuiness both produced automatics and pointed them at Jergens.

"Now, look you," I said. "Nobody knows we're here. We are going to shoot you and leave you lay. Your body won't be found until Monday morning, and nobody will know what happened except Doctor Schuler, who has a good story to tell of having left you here to meet an unknown contact at your request. So you . . ."

At that point I was interrupted by a resounding crash. Jergens had fallen off his chair in a dead faint!

For once I was confronted with a situation I couldn't deal with. I tested Jergens ungently with my boot. He was not shamming. Then I dashed to consult Schuler, who was in another office: "He's fainted, what do I do now?"

"Don't let it worry you," the lawyer said. "Take this pitcher of water and throw it over him."

I went back and emptied the water on the prostrate profiteer, who came to, spluttering. We propped him up in the chair and continued the discussion. He was very cooperative. We figured out how much twenty thousand pounds was in marks — it came to billions — and he drew us a check for it. I told the boys to hold him, and took the check in to Schuler.

"This won't do," he said. "It's probably good, but the banks are closed by now. I'll draw up a document for him to sign."

He hastily drafted a paper in which Jergens admitted receiving the deposit of twenty thousand pounds for the purchase of arms. That would at least put him in an illegal position. Jergens was so upset at being left alone with McGuiness and Kenny that he could hardly hold a pen, but he signed. Then we let him go.

Doctor Schuler was a very astute lawyer indeed. He started a suit against Jergens immediately, and got a judge he knew to put it on the calendar for the following morning. A subpoena was served on Jergens that night.

Early the next morning, Schuler lodged the check at his bank, and asked them to get cash for it as quickly as possible. Then we all went to court. Dowling was prepared to admit everything, including his forged passport, as Schuler felt that honesty was our best chance. In the somber, dirty-windowed courtroom our names were called, and Schuler replied that we were present. Then Jergens's name rang out. I saw him sitting in the back of the room, but he did not answer. Again the bailiff shouted, "Herr Jergens!" Still our man sat quiet as a frightened mouse.

The court then accepted Schuler's plea to make the agreement a rule of the court. Nor was Jergens's check stopped. We got every shilling of our money back. It is in my mind that the poor fellow thought it worth twenty thousand pounds to be rid of us.

It was just before this that our little company was reinforced by Charles McGuiness, master mariner. The dribs and drabs of arms we were sending over were not enough, and we had decided to buy a ship or two. Captain McGuiness reported to command our merchant marine. The sealed orders he brought me from Liam Mellows were most peculiar. In them I was instructed that McGuiness had an anchor tatooed on the back of his left hand and a ring worked on the fourth finger. Since these marks were known to the British Secret Service I must have them removed.

I was further informed that though McGuiness was a Catholic, he had not been to confession for fourteen years, during which time he had committed just about every sin in the calendar. Since he was to command a desperate undertaking, Mellows ordered me not to send him into danger until he had absolution.

I was to see to it that he was put in a state of grace.

Sure this was a strange assignment for me, but it was typical of the devout and devoted leaders of the Irish Revolution. They thought nothing at all of risking a man's neck; but under no circumstances would they endanger his immortal soul.

Mellows also warned me that I must handle McGuiness gently for he had a terrible quick temper; but if once I won his confidence, he would stop at nothing to help me.

Charley McGuiness was, in fact, the toughest character I have ever met. He was a short, barrel-chested, wide-shouldered man, who always walked with his elbows out and his hands up ready for a fight. He had a big, baldish head and a great fleshy face that was scored and burned by the winds of all the oceans. The tattoo on his hand was nothing. When naked he was spectacular. From the soles of his feet to his neck he was a picture gallery, with everything from mermaids to alligators. Just to show you the kind of man he was I will tell you one anecdote.

Charley and I were in a dockside saloon in Hamburg frequented by sailors of all nationalities. I saw a man come in who looked familiar, and stared at him. There were four Swedish sailors at a nearby table, one of whom thought I was staring at him and took offense. He came over to us in a very belligerent way. It looked like a roughhouse might develop, but I explained civilly that I was looking at another man altogether. McGuiness helped placate the Swede and when he left peacefully, Charley expressed himself as being happy that he had helped avert trouble.

After a bit Charley finished his wine, stood up and went over to those four Swedes. He tapped one of them on the shoulder and said, "Well, gentlemen, if it's trouble you're wanting, I am willing to oblige."

Waiting for no more than the look of amazement on their faces, he knocked his man off his chair. The other three were up like a flash, and the fight was on. While I was still wondering whether to risk breaking security by helping Charley, he knocked down the other three Swedes. They were spread like a starfish around the table. Looking down at them, Charley said, "Now, gentlemen, I think we understand each other. Good afternoon."

You may imagine how worried I was about carrying out Mellows's orders with a character like this. I consulted a number of German doctors about removing the tattooed anchor. None of them gave me much help until finally, in Hamburg, I discovered one who was sufficiently shady for me to confide in. This chap examined McGuiness, and stated that he could do the job; but he pointed out that to do it properly, he would have to cut most of the skin off the back of the hand, as you'd cut a pattern from a piece of cloth. This would be very painful as he had no means of giving a proper anaesthetic, and a local would not help much.

With no hesitation Charley said, "Get on with it!"

We made an appointment for the next morning. McGuiness was as carefree as though he were going to a bar for a drink. In the horrid little surgery, Charley was laid out on a couch. The one cheerful appurtenance was a very pretty nurse. She stood on one side of the couch dabbing with iodine, while the doctor was making his incision and cutting off the skin.

Sitting in a chair in that little hot room, listening to the grizzily sound of scissors cutting flesh and tissue, I felt like vomiting, but Charley gave no indication of suffering. Right in the middle of the operation he winked at me and gestured with his head. I looked around, and found that he was caressing the nurse's legs under her skirt with his free hand, and evidently enjoying this counter-operation.

The doctor finished up by pulling the flaps of skin loosely together and sewing them up, leaving a straight, puckered scar down the middle of Charley's hand. The bit taken away from his finger was left to heal itself.

On the way back to our hotel, Charley seemed very irritable —he must have been in great pain. He got it into his head that the chauffeur was taking us a long way round. "We'll not let the —— think we're fools," he said. And without any further discussion, he put his right fist through the glass partition behind the driver's head.

As a result of this, I had to take him back to the doctor, for his right arm was torn from knuckles to elbow. Then with *both* hands heavily bandaged, I brought him back to the hotel to lie up and cure himself for the work ahead.

Saving the Soul of Charley McGuiness

McGuiness was primarily concerned with ships. He was not only to command one, but to be my adviser for the examination and selection of vessels to meet our purpose. I had already made contact with a Captain Brauner, a German ex-naval and merchant marine officer, who was now a ship's broker and chandler with an office in Bremen. Brauner slept in a bunk in his office, which was fixed up like the captain's quarters of a ship. He was a queer, gaunt, cadaverous-looking man. McGuiness did not like the looks of him, but I must say he proved more than trustworthy. He kept his business with us absolutely secret.

By now I had acquired sufficient stock of munitions to fill a small boat. We told Brauner what we wanted, and he came up with an ideal vessel. She was a small trawler, with a large fish well in her bottom under the deck boards, which could be filled with rifles, revolvers and ammunition, and still leave room for her crew and the stores necessary for a voyage from Bremen to Ireland. Her name was *Anita*. McGuiness fell in love with her. The price was comparatively low because of the advantageous rate of exchange between pounds and marks, so I bought her.

We wasted no time. Charley signed on a crew and brought *Anita* around to the Free Port of Hamburg. Goods could be sent by rail or canal boat to the Free Port from all over Germany; and then shipped abroad without customs inspection. I had taken part of a warehouse there and filled it with munitions of all sorts. *Anita* was brought alongside the quay close by this warehouse, and we loaded her until she lay deep in the water with arms and ammunition.

In a matter of hours, she was ready to start down the river to Bremen which would be her port of exit. I was standing on the dock, and Charley was just going aboard, when down on us like green divils came the Gippo — the green-coated, black-helmeted police of those days. They swarmed all over *Anita*, blowing whistles and yelling — especially when they found the guns.

Charley and the crew were loaded into a big black paddy wagon and carted off to jail. Nobody spoke to me. I must have looked like the innocent bystander.

Though I was free to go, I was badly worried. There must have been some slip, the Gippo probably had been tipped off by the British C.I.D. Meanwhile, all our work was lost, the arms gone and *Anita*, too. And poor Charley maybe sentenced to jail for years. I was determined at least to save Charley.

Back to Doctor Schuler's little office, where we had held up Jergens, I went. When the lawyer saw me, he said, "Have you been taken again?"

"By the police," I answered. "We're in real trouble this time." And I told him my story.

Schuler was a man of infinite resource. He immediately propounded one of his extra-legal schemes to rescue Charley. "I think we can get him out," he said. "You must pose as the Irish Republican consul in Hamburg. I think you can get away with it. We Germans are rather sympathetic to your cause, and won't ask many questions. Then we'll get him a quick trial."

I put on my best dark suit and my most pompous manners and went to the jail. An authoritative manner went a long way in a country as chaotic as post-war Germany where nobody was sure at all who would be who tomorrow. The officials were positively deferential. They took me down to a great stone barn of a room which had two big iron cages full of prisoners — men on one side, women on the other. It was like a scene from Hogarth, with doxies and filchers having a great time yelling bawdy remarks at each other from their cages.

Waving my turnkey back, I went up to the men's cage. When Charley saw me he looked thunderstruck. He rushed to the grill and said in an echoing stage whisper, "For God's sake, you vamoose!" That was a favorite word of his.

"I've come to get you out."

"Vamoose!" he repeated. "I'll probably get a few years, but if you get mixed up in this we'll both be locked up. You have a wife and child, and anyway you're much more important to the work here than I am."

This was indeed loyalty!

I said, "No, Charley. I've talked with Schuler, and we're going to get you out of this. He'll be coming to see you. Be absolutely frank with him. When you're brought to trial you'll have to admit that you were loading a ship with arms for the Irish Republican Army. I think you'll find that the judge won't regard that as so great a crime."

Schuler worked fast. The next morning Charley was brought to trial and made a full confession. Of course, he was traveling on a forged passport as "Captain Charles Thompson," but since it was a very good forgery we did not bother to mention that.

The judge assumed an outraged air, and imposed what he considered a heavy fine — fifteen thousand marks. That was only a few pounds and Schuler promptly paid it. But we were still out one ship and a cargo of arms.

Well, as it happened we not only saved the ship, but the cargo, too. In fact, the sympathetic authorities did not even impound the *Anita;* but, of course, under the Treaty of Versailles, the arms had to be destroyed. So they were loaded into a lorry to be carted off to a suitable place; and somehow it happened that the lorry never reached its destination; but instead went around the block to the back door of my warehouse. Those Germans did not like the British at all.

However, we were right back where we started, and very worried, too, for it was sure now that we were being watched. We lay quiet for a while, cooking up a new scheme to get a large shipment of arms out. Naturally, my small-scale smuggling racket was working beautifully; but what a few men could carry on their persons was just a tiny trickle.

Meanwhile, I still had in mind the perilous condition of Charley's soul. So I paid a call to a Franciscan Order which had a mission to seamen. There I luckily found two Irish priests. One of them was a large robust, round-faced happy friar, and his partner the opposite of him, being thin, frail and esthetic-looking.

"Sure it is simple," said my jolly friar. "Just have a drink with him at the Triere Café. We'll come in and make your acquaintance. The rest you can leave to us."

For the Life of Me

It was no trouble whatever to get Charley into a saloon. We had been there a short time when the two friars came in. I paid no attention, until Charley noticed them, and made a joke about Brother Mutt and Brother Jeff. They stopped at our table and one of them said, "You sound like men from Ireland."

"That we are," Charley exclaimed. "Won't you sit with us, and have a bit of drink?"

Of course they did, and the talk ran on Ireland until I could see they were making McGuiness homesick. It ended with them inviting us to come to their monastery for tea the next day. Charley needed no urging.

It was a bare, dismal place where they lived; and the refreshments no more than weak tea and very hard, dry bread. But Charley enjoyed himself. We chatted some more about Ireland, and then the fragile friar asked Charley to walk around the grounds. They went out together, and I was left with my Friar Tuck.

Minutes and hours went by. I drank that miserable tea until it was up to my gullet; and we talked until the springs of our brains ran dry. But it was in a good cause. For finally Charley burst in through the door in high good humor. With a great grin, he said, "You know, Bob, I think this was something you put over on me. But you can be happy. I've made me confession, and am all right and ready for anything now. Only I hope you've been converted and confessed *your* sins. It would be only fair if you had to do penance as I have."

So there at least, was one mission accomplished. I wrote to Mellows, "You will be glad to know that Charley is now in a state of grace. But for how long — that is another question."

CHAPTER X
The Guns Get Through

Aᴠᴛᴇʀ the capture of *Anita*, Charley and I decided that it would require a much more elaborate subterfuge to get our arms out of Germany. We were also somewhat worried about our safety. We believed that the British Secret Service had marked us; and Charley thought that they might try, as he put it, "to do us in." So we got two automatics from our stock, and always carried them.

Our Irish "Ambassador," John T. Ryan, also got into a flap, and asked me for a revolver to defend himself. I gave him one, but since I hardly felt that Jetter had nerves of steel, I carefully gave him the wrong size ammunition — I did not want him shooting any sympathetic Germans. Jetter found out about my deception. He never forgave me.

Meanwhile, I was putting our new plan into execution. Through Brauner, I agreed to purchase a three thousand-ton tramp steamer, named, of all things, the *Karl Marx*, on condition that she be put in drydock for inspection, and then be given a trial run. For all this I paid five hundred pounds down. It was all I ever intended to pay.

But a big ship like that needed to be handled by a tug; so I purchased a staunch, seagoing little towboat called *Frieda*. I also bought a large number of barrels of cement.

After drydocking, we loaded old *Karl Marx* up with cement, preserving an ostentatious secrecy. On the day appointed for the trial run, I boarded her with a captain and a skeleton crew. Charley McGuiness, at the wheel of *Frieda*, towed us up the river and out to sea. Only a very acute observer would have noted that *Frieda* lay remarkably deep in the water.

For the Life of Me

We seemed to have a bit of trouble getting steam up in *Karl Marx*, and she was quite far out at sea by the time her old engines began to clang and bang turning the screw. A long blast on the whistle signaled Charley to cast off the lines. Three cocky toots from *Frieda* bade us farewell, and in a slashing circle of foam she swung around and headed *westward*.

For two days, I had *Karl Marx* sailed up and down the North Sea. Later I learned that half the British Navy was watching her. Meanwhile, a shabby little tug was puffing along in the direction of Ireland, cram-jammed with combustible contraband.

However, I had a worrisome time for the next ten days. Dispatches from Ireland, brought no mention of the *Frieda*. I began to fear that either His Majesty's Navy was smarter than I thought, or that Charley had overestimated his seamanship. The fact that we had probably lost the *Frieda* and her precious cargo was bad enough; but I was haunted by the thought that I had sent Charley and her crew to their deaths. At night I tossed beside Lily wondering what mistake I had made; whether I should have consulted some naval authority as to *Frieda's* ability to make the trip. By the end of that ten days I was convinced that Charley was no more. As it turned out I was right to be anxious.

On her run down the Dutch Coast, *Frieda* stuck her blunt nose into a gale. She labored and bucked, and buried herself almost up to her tall stack in those roaring seas. A man with more brains and less bravery than Charley would have put into a Dutch harbor. He kept on and rode it out; but he had burned a terrible lot of coal. As *Frieda* swung around Lands End into the Irish Sea, the stokers' shovels were scraping the bottom of her bunkers.

McGuiness put the crew to work with axes chopping up everything burnable to keep up steam, like Phileas Fogg on the last leg of his world tour. First the furniture went, and then the crates in which the guns were packed. As they neared the Irish coast, they went to work on *Frieda's* wooden cabin, smashing up partitions and feeding them to the furnace. At dusk, as Charley had reckoned, they came to Waterford Harbor.

No one apparently took notice of a little, battered tug steaming up the winding Suir Estuary to Waterford City, though it is a miracle they did not. For the varnished wood they were feeding her sent a comet's tail of golden sparks streaming out of her stack, and she must have looked like those American prints of a steamboat race on the Mississippi River.

Charley tied her up at Passage, just below Waterford, and scouted around until he found Doctor White, a famous physician and a great Irish Republican, though later he went Free State, which was a pity. White thought Charley was crazy; but finally put him in touch with the local brigade people. In scows and rowboats, they came to *Frieda* in the night, and by first light, she was empty and innocent.

Now there we had *Frieda,* who had run her course. She had cost us over one thousand pounds. What to do with her? Charley was equal to the problem. He sailed her empty down to Cork and sold her there to a Captain Collins, who had a contract to supply the British ships at Queenstown Naval Base with coal. So *Frieda* ended her days carrying coal to His Majesty's Navy. The price she fetched was two thousand pounds. A nice little deal.

After *Frieda's* successful voyage, we felt much better, but we did not relax. Instead we ventured into a new field. Nosing around among his seafaring friends in Ireland, McGuiness heard that an ancient two thousand-ton tramp steamer called the *City of Dortmund* was on her way to the scrap heap. He looked her over and decided there was a little life left in the old girl. With Liam Mellows's approval he bought her from her owners, Palgrave, Murphy and Company.

A new firm called International Shippers, Limited was quickly formed, McGuiness and I being the nominal owners. We decided that the *Dortmund* should not be used for arms smuggling, but run clean in general cargo between Hamburg, Bremen, Belfast, Cork and Dublin — her home port. However, and a great, huge however it was, she would have an all I.R.A. crew, and be available for a grand coup if a sudden emergency should arise.

In this way we could train men for the smuggling business, and also have a fairly safe means of transporting wanted men out of Ireland, or landing *unwanted* men there. Nor was *Dortmund's* cargo all as innocent as it seemed. For it had been in my mind that, rather than transport explosives through the blockade with all the attendant risks, we could safely send their chemical components separately and assemble them into a lethal compound after their arrival.

The ship finally came into service in the winter of 1921. As her agents in Germany we appointed Paul Gunther and Sons, an old German firm of high repute, who could get us general cargo.

As to the chemicals, that was another story. There was a very well-known firm of chain store chemists (drugstores) in Dublin called Hamilton, Long and Company, who had a splendid reputation with the British. The I.R.A. had a man working in one of their shops. We had him get us some of their order forms, and filled them out requesting so many tons of certain items, including such harmless drugs as bicarbonate of soda. Paul Gunther and Sons supplied us with the necessary bills of lading and other documents.

When the *City of Dortmund* tied up in the Liffey on her first run from Hamburg, a lorry appeared on the dock to take delivery of the goods consigned to Hamilton, Long, as per bills of lading which the driver produced. Everything was in perfect order, and of course the British would never suspect the firm of Hamilton, Long of any monkey business. Indeed, Messrs. Hamilton and Long, if they had known, would doubtless have had apoplectic fits.

The lorry was cleared and lumbered off. As far as the port authorities were concerned the goods had been delivered to Hamilton, Long; instead of which they naturally went to several secret rendezvous, where they fell into the hands of people who knew how to combine them in such a way as to give the British a maximum amount of trouble.

Since nothing was ever suspected about the operation, this means of supply never broke down. We also worked it with another type of contraband consigned to the English affiliate of the General Electric Company.

Still another method of smuggling was employed by Kenny, Murray using regular cargo ships. They ordered from Germany a large quantity of old-fashioned mangles. These were nothing more than big solid wooden rollers turned by a crank for squeezing the water out of large pieces of cloth. They were ordered by Kenny, Murray for the highly respectable laundry supply house of Messrs. Parkes of the Coombe, Dublin.

But the rollers we sent were hollowed out and stuffed with ammunition. The ends were carefully replaced with no noticeable cracks. Of course, Kenny, Murray saw to it that they got to an appropriate destination; and delivered other mangles to the Messrs. Parkes.

These operations sound as smooth as silk, and so they were, but they were not carried through without some tense moments. For example, the second time *Dortmund* docked in Hamburg we had a mutiny. Since Charley was the only master mariner available to us, we had engaged a retired sea captain to command the *Dortmund*. Captain Martin was the only man aboard who was not a member of the I.R.A., and who was *not* in the know, so our seagoing soldiers were not very respectful of him. In fact, when in port, they considered that he was not their officer.

That time when *Dortmund* arrived, the whole crew decided to take shore leave together. As everyone knows, you can't go off and leave a ship with the captain alone aboard. There is a lot of maintenance to be done, attending to the engines and the like. Captain Martin called on us for help.

Charley McGuiness and I hurried down to the quay and found the poor old captain in a state of helpless agitation. This was the sort of situation that brought out the best in Charley, so I let him take command.

"Assemble the crew on deck," he told the captain. And to

me he said, "Take this pistol and go up on the bridge with Captain Martin. I'm going on deck to talk to the crew. If they rush me and I go down, you know what to do!"

"That I do!" was my answer.

I went up on the bridge and looked down on the forward deck where the crew were gathering in little discontented knots in the shifting lights and shadows of swinging, naked electric bulbs. It would be hard shooting in that tricky light, but I was in good practice. I leaned on the rail with the gun ready.

McGuiness walked out on the deck, his gait between a roll and a waddle, his great arms hanging loose and ready.

"Now listen, you bastards!" he bellowed.

That got their attention, and for five minutes he gave them the rough side of his tongue, which was like an iron rasp.

"Now hark to this!" he wound up. "There is one boss on a ship, at sea or in port. Captain Martin is your boss. If any of you bums don't like it, now is the time to say it.

"But," he added, "before you do, I'll tell you I have a nice iron belaying pin here and I know how to use it! Now, gentlemen, if you want to sort this thing out with me, just step forward!"

The leader of the mutineers tried to put up an argument, but he was halfhearted about it. In about five minutes strict discipline was restored.

After *Dortmund* had been in service a short time, a message came to me from Collins. Heavy fighting had developed in Cork, and it was essential to get one hundred Parabellum or Peter the Painter pistols there at once. They must be sent in the *City of Dortmund*. Although I felt that the ship should be reserved for a greater effort, a more desperate emergency, this was an order and must be obeyed.

I met the *Dortmund* at Hamburg and conferred with one of her crew named Seamus Dolan, who was an experienced I.R.A. man — McGuiness was not available. Dolan and I concocted a scheme that sounded promising. I managed to get about two hundred pistols from our arms dump aboard *Dortmund*. I also ordered a large number of sacks of potatoes to be put aboard her. The cook, who was our man, was instructed to shuck about half the potatoes out of each sack, replace them with pistols, and pile potatoes back on top — a sort of potato-pistol sandwich.

When this was arranged, I ordered the captain to make a slow voyage to give me time to get there, and headed for Cork via London, Holyhead and Dublin. I knew nobody in Cork, nor how I would make contact with our people there, so I stopped a night in Dublin. I stayed in the Woods's little brick house on Morehampton Road, sharing the familiar double bed with Liam Mellows. We slept not at all but talked the night away, he giving me instructions, and then telling me the news. It was glorious. All over Ireland we were winning. Our guerrilla war had the British tied up in their forts and barracks. They could only hold the big cities.

In Cork I went straight from the station to a certain tobacconist and news vendor, where, according to plan, I asked for a long list of specific items — certain papers, a particular brand of tobacco and other things. The girls behind the counter looked scared as I rattled off my wants, but they kept their nerve. When I had completed the full list, one of them said, "You'll have to wait a bit, while we sort and pack these things for you."

This, too, was according to plan. Meanwhile a message was sent to the local brigade. While I waited, customers were coming in and out, being waited on; and I was getting my items singly and slowly. Next thing, two men came in, Sean Hegerty and Tom Crofts, though I did not then know their names. Sean said quietly, "Follow us."

With my arms full of parcels, I obeyed.

Cork was a strange city to me; and dangerous it looked. For the British were making a tremendous effort there, it being so close to their great naval base at Cobh — Queenstown, as they called it. The broad main street was full of armed men in uni-

forms patrolling in pairs. I saw the khaki of the British Auxiliaries, the nasty black berets of the Black and Tans, and the
familiar helmets of the Royal Irish Constabulary.

My men turned into a steep, narrow street toward the harbor, and fell back so I came up between them. "Now who are ye,
and what have you got for us?" asked Hegerty in his broad Cork
accent, which sounds like stage Irish.

"I'm Captain Swift," was my answer, "and there are two hundred Parabellums for you aboard the steamer *City of Dortmund*."

Then I told them where the guns were hidden and of our
plan for getting them ashore.

"Very well," said Hegerty, "when will she be due?"

"Tomorrow most likely."

"And where will ye be?"

"At the Imperial Hotel, under the name of Briscoe."

They raised an eyebrow at that, for the Imperial was the
hangout of the Black and Tans. Nonetheless, they said, "all right,
we'll keep a watch for the boat. We'll be told when she enters
the river, and will send you word."

Like a flash they turned a corner and were gone.

The next day a message was slipped under my door that *Dortmund* was coming up the river. Three hours later the same pair
came for me. They had two horse-drawn cabs waiting, one for
them and one for me. It was evident that these gentlemen did
not trust me far. Later I heard it was because I "looked too
much of a swell" to be one of them. It seemed they had things
arranged so that if this were a trap, they would make short work
of me.

The sun was still high when we got to the docks, for in early
June, it does not set until nearly eleven, and there is very little
time of darkness. The familiar, rusty old ship loomed respectably
large at the little Cork quay. The sheds were crowded with customs men and military.

Standing alongside *Dortmund*, abeam of her galley, I heard
the cook making bitter complaint of the quality of the potatoes
the ship chandler had put aboard. "They're not fit for pigs, let

alone honest seamen," he howled. "I'll not have them on me ship. Off they go, and let that Dublin crook fitch them or not as he pleases!"

A sack of potatoes was manhandled down the crew's gangway and dumped at my feet with a thud — oh my precious Parabellums! Others were thrown into a disorderly heap on the deck. Behind the last came the cook, still raging. I had a quick word with him and Hegerty.

The sacks just lay there with nobody paying them any heed; the customs men being busy with the regular cargo as it was hoisted out with a great clatter of blocks and puffing of the old-fashioned donkey engine. Soon a lorry drove onto the dock. Men quickly hove the sacks into it, and off it went. Then I had nothing more to do than get my receipt from the I.R.A. men for items delivered as per specifications.

As there was no train from Cork that night, I went back to the Imperial. I was sitting in the lounge reading to rest my jangled nerves. The place was crowded with Black and Tans taking their ease off duty. It must have seemed a night for celebrating to the I.R.A. They came roaring in to raid the hotel. The Tans were quick off the mark, and in a second I was in the center of regular fusillade — the whiz-wack of bullets maybe coming from my own guns.

The battle raged all around me, the Tans shooting at people in the entrance, and they shooting back. I had to stay where I was, frozen in my chair. I was not in any position to move, because where would I go? And what would I do?

I waited until the whole barrage concluded. Even then I dared not satisfy my anxiety about who among our people might be killed or wounded. I therefore thought it best to go to bed; and finally slept to the accompaniment of single gun shots and rattling bursts of machine gun fire echoing still through the empty streets of Cork.

Incidentally, we continued to run the *City of Dortmund* after the Truce and I believe that she was the first ship ever to fly the green, white and orange tricolor of Ireland.

The most ambitious attempt we ever made at gunrunning was early in that summer of 1921. For it we bought a new ship, the *Hannah*, a motor auxiliary like *Anita*, but rather larger. She was loaded with five hundred pistols and two hundred rifles. The latter were originally German military guns, which had been rebored and made into sharp-shooting, double-trigger sporting rifles — "elephant guns," the Germans called them. Though they had short stocks and a huge bore, they would suit our purpose very well.

In addition to the small arms, the *Hannah* carried a few machine guns and approximately a *million* rounds of ammunition.

So large a movement of arms meant great risks but also promised great opportunities for our fighting men. Special precautions must be taken. Pax Whelan, the brigadier at Dungarven in County Waterford, was alerted to form a plan of operations, and I felt that I myself must go to oversee the landing.

Whelan was a most ingenious man. He sent word by a courier that his plan would be for the *Hannah* to sail close in to Dungarven on a course that would appear to by-pass it. Then she would suddenly stop and send up signals of distress. Whelan would have I.R.A. people disguised as fishermen in boats ready to rush out and tow her in, and in the towing they would bring her to a place far from the docks where police and customs men abounded. Arrangements would be made to unload her quickly before suspicion was aroused.

The *Hannah* started from Hamburg with McGuiness in command and my prayers for her safety. The voyage was expected to take seven or eight days, and I hastened over my familiar route — London, Holyhead and Dublin — and then by train to Dungarven.

Despite the risk and strain of it, that was a happy occasion for me. It was grand to be back on the coast of the Irish Sea with all the fine familiar smells of sweet meadows and salty shingle and the breath of ocean blowing into my lungs. That was the time I have told you about, when Ben McCarthy took me for a spy, but since I never knew of his unpleasant intentions, they did not trouble me.

Pax Whelan, when I finally met him, turned out to be a splendid fellow, and I liked all his staff; Ben McCarthy, the vice-commandant; his brother who led a flying column and Mr. Spratt, the transport officer. They were a glorious, high-spirited lot, and while we waited for the *Hannah* we had one of those uproarious good times that sometimes happen in the midst of war.

First of all, Whelan was wonderful about my security. He would not allow me to remain in one place for long. Each night I slept in a different farmer's house. I remember on the second night getting up at dawn of morning and looking out of the little lattice-paned window of my room. I saw two heads across a fence, and was sure these men were spotting me. It seemed wise to see if there was an escape way in the back, so I stole down to the kitchen and looked out the back door. Sure enough, on the other side of a hedge again a cap on top of a head. There was no use trying to get away, so I waited quietly until Pax Whelan arrived about eight o'clock. I said to him, "Did you notice any men outside?"

"Why?" he asked.

I told him my worry.

He roared with laughter, and going to the door, whistled sharply. One of the men came out from behind the fence.

"Have you been on duty all night?" Pax asked him.

"I have, sir."

"What were your instructions?"

"My instructions, sir, were that if this house was raided, we were to see that this man escaped. No matter what happened to us he was not to be caught."

"And why were you given those instructions?" Pax asked, smiling.

"Well, sir, you told us last night, this man is an Irishman by conviction. He could have chosen to be otherwise. Not like us; we have to be Irish."

For the Life of Me

I was **much touched** by this tender protection Pax was giving me.

Those three days were a time of laughter too. One night Mr. Spratt had a drop or more of poteen and felt like singing, for in this farmer's house there was a piano, and the farmer's daughter could play it. Spratt only knew one song, but he knew it well — all eighty verses of it. Along about the fortieth verse I decided to go to bed, but even there I could hear Spratt roaring out increasingly indelicate adventures in "The Foggy Foggy Dew" — he pronounced it "djew."

The following morning Spratt came humbly up to beg my forgiveness.

"For what?" I asked.

"For what I did last night."

"And what did you do?"

"Well," said Spratt, "if I had known last night that you were a Jew I certainly would not have indulged in that song."

That same day Pax Whelan came to say he was taking me to a court-martial of one of his men. Someone from G.H.Q. would be sitting in to be sure justice was administered. Spratt was both a witness and a principal in the case.

The court convened in the parlor of another farmhouse with great solemnity. This was a very serious matter. It appeared that shortly before my arrival in Dungarven the Waterford Brigade had arranged a tidy little ambush of a British column, in the course of which there had been an incident that held implications of black treachery.

First off, the court moved to inspect the scene of the ambush. Here was a road curving through slightly rising ground. The road had been mined, and Spratt was placed behind a hedge at the curve, where he could see the British coming, and signal to the man with the plunger to detonate the mine when a vehicle was over it. Other men were placed on the gentle hillside to fire down on the British.

The ambush worked beautifully. A British lorry was totally wrecked by the mine, and they had been forced to retreat in

114

their remaining vehicle under a storm of fire with nobody knew how many killed and wounded. There was only one I.R.A. casualty — Spratt.

But here was the dark fact. Spratt had been shot in the back, or more exactly, in the backside, by a shotgun — even to this day he occasionally feels a pellet finding its way out of him. Now no enemy was behind Spratt, and British troops do not use shotguns. It was evident he had been shot by one of his own men. The man who had been stationed behind him was the prisoner before the court.

After thoroughly inspecting the ground, the court reconvened in the farmhouse. All the facts were established. The prisoner was then brought before the court, and duly sworn. I remember him well, a country boy, with bright red hair and a wind-red face with great round blue eyes in it. It was a face of innocence, which made his crime even worse.

Pax Whelan told him that he must now tell his story, and the silence was thick with tension as he began.

"Brigadier," he said in his deep country brogue, "how could you think I would do such a thing by design? It was pure accident and this was the way of it. I was there up the hillside behind Mr. Spratt, looking down at the bend in the road. It was terrible dark, and then the shooting began. Now, sure, I did not know that Mr. Spratt's trousers were split in back. When he bent down to look through the hedge at the corner, the trousers parted. How else could I think but that it was a face looking up at me? So I let him have it."

I heard no verdict given. The court collapsed in laughter.

In the evening of the third day, our lookout, lying flat on the turf on Helvick Head, sighted a motor auxiliary. I hurried with Pax to the cliffs, and stared at the little speck of a boat crawling over the blue water with so much of our hopes aboard. Through my field glasses I was able to identify her as the *Hannah*. Pax immediately sent couriers flying off in all directions to put our plan into operation.

It was a beautifully organized military operation. Every road leading to Dungarven was mined and guarded by men in the slouch hats and trench coats that were almost a uniform of the I.R.A. They lay concealed behind hedges and walls. All the bridges were also mined. Even though the British discovered our plot, they would have a hell of a fight to break through our lines.

We on the headland watched *Hannah* slowly sail past the mouth of the harbor; saw her drift to a stop and lie dead in the water, while the German ensign was hoisted to her gaff upside down. Pax waved to the two little motor fishing boats that were waiting, and off they went. Across the harbor at the British installation there was no sign of activity. Anxiously we watched the two small boats chug toward *Hannah*. They reached her at last and put lines aboard. Then began the long haul in. It was so desperately urgent and so agonizingly slow, like the laborious movements of a man in a nightmare. Sweeping our glasses across the harbor we saw that all was quiet there. If anyone was watching they evidently thought, as we had intended, that a broken-down fishing boat was getting a tow.

Pax had chosen the landing place well. It was a cove on the far side of the harbor called Ring, where during the war the British had planned a submarine base. It was deserted now, but the sturdy dock they had built still stood.

As the *Hannah* was being towed in, a strange assortment of transport began creeping over the small roads and hill paths toward Ring. There were farm wagons half loaded with hay or vegetables, horse-drawn cattle trucks, outside cars, pony carts, and two-wheeled platforms pulled by little small donkeys, all moving through the long dusky twilight under a sky still red from the afterglow.

Pax and I and the brigade headquarters staff hurried down to the dock. The dim red and green running lights of *Hannah* and her towing boats crept toward us across the slick dark water. She was swung expertly and bumped against the side of the dock. As men hurried up with oil lanterns, Charley McGuiness jumped ashore and grabbed my hand.

In a minute the hatches were off and men swarming aboard, in and out of her like ants in the yellow glow and deep shadow. Everybody lent a hand, soldiers with Sam Brown belts over civilian clothes, farmers in muddy boots and shirts, all the officers led by Pax, and I in my foolish-looking city suit, toiling like demons.

As the carts and carriages were loaded they moved off, scattering through the hills into the deep country where the British dared not go. They would later transfer their load to another seemingly innocent vehicle to be hauled up the coast to Dublin; for these arms were mostly intended for the Dublin brigades and a great effort in the capital. The whole job was completed in a few hours; and all the men and carts and animals melted into the night with the largest single arms shipment ever to reach the Irish Republican Army.

Of course, not all the guns arrived at their proper destination. So desperate were our people for arms that many a case was cracked open and guns and cartridges taken. It was stealing if you like, but an honorable sort of theft. For they were taken for no personal gain, but by men wanting to arm themselves to fight for Ireland's freedom.

Despite the looting, a great quantity of material reached the Dublin brigades. All this happened on the eve of the Truce with England — the Truce which they begged of us; and the Treaty that brought not peace but a more terrible war. Had I known the use to which these weapons would finally be put, I would have been heartsick.

CHAPTER XI

The Truce and the Treaty

Nᴏɴᴇ of us of the rank and file had any idea how close we were to winning the war against England. I doubt if the top brass, even President de Valera himself, realized it.

In December, 1920, the Chief had returned to Ireland. Again he crossed on a British ship, with the appropriate name of the *Celtic*. Her crew concealed him in her lower depths behind a bin of potatoes. When the British found he had left New York they set up a great hue and cry. All the liners landing in England were searched, but Dev was ghosted ashore in Liverpool under the very noses of the police; and thence to a small cross-channel freighter which tied up in the Liffey close to the customs house. From her Dev stepped onto a quay in the very heart of Dublin. It was Christmas Eve.

During the remaining months of the winter of 1921, de Valera functioned as President of Ireland on-the-run. Difficult as it was to disguise his tall, lean figure, bold, jutting nose and brilliant eyes, he managed to bicycle around Dublin without detection. He conducted the affairs of the government from a secret office in Mount Street off Merrion Square.

Other departments of the Republican Government were scattered in cubbyholes throughout the city. The cabinet seldom dared to meet. They could not communicate by telephone or mail, which were subject to censorship. Many of the communications between them were carried by little Irish boys and girls skipping, apparently light-hearted, through Dublin's crowded streets with dispatches that could hang half the cabinet concealed in the soles of their scuffy shoes. Yet the Republican Government was, in fact, the only functioning government of the country. King George V of Great Britain and Ireland and Emperor of India was mournfully informed by his Prime Minister, Lloyd George, that "The King's writ no longer runs in Ireland."

The English people were growing very tired of the war. Large and vociferous sections of public opinion were revolted and appalled by the brutalities of their forces in Ireland. Great English newspapers such as the *Manchester Guardian* and the *London Times*, condemned the policy of "ruin and rapine" in Ireland. Officers of the British Army ordered to Ireland did everything in their power to avoid the duty — some resigned rather than take it. Even the Black and Tans were getting tired of blood and murder, and danger without glory.

The immense difficulty of fighting against a guerrilla army, which materialized in the hills at night and dissolved into ordinary civilians by day, and which was backed by almost the whole population of the country, confounded the British generals. In May, 1921, Commander-in-Chief Sir Neville Macready, informed the British Cabinet that the eighty thousand troops they had in Ireland were not enough. On his advice Winston Churchill, Minister for the Colonies, informed Lloyd George that "a hundred thousand new troops and police must be raised," to reconquer the country.

There were two happenings that really rocked the British Government. The first was the elections of May, 1921. On May 3 a law, previously passed by the British Parliament and ironically called "The Better Government of Ireland Act," came into effect. It partitioned Ireland into two areas or "dominions," the six counties of the Northeast and the twenty-six counties of the South, and set up two parliaments. This partition was against the will, not only of the Southern counties, but even of the Unionists of the North who sided with England. In accordance with this law elections were held for the two parliaments; in the South on May 19, 1921, and a week later in the North.

The result of these elections really shook up Lloyd George. In the South every one of one hundred and twenty four Sinn Feinn candidates was returned *unopposed;* not a single man in Ireland would run against them. In the Protestant, pro-English North nearly twenty-five per cent of the Sinn Feinn or Nationalist candidates won, including such Republicans as de Valera for South Down — he was also elected for Clare in the South — Michael Collins for Armagh, and Eoin MacNeill and Arthur Griffith, who were both in English jails. The elections proved conclusively that in spite of terror and propaganda, the people of Ireland were solidly behind the Irish Republic.

The other disaster to British rule was a military operation in the heart of Dublin. On May 25, 1921, one hundred and twenty men of the Dublin Brigade seized the beautiful old customs house on the bank of the Liffey and, holding the streets around it, burned it to the ground. The soaring flames, which sent the great copper dome crashing down between the tall marble columns, consumed tax records and files of the government. This reduced the British administration in Ireland from confusion to chaos.

During all the early months of 1921, there had been unofficial British peace feelers — Lord Derby had even arrived in the childish disguise of a pair of horn-rimmed glasses and attempted to negotiate. To all of them de Valera had replied that he would parley with no one except on an official basis and as the head of a sovereign state. He did not think Lloyd George would meet these conditions.

But King George, who went to Belfast to open the rump parliament of the North in June, said, "I appeal to all Irishmen to pause, to stretch out the hand of forbearance and conciliation, to forgive and forget, and to join in making for the land they love a new era of peace, contentment and goodwill. . . ."

On the afternoon of June 22, a squad of the Worcester Regiment, then garrisoning Dublin, made a routine raid on a large brick house called "Glenvar," in the suburb of Blackrock. They surprised several Irish gentlemen chatting in the garden — it was a meeting of the Republican Cabinet. The troopers let all the men go except one who seemed to be wearing a disguise. Him they marched off to Portobello Barracks. There they discovered that they had captured the President of the Irish Republic.

Instead of being received with rejoicing in London, the news caused a panic in the Cabinet. For that very day Lloyd George had decided to negotiate. The Under Secretary of State for Ireland, A. W. Cope, sent a frantic message to Dublin Castle. The following morning, de Valera prepared himself for the dreary resumption of prison life with a high probability of being shot. Instead the Commanding General called to tell him he was a free man. Dev was dumbfounded.

"Go to your own house at Greystones," he was told. "You will soon receive a very important communication."

On June 25, a letter bearing the seals of His Majesty's Government was delivered to him. It began:

> Sir:
> The British Government are deeply anxious that . . . the King's appeal for reconciliation in Ireland shall not have been made in vain. . . .
> I therefore write to you as the chosen leader of the great majority in Southern Ireland and to Sir James Craige, the Premier of Northern Ireland:
> That you should attend a conference here in London with Sir James Craige to explore to the utmost the possibility of a settlement. . . .
> . . . We ask you to meet with us, as we will meet you, in the spirit of conciliation for which His Majesty appealed.
> I am, Sir,
> Your obedient servant,
> D. Lloyd George.

This letter was not quite the official recognition of a sovereign power that de Valera had demanded, but it was too conciliatory to be turned down. Almost immediately upon receipt of it, the President and all the cabinet members moved their offices to the beautiful, eighteenth century Mansion House of which I have such fond memories. As they drove up, the people packing Dawson Street cheered wildly at the public appearance of the men who had fought so long in secret.

Inside, the cabinet gathered in the long, carved paneled Oak Room, hung with the coats-of-arms of all the Lord Mayors of Dublin, to consider their reply. Every little while they broke off joyfully to greet old friends released from British jails as a token of her government's sincerity. Arthur Griffith came, who had been taken when he was Acting President, Bob Barton, Eamon Duggan, Michael Stanes, and many others, wearing still the ragged, dirty clothes of long imprisonment.

De Valera sent a cautious message to Lloyd George promising a full reply later, and invited the leaders of the North to confer with him on "the reply which I, as spokesman for the Irish Nation, will make to Lloyd George."

Sir James Craige obdurately refused; but the others came, headed by the Earl of Midleton. The meeting was held at the Mansion House on July 4. The arriving dignitaries walked through the graceful portico above which flew the green, white and orange tricolor of the Republic, and the Stars and Stripes in honor of America's Independence Day.

De Valera's first condition was that a truce should be declared before negotiations started. The British at first refused, but Unionist Lord Midleton induced them to accept. On July 5, South Africa's great elder statesman, General Jan Smuts, arrived from London to lend the voice of his experience and persuasion to the Council. The Conference ended on July 8, and de Valera telegraphed Lloyd George that he would come to London to discuss with him "on what basis . . . a conference can reasonably hope to achieve the object desired."

On July 11, 1921, was proclaimed the Truce which ended our centuries long war with England, though no man could be sure that this would be its result.

I was in Germany while all these great events were taking place, and only gleaned a little of them until the news of the

The Truce and the Treaty

Truce was published. Like all Irishmen everywhere my heart blazed with the fires of exultation. Second thoughts damped them down; for it was a long road from a truce to a treaty that would give us a free, united Ireland.

Nevertheless it was a fine thing to come back to Dublin in that summer of 1921. Just as the spring sun breaking through the long, heavy clouds of our Irish winter seems never more brilliant; so did the light of peace touch the old city with new glory. To walk her streets free and unafraid, greeting old comrades in their spic-and-span new uniforms was a great joy. Every night, with the curfew gone, the streets were crowded with laughing people; and in the squares were bonfires, with young folks and old dancing around them to the Irish pipes and shouting, "Up the Republic! Up Dev!"

Indeed, every village of Ireland lighted its victory blaze, so that from the air the land must have looked like a garden bursting with fiery blooms. But the Irish Republican Army were not so confident of peace. Realizing that victory celebrations were premature, they doused the bonfires and told the people to wait. De Valera also warned the people that they must maintain discipline and keep "an unbending determination to endure all that may still be necessary, and fortitude such as you have shown in all your recent sufferings. These alone will lead you to the peace you desire."

The Army heard him and obeyed; keeping up their drills and practice marches, and preserving their wonderful discipline and endurance. But the people of Ireland had been too long deprived of any comfort or delight. As suffering could not do, joy sapped their fighting spirit.

As for me, after a brief stay in Ireland, during which I conferred with Arthur Griffith, Cathal Brugha and Mellows at the Mansion House, I was quickly sent back to Germany to continue my operations. For as we understood the Truce, it did not forbid the importation of arms. However, the Germans, unwilling to upset the applecart, stopped one of my shipments.

123

Also, there appeared to be a worrisome division in the Army command. Orders I received from Liam Mellows might be countermanded by Collins. And of course I knew very little about the alarms and discursions, the telegrams and letters, the crises and capitulations that went on during the summer about the terms on which a peace conference could even begin to confer.

However, all the world knew when it finally met on October 11, 1921. De Valera had decided not to go himself. Since he was both Chief of State and the executive head of the government, like the American President he feared he might be pressured into snap decisions. To head the delegaton he chose Arthur Griffith, the Foreign Minister, who accepted with forebodings that he would not be able to bring back a Republic. Then came Michael Collins, next to Dev himself the most powerful man in Ireland. Collins did not want to go unless Dev did. The President pleaded with him for hours, before he consented. The other commissioners were Robert Barton, Minister of Economic Affairs; Eamon Duggan, a legal expert; and Gavan Duffy, who had been Roger Casement's legal counsel and friend. Erskine Childers, the man of English birth who had taken our side, and run the first arms for the Volunteers in on his yacht back in 1914, was named Secretary of the Delegation.

De Valera felt that he had chosen well. Griffith was a moderate and a compromiser, but he was the founder of Sinn Feinn. Michael Collins seemed a man of steel. The others were brilliant and devoted patriots. He forced Dáil Eireann, somewhat unwillingly, to name them "plenipotentiaries" in accordance with English insistence. But he instructed his envoys that, "It is understood before decisions are finally reached . . . that a dispatch will be sent to members of the Cabinet in Dublin, and that a reply will be awaited by the plenipotentiaries before final decision is made."

To meet their group the British put their first team in. Headed by Lloyd George, who was the slickest statesman in Europe, it included such masters of the art of diplomacy as Joseph Chamberlain, Lord Birkenhead and Winston Churchill. The inexperienced Irish envoys were simply not in that class.

The negotiations lasted for nearly two months. During that time Collins came back a dozen times to confer with de Valera. Griffith came once. As the latter had warned, the British would not accept a Republic; nor would the North of Ireland. To avoid partition and bring Ulster in under an All Ireland Parliament, de Valera, against the wishes of ardent Republicans like Cathal Brugha and Austin Stack, proposed the compromise of "External Association." By this plan Ireland would acknowledge the King as head of an association of states, but *not* as King of Ireland. That was as far as he felt he could go. As for the name of the government it could be *Saorstat*, which to the British means free state, but is equivalent in Irish to republic. He would under no circumstances accept partition.

On December 3, 1921, Arthur Griffith brought back England's final offer which amounted to something less than full dominion status. At a full cabinet meeting — Collins and Barton being absent in England — de Valera declared it not good enough. He decided to go to England himself to break off negotiations. Griffith dissuaded him by promising not to sign the agreement unless its terms were changed to meet the President's wishes.

On the Sunday of their return the envoys presented de Valera's new offer of External Association to the British Cabinet. Within a few hours it was contemptuously rejected. The next day there were further conferences at which the British made a few minor concessions and Lloyd George accepted a slightly modified oath of allegiance which Collins drew up. That same night at 7 P.M., the Irish envoys were given an ultimatum. They must all sign the articles of agreement by ten o'clock or England would declare total war against the Irish Republic. Lloyd George's solemn words were, "The man who is against peace must bear now and forever the responsibility for immediate and terrible war."

Lloyd George was clever. He struck like lightning, giving our people but three hours; scarce time even to think; no time they believed, to refer the decision to the Chief; though I blame them bitterly for not even trying to telephone their President.

First Griffith, the man of peace, agreed to sign. Then Collins cracked. Winston Churchill, describing that moment wrote: "Michael Collins rose, looking as though he were going to shoot someone, preferably himself. In all my life I never saw so much suffering and passion in restraint."

After Griffith and Collins signed, Duggan and Duffy followed. Only Robert Barton refused to sign. Barton belonged to what we call the ascendancy class; a Protestant, an English aristocrat, slim, elegant, correct; and, having given us his allegiance, fearlessly devoted to Ireland's cause. Only Barton held out. But Lloyd George said they all must sign or there would be war. I think Lloyd George was bluffing, but Barton did not. He described the scene thus:

"Speaking for himself and his colleagues, the English Prime Minister, with all the solemnity and power of conviction that he alone of all men I have met, can impart by word and gesture — the vehicles by which the mind of one man oppresses the mind of another — declared that the signature of every member of our delegation was necessary or war would follow immediately."

So Barton also signed. He gave his reason in his speech in the great debate in the Dáil, saying: "I do not seek to shield myself from the charge of having broken my oath of allegiance to the Republic . . . That oath was, and is still to me, the most sacred bond on earth . . . For myself I preferred war. I told my colleagues so; but for the Nation, without consultation, I dared not accept that I myself, and of my own choice, must commit my nation to immediate war. . . ."

On Tuesday, December 6, word came to Dublin that the Irish plenipotentiaries had signed a treaty with England. That same evening the Articles of Agreement were published. The President of the Irish Republic was not consulted.

The Truce and the Treaty

These things I have told you, though I did not learn them until later, but now I speak of my own knowledge. For on Wednesday morning I read the terms of the Treaty with despair in my heart. I was confounded and stricken by what seemed like the treachery of our envoys, or such misfeasance as to be criminal negligence.

For these Articles of Agreement gave us even less than dominion status. We were to be still part of the British Empire, still subjects of the English King to whom our officials must swear allegiance. Furthermore, the British kept the right to use our harbors as naval bases. This could force us into another war whether we thought it just or not. Finally, and perhaps worst of all, the six counties of the North were given the right to vote themselves out of the nation, to become a separate country. This partition would forever sunder Ireland into two antagonistic states, weakened by an artificial division contrary to geographical fact, inseparable economic interests and the national kinship of all Irishmen.

Thus had Ireland lost all she had won by five years of war. The waste of it! Dominion status with partition we could have had without ever firing a shot. So many loyal men, my friends and fellow countrymen, had died, it seemed, for nothing — Pearse and Connolly, Clarke, MacDonough and Count Plunkett; Terence MacSwiney, Lord Mayor of Cork, whose martyr's death from a hunger strike in Brixton Jail had steeled Irish hearts to a superhuman effort; and thousands of unnamed Irish lads, dead in country ditches, and the gutters of our cities; shot against prison walls or in the very doorways of their homes. This treaty made vain the sacrifices of the people of Ireland valiantly enduring five years of misery and suffering and death that stalked down dear familiar streets. And what of the Irish women, weeping for their men, who had died to earn a victory thrown away at the council table?

So this treaty seemed to me a shameful surrender of all that we had gained. So it seemed to my Chief, President Eamon de Valera, and to the staunch defenders of Ireland's freedom. But when I came home, I found that this was not true of the Irish people.

The streets and avenues of Dublin were bright with the cheer of the first truly peaceful Christmas in five years. Carefree people surged in and out of the gaily decorated shops on Grafton Street, brimming with luxuries they might now hope to afford. The churches were crowded with the devout offering prayers of thanksgiving that the strife was over. Joyful families were greeting husbands and sons and fathers released from English jails; and in their homes, for the first time in that long era of discontent, the people dared to give themselves over to an untroubled Christmas spirit.

For they did not fully understand the implications of this document their chosen representatives had signed. All they knew was that Ireland had been given the appearance and form of freedom; that a treaty had been made with England ending fear and bloodshed and suffering; ending war with honor. So they thought. They could not understand or realize what had been lost.

For the Treaty was presented to them as a victorious accomplishment. The newspapers published the Articles of Agreement on the front pages. They were gaily festooned with shamrocks and holly berries in green and red; and applauded in half a hundred editorials. In that guise the Treaty seemed to glitter like the star of Bethlehem bringing glad tiding of peace on earth and good will toward men.

In the midst of this rejoicing, came President de Valera's solemn announcement:

> My friends, Irishmen:
> I feel it my duty to inform you immediately that I cannot recommend the acceptance of the Treaty. . . .

It was virtually disregarded by the public.

I learned that there had been a despairful cabinet meeting in the Mansion House on Wednesday, December 7. Cathal Brugha and Austin Stack had proposed dismissing Collins and Griffith from their ministries immediately. William Cosgrave urged that they must first be heard in their own defense. President de Valera cabled ordering them home.

There was a violent storm in the Cabinet on their return. They told their story to the crag-faced President and their angry colleagues. For five hours they stormed and pleaded, argued and quarreled. In the end Cosgrave was won over to the pro-Treaty side. And so they voted; Griffith, Collins, Cosgrave, and Barton to recommend the Treaty to the Dáil; de Valera, Brugha and Stack against. So was Republican Ireland split down the middle. Hot-headed patriots in the Army wanted the President to reject the Treaty and arrest the signers for high treason. De Valera said, "There is a constitutional way."

The Treaty itself provided that it would not take effect unless ratified by the Dáil and Parliament. The President called the Dáil into emergency session.

CHAPTER XII

The Fissure Widens

Dáil eareann met on December 14, 1921. The British Parliament met that same day and ratified the Treaty in forty-eight hours.

Usually, except when it was on the run, the Dáil held its sessions in the Round Room of the Mansion House, a large circular annex attached to its rear, which was admirably suited to parliamentary deliberations. But this excellent forum was now decorated with evergreens and holly and filled with the booths, displays and jollity of the *Aonach* or Christmas fair. So the Dáil was summoned to meet in the Convocation Hall of University College on Earlsfort Terrace off St. Stephen's Green. A worse place to hold a parliamentary meeting is hard to imagine.

Though I was not a member of the Dáil, I attended many of the sessions during the Treaty debate. The scene of them is branded on my brain by the heat of passion. University College — now the National University — was a long granite building in classically, columned Greco-Roman style. You entered an impressive marble hall from which two broad stairways branched upward to the gallery on the second floor outside the Council Chamber. The room where the Dáil met was immensely long and narrow, about one hundred feet in length and perhaps thirty feet wide. It was lit by electric globes hanging on iron standards from its comparatively low ceiling. There was a little platform at each end surrounded by balustrades. The Speaker, Eoin MacNeill, presided at the south end of the room, and the deputies sat on folding chairs interspersed with tables all higgledy-piggledy down the long room. Because the ceiling of the Chamber was so low its acoustics were nearly nonexistent. Not only was it almost impossible for members in the back of the hall to hear what the orators were saying, it was difficult even to see who was speaking.

On the day of the opening session Earlsfort Terrace was packed with people as far as the eye could see, held back by police and the Irish Republican Army ranged along the stone balustrades outside the College. As the leaders of the opposing parties came into sight they were greeted by storms of cheers and boos. Some arrived on foot, pushing through the crowds. Michael Collins drove up in an open automobile, jauntily acknowledging a cyclone of cheers and catcalls. Arthur Griffith, arriving in an old-fashioned, two-wheeled jaunting car, drew tremendous cheers. Cathal Brugha pedaled up on a bicycle. There was a tense respectful silence, broken by occasional shouts of "Up Dev!" as President de Valera drove up in a black limousine and stepped out between the saluting soldiers.

In the Council Chamber the cabinet ministers took the places they would occupy throughout the debate — Arthur Griffith, Cosgrave and Collins in folding chairs on the floor to the Speaker's right, Stack and Brugha on his left. Last to arrive was President de Valera. He came into the Chamber looking terribly gaunt and stern, and immensely tall in his dead black overcoat. With a slight inclination of his head to the Speaker, he sat down next to Austin Stack. Thus were the lines drawn. The men who had worked and fought so long together now sat somberly regarding each other across an invisible barrier.

Throughout the days of hot debate that followed, the fissure that had sundered the Cabinet spread down through all the strata of the state. Sinn Fein was broken by it. The Irish Republican Brotherhood split; though Michael Collins, Chairman of its Council, managed to bring the majority of the Brothers to favor the Treaty and work underground for its approval. The Army Command parted down the middle. Minister of Defense Brugha, Austin Stack, Liam Mellows, Rory O'Connor and most of the younger brigadiers opposed the Treaty with anguish and passion. Chief of Staff Richard Mulcahy, Assistant Chief of

Staff, J. J. O'Conell, O'Duffy, O'Hegarty, and, of course, Michael Collins, were for approval; not because they liked it, but because as Collins said in the Dáil, "Rejection of the Treaty means your national policy is war. If you do this . . . as a national policy, I for one am satisfied. . . ." And General Mulcahy, speaking with all the authority of his position, added, "None of us want this Treaty. None of us want the Crown . . . [but] I see no alternative. . . .

"We are not in a position of force . . . We have not been able to drive the enemy from anything but a good-sized police barracks. . . ."

Cathal Brugha answered that England's position was weak; Ireland's strong; [but] "If instead of being so strong, our last cartridge had been fired, our last shilling spent, and our last man was lying on the ground and his enemies howling around him and their bayonets raised ready to plunge into his body . . . if they said to him: 'Now will you come into the Empire?' he should say, and he *would* say: 'No, I will not!'

"That is the spirit that has lasted all through the centuries . . . [and] the British Government and the British Empire will have gone down before that spirit dies in Ireland."

For eight days the Dáil debated as rising passions opened the national wound ever wider. On December 22, Michael Collins, hoping, perhaps, that Christmas would calm angry spirits; fearing, perhaps, that the Treaty would be lost by an immediate vote; wanting, perhaps, more time to work underground for its approval; proposed an adjournment to January 3. Fear, hope, cunning and reason all moved the deputies according to their natures to vote "Aye!"

Soon we saw that the adjournment was a mistake. So many forces were working against the Republic for which we stood. The whole press of Dublin was against us, using scare headlines to frighten the people. The clergy from their pulpits preached a peaceful acceptance of the enemy's terms. Thousands of men returning weak and ill and broken from English prisons and concentration camps reinforced the argument against risking further war. And the very spirit of Christmas undermined the stern morale which had made our people unconquerable.

We were working hard to counter these things; using all our influence and eloquence; buttonholing those deputies who were still uncommitted; arguing and pleading with them to remember their sacred oath to the Republic. Some we won over; some whom we thought safe, voted against us in the end. One of these was Pat McCarton, who had come to me in Germany to get him home in time. I told him if there was no other way I'd send him in the *Dortmund*. As it happened, I enlisted the help of a good friend, a chemist from Athlone, whom I persuaded to risk exchanging passports with McCarton so he would not be delayed. You may imagine what kinds of a fool I called myself when McCarton voted for the Treaty.

Nor did the "cooling-off period," disarm the tempers of the times. Those who stood by our oath to the Republic and were willing to risk everything for freedom were viciously abused as "irreconcilables," "radicals," "gunmen." In turn our bitterness against the plenipotentiaries who had betrayed their trust increased.

Our anger was greatest against Michael Collins. We could understand how the others came to fall. Arthur Griffiths never had been a fighter. He had been swept into the physical force movement and was at heart a parliamentarian; a sort of Home Ruler whose panacea was a dual monarchy like Austria-Hungary with separate countries owing allegiance to a single king. No wonder he had been confounded by the specious arguments of Lloyd George!

Duggan and Duffy were followers not leaders. Bob Barton disarmed us by his manly explanation of the terrible pressure put upon him to sign.

But Collins, our man of steel and granite, our fearless fighting leader, trusted and beloved; what strange malaise had weakened Michael Collins? Had it been the strain of those long conferences for which this man of action was unused and ill-prepared?

Had the practiced subtleties of English diplomats seduced his mind? Was there some personal reason or physical illness? Or could he have betrayed his country for personal ambition? We could not understand the man at all.

But whatever the reason, once committed, Collins was the most active and the most effective advocate of the Treaty. Without him it would never have been approved. His argument that this agreement was but a steppingstone to our ultimate objective — a free Republic — won many votes. *But there were those who thought it a dishonor to sign a Treaty meaning to break it.* Collins also pleaded that since he had signed the Treaty, to vote against it would be to discredit him. But his most effective weapon was the trust our people had in Michael Collins. Man after man would say, "What's good enough for Mick is good enough for me."

Therefore those of us who stood with our great Chief, de Valera, and Brugha, Stack, Mellows, Rory O'Connor, and the wonderful women deputies, Countess Markieviez, Mary Mac-Swiney, Margaret Pearse, who voted every one against the Treaty — we, who kept to our oath, focussed all our bewildered bitterness on Collins. Him we could not forgive — even in death. The greatness of our love and trust was the measure of our abiding anger.

When the Dáil reconvened on January 3, 1922, we knew in our hearts that we were beaten. There were still moments that uplifted our spirits. Sean T. O'Kelly, our little game cock, so short that you could hardly see where his brave voice was coming from, saying, "It is a Treaty of surrender, subjection, servitude, slavery, and I appeal to you . . . to drive it from approval to rejection, and from rejection to the oblivion from which it should never have emerged."

And Liam Mellows! I remember him standing there facing that long room, square and sturdy, with his gold hair lighting the gloom and his blue eyes like stars of constancy. He said, "To my mind the Republic does exist. It is a living thing for which men gave their lives . . . for which men were hanged . . . for which people suffered . . . for which men are still prepared to give their lives. . . ."

He said that the people were being stampeded into favoring approval by the belief that there was no alternative but "immediate and terrible war . . . That is not the will of the people, it is the fear of the people," he shouted.

As to the economic advantages of joining the Empire, "That was not the ideal that inspired men in this cause, and it is not the ideal that inspires us today. We do not seek to make this country . . . materially great . . . we would rather have the people of Ireland eking out a poor existence on the soil as long as they possessed their souls, their minds and their honor."

Then he spoke like a prophet, telling the world, and Ireland in particular that nothing done here would bind future generations of Irishmen to limit their freedom. No matter what we did here, new people would arise, and they would take up the struggle where we left off. And he foretold that this Treaty would not bring peace to Ireland, but would make her a cockpit of future wars.

Liam Mellows's great oration, read in the light of present knowledge, sounds like a prophecy fulfilled.

There were many other speeches, for virtually every member of the Dáil arose to explain why he would vote as he did. Some of them were dull, spoken to a half-empty room. But when our Chief spoke the place was crowded beyond breathing for all the world hung on his words.

At the very beginning of the debate he had set his position clear. He said, "We were elected by the Irish people, and did the Irish people think we were liars when we said we meant to uphold the Republic, which was ratified by the vote of the people three years ago, and was further ratified — expressly ratified — by the vote of the people at the elections last May? . . .

"I am against this Treaty because it does not reconcile Irish national aspirations with association with the British Government. I am against this Treaty, not because I am a man of war, but a man of peace. I am against this Treaty because it will not end the centuries of conflict between the two nations of Great Britain and Ireland. . . .

"A war-weary people will take things which are not in accordance with their aspirations . . . but I will tell you that Treaty will renew the contest. . . .

". . . And are we in this generation, which has made Irishmen famous throughout the world, to sign our names to the most ignoble document that could be signed?"

Throughout the grand debate, the President had for the most part sat in troubled silence; rising only to refute a specious argument, using his great influence to limit personal abuse and hot-headed calumnies by both sides; and by the power of his own prestige keeping the discussion on a high plateau.

On the re-convening of the Dáil on January 3, he tried to introduce his own compromise proposal of "External Association" with the Empire, which became known as Document Number 2. It was contemptuously dismissed by the opposition and the press as a mere quibble, not worth fighting for.

On January 6, seeing how the tide ran, the President of the Irish Republic offered his resignation. He said that his duty as Chief Magistrate was to preserve the Republic. "I can do that no longer . . ."

He spoke of his fundamental belief in the right of the Irish people to govern themselves. "Anything that takes away from . . . [that right] is absolutely against my principles, and I hold that it would be a subversion of nationality. . . ."

It had been proven, he said, that the men of the Easter Rising, "did represent the hearts and souls of the Irish people. I say that no election taken under duress will disprove that today. . . .

"I have been brought up among the Irish people. I was reared in a laborer's cottage here in Ireland . . . I stand definitely for the Irish Republic as it was established — as it was proclaimed in 1916 — as it was constitutionally established in 1919, and I stand for that definitely; and I will stand by no policy whatever that is not consistent with that. . . ."

Then he made his grand defiance. If the Dáil approved the Treaty and then re-elected him President, "we will deny the right, we will oppose the will, of the British Parliamentary power to legislate for Ireland; and we will make use of any and every means to render impotent the power of England to hold Ireland in subjection by military force or otherwise."

The Dáil was stunned. It was as though George Washington had offered to resign in the camp at Valley Forge. Collins and Griffith leaped to their feet protesting. The President was adamant. Finally Griffith privately begged him to withdraw his resignation until after the vote on the resolution to approve the Treaty. "Very well," said de Valera, "on condition that the vote is taken within twenty-four hours."

On the afternoon of January 7, 1922, I was not at the Dáil, but at Army Headquarters in Parnell Square. To us there a man came running, saying in a broken voice, "They voted for the Treaty! They voted sixty-four to fifty-seven for the Treaty!"

Though I knew it would happen, the news was like the shock of a .45 caliber bullet in my belly. By seven votes we had lost; Ireland had lost! What had we left undone? How had we failed by such a narrow margin? We men of the headquarter troop stood not speaking. Looking dumbly at each other.

Then fear gripped us; fear for the Chief, and for our leaders. There had been rumors that attempts upon their lives might be made. The opposing leaders had the same fear. What was happening now in the Council Chamber? Buckling on our revolvers, a band of us started for Earlsfort Terrace.

The Barracks Quartermaster, Sean Nolan, was with us; Tony Woods, Ned Kellerher and others whom I cannot remember. It is hard to recall the faces. There was a mist before our eyes . . .

The throng in Earlsfort Terrace was the greatest I have seen; extending back and filling Stevens Green; an excited but somber crowd it was. We abandoned our car in the street, and shoved our way through — as a rugged old football player I could buck a line. The great marble lobby was crowded with people; they were on the stairways, packed like cattle in a slaughter yard, uneasily moving and pushing. We jammed ourselves through them up to the gallery; and then by main force through the roiling people into the Council Chamber.

The confusion in that room was indescribable; it must have been a little like a scene in the States-General during the French Revolution. The deputies were all on their feet milling around. Little bands of armed men like ourselves were gathering protectively around the leaders of both parties in fear and anger. There was not much noise, but the hissing, rumbling, muttering of hundreds of angry men was more ominous than roaring and shouting.

The tension was terrific. The minds and emotions of men were stretched to the point of breaking. Next to me in the crowd, jammed body to body, stood a noted member of the famous active service unit; and I saw his hand constantly caressing the butt of his revolver. A single shouted epithet, perhaps even the wink of an eye, could have been the flash to fire that powder train. The war of Irish brothers could have started right there with a holocaust of the people's representatives shooting it out in the Council Chamber.

President de Valera had left the room after the vote. Now he came back into it, and incredibly the tension stretched to a higher pitch. He went to his regular seat; and then stood up signifying that he wished to speak.

Almost instantly all sound died away. It was unbelievable that so many men could be so quiet — they seemed even to have stopped breathing. That acute silence lengthened unbearably, as the Chief stood there towering over the lesser men, seeming to grow taller, gaunter and more overpowering. But his face no longer had the granite self-control to which we were accustomed; its formidable features were working in a fight for self-control and his tall body swayed in the wind of emotion. At last he mastered himself; though his voice sounded as harsh as though the words were forced from a rusted throat:

"I would like my last word here to be this," he said. "We have had a glorious record for four years . . ." he gasped and recovered himself. "It has been four years of magnificent discipline in this nation. That discipline must be preserved. The eyes of the world are upon us. . . ."

Then Eamon de Valera broke. Burying his face in his arms to hide his tears, he sank back onto his little chair.

At the collapse of our great Chief, who had led us through those terrible years of war and never before had faltered, the tension went out of the room in a great sigh. All we wanted to do was get out of there. We hardly heard Cathal Brugha shout that the Army would hold to its discipline. In no more than a moment we were all streaming out of that place in a disorderly rush. Many a man walked blindly with tears streaming from his eyes. Nor was there any exultation of victory in the faces of our opponents — Arthur Griffith, dark eyes and full mustache startlingly black against the gray pallor of his skin, looked to feel the hand of death on his shoulder. There was no devil in Michael Collins' eyes, just a grim blank stare and the mouth of him like a slit in a visored helmet. For the most part the faces of those men pushing down the stairways were all blurred and crumpled and streaked with tears.

I kept telling myself that I was a soldier of Ireland still, that I must not weep, but if I had to speak a single word I would have burst out bawling like a child that knows there is none to comfort him. I felt as I had when my dear Pappa was felled by his final stroke, and lay for some days dying — I was helpless to talk to him, so much though I wanted to; and he was helpless to speak to me.

To tell you the truth, it was not so much of Ireland and her future I was thinking as of my comrades and beloved leaders; about Dev and Mellows and Seamus Robinson, about Eamon Martin and Sean Noonan, Sean McEntee and Sean Etchingham,

139

about these men who I knew saw the terror and the disaster that was looming up in front of this nation . . .

So we came out of that building into the crowded street. The people parted silently to let us through. Grave and respectful they were, like men watching the funeral procession of some beloved person. And so they were; for I felt that I had just left the dying bed of Ireland and her people.

CHAPTER XIII

The Choice

THE day after the Treaty was approved we had a gloomy little gathering. Mellows was there and Seamus Robinson; I forget who else. We were as despairful as only ardent young men can be; for the cause which had been the mainspring of our existence seemed forever lost and life had no more meaning. "What next? What next?" we asked each other and ourselves.

We were agreed that none of us wanted to remain and watch the chains that bound us to Britain re-forged by Irishmen. We felt that it might be better for us all to leave Ireland and go somewhere else where we could carry on the fight against the Empire.

Seamus Robinson proposed India, where rumblings of discontent were a prelude to her fight for independence. "Let's go there," said Seamus, "and teach the Indians all we have learned about guerrilla warfare and British tactics. With their vast population we'd have a chance to strike a real blow for freedom."

His suggestion provoked an outburst of genuine enthusiasm; so volatile are we Irish that it takes but a spark of courage to rekindle hope. However, it went no further because developments at home took another shape.

The fact is that on January 8, 1921, all was far from lost. Indeed, it nearly was regained the next day in the Dáil. On January 9, President de Valera resigned. After a short debate the motion was put "that Mr. de Valera be re-elected President of the Irish Republic."

In effect that was another vote on the Treaty. The motion was defeated by 60 votes to 58; the Chief not voting. This time we had lost by two votes. De Valera and the anti-Treaty deputies then temporarily withdrew, and Arthur Griffith was elected President. But president of what? Since he was committed to disestablish the Republic, nobody — not even Griffith — seemed to know!

Griffith promptly appointed a new ministry with Michael Collins as Minister for Finance, Liam Cosgrave for Local Government and General Mulcahy, Minister of Defense. After that de Valera and his party returned to their seats, and the Chief promised that when Griffith was acting in his capacity as President of the Republic, the anti-Treaty party would not stand in his way, but when he functioned as head of a provisional government, "We will have to insist . . . that the government is not the legitimate government of the country until the Irish people have disestablished the Republic, and we shall do everything in our power to see they do not disestablish it."

Thus we found that though we had lost the first two skirmishes, we had not lost the battle. All parties agreed that the vote of approval in the Dáil at most, merely gave the Executive the right to establish a provisional government. Only the Irish people in a general election could ratify the Treaty.

With amazing rapidity the political maneuvering began on that basis. De Valera formed a new party called Cumann na Poblachta — the Republican Party. To support it Erskine Childers started a small weekly newspaper which he named *An Phoblacht na h-Eireann* (The Republic of Ireland) designed to expose the worst features of the Treaty and appeal to the loyalty of the Irish people.

Meanwhile a provisional government was quickly and illegally formed at a meeting of the "South Ireland Parliament," which was a figment of British imagination and consisted only of the pro-Treaty members of the Dáil — our people would not attend. Michael Collins was named Chairman of the Provisional Government — Griffith wanted to keep the presidency non-political. The other ministers took office in the new government. On January 16, Collins received the "surrender" of Dublin Castle from the Lord Lieutenant. British Army Headquarters were moved to Phoenix Park; and British troops began to pull out, their regimental bands playing a tune with the appropriate if somewhat sinister title, "Let Erin Remember."

Most of all we were worried about the Irish Republican Army. Would the Provisional Government keep it intact? General Mulcahy promised that "The Army will remain occupying the same position in regard to the government . . . and the Minister of Defense . . . as we have had up to the present." But we did not trust him. And right we were!

On the surface Mulcahy did everything to fool the Army into believing that it was still the I.R.A. They were issued the green uniforms and the badges worn in the Easter Rising of 1916, and the tricolor flew over their barracks. On January 31, when Beggars Bush Barracks was handed over by the British to be their headquarters, the Army marched down Dame Street with Michael Collins taking the salute from the steps of the City Hall, and Mulcahy spouting hypocritical gibberish about "going ahead under the old flag . . . still guarding the old ideals . . . the burning spirit of patriotism . . ." and (most blasphemous phrase of all) "the fires of Easter week"(!)

We were not taken in. Even before the formation of the Provisional Government, Rory O'Connor, Liam Mellows, Oscar Traynor, and Liam Lynch had called for a convention of the Irish Volunteers, which it was their right to hold, Mulcahy stalled it off by insisting it would bring the British evacuation to a halt. The best they could get for the time being was a vague promise of a convention in two months, and permission to send two Republican observers to the Army Council to make sure Republican aims were "not prejudiced." The men chosen were Traynor and Earnán O'Malley, commander of the Second Southern Division. When his entire division resigned from the Free State Army, O'Malley withdrew and Andrew MacDonnell, Commander of the Wicklow Brigade, replaced him.

This Andy MacDonnell was a great friend of mine and one of the best commanders in the I.R.A. He had been out in the

Easter Rising at the age of sixteen, one of the youngest of that youthful band. When the fighting began again his courage and cunning soon brought him command of the Wicklow or South Dublin Brigade. He was a wee, small fighting fellow with a rosy baby face that concealed his guile.

I remember how, in the days of the British, Andy met the famous Major Bryan Cooper, one of England's most active intelligence officers. Andy needed a car for some nefarious business or other, so with a group of his boys he paid a call on Major Cooper at "Khyber Pass," as the major called his magnificent mansion at Killiney. Andy and his men just knocked at the door, and when a maid opened it, they rushed in and held Major Cooper up in his study. "I'll be needing to borrow your motor car for a bit," said Andy. "My men will keep you company until I bring it back."

He went off on his errand, while the men sat there with guns pointing at the major, who was too wise a man to make a fuss. After some hours Andy came back. "Your car's back safe and sound," he said, "and now we'll be taking our leave with many thanks."

"Not at all," said Cooper. "But I say, are you really the commander of one of these I.R.A. units?"

"That I am!"

The major's face was a study as he drawled, "Now I understand the saying 'And a little child shall lead them.'"

MacDonnell had great care for his men. When they were operating against the British among the wild Wicklow Hills just south of Dublin, he came to an odd arrangement with Lord Powerscourt, who was, of course, one of the British Ascendancy people. His Lordship held one of the most magnificent desmenes in Ireland, with a great stone Georgian mansion and several thousand acres of land with herds of cattle and flocks of sheep. It would have been easy for the Wicklow boys to take it and burn the house as was done in many cases. Instead, at Lord Powerscourt's request, Andy stationed a permanent I.R.A. guard on the premises which kept it safe. In return for which Lord Powerscourt never counted his sheep, and the Wicklow Brigade always ate well.

Despite General Mulcahy's fiction that the Army would be kept intact, he right away began seducing it to the Free State. He started recruiting men who were never in the Republican Movement at all; many of them had served in the Irish regiments of the British Army as British soldiers. Influenced by Michael Collins the Irish Republican Brotherhood took a hand in the subversion of the Army. The new headquarters staff put pro-Treaty men into the key positions and did everything possible to make posts in what was becoming a new professional Free State Army attractive to our best people.

They were after me all the time; for they realized how much I had done toward arming our people and how valuable my contacts would be for bringing munitions to the Republicans if I remained with them. I was offered a commission as colonel in the Quartermaster Corps if I would come in to Beggars Bush. Most uncivilly I told them the exact location where they could put their commission!

Seeing the way things were going, the staunch Republicans held together. Thus a cleavage spread right down through the Army by brigades and smaller units. Soon there were certain units of the Army that were definitely known to be Free State, and others — many others — who stood by their oath to the Republic. As the British troops were withdrawn from different parts of the country, there was a wild scramble of units from both sides to seize their vacated barracks. Later the Dublin brigades seized various buildings in the city and fortified them, and brought in members from the country who previously had merely been on call. The buildings we held in Dublin included the Ballast Office, the Masonic Hall, Lever Brothers and, ironically, the Kildare Street Club, a great gloomy old place which had been the social stronghold of the English aristocracy.

While all this was going on there were some amusing happenings. Andy MacDonnell, ever thoughtful of his men, heard that the Free State was issuing uniforms and arms to commanders who applied at Beggars Bush Barracks. He promptly marched some of his loyal Republican men up there and got them resplendently outfitted at the Free State's expense. Unfortunately the Staters caught on before he could bring in the rest of his command.

I recall the first time I saw Andy in his fine new general's uniform. I went down to see him at Bray, and was directed to Brigade headquarters in the former police station. It was heavily barricaded. I knocked on the door. The letter box in it flew open and two revolvers appeared pointed at my gizzard. I said *very* politely, "I'd like to see the brigadier."

"You can't see him."

"Why can I not?"

"He's not here. He'll be back in a few hours."

Not liking to argue with two revolvers with no face behind them, I went away.

Strolling on the Promenade at Bray, I observed MacDonnell. He looked magnificent in his new green uniform with bright badges, gold braid and a general's shoulder bars. He was accompanied by the equally resplendent figure of his adjutant, a former British officer.

"Hullo, Andy," I said. "I want a word with you."

Andy tried to make his youthful face look stern, and the adjutant said stiffly, "If you wish to speak to the brigadier, you should address him through me."

My mouth opened wide. "Holy God! Is this what we fought for?" I gaped. "All this imitation of British rules, regulations and military manners?"

Andy soon dismounted from his high horse, and told me how he had acquired his uniform.

Since the Provisional Government had authorized the use of Republican badges and symbols in their army, our men began sewing purple patches on the collars of their uniforms to indicate the difference. Thus there was practical proof where people stood in this argument — with Griffith and Collins or with de Valera and the I.R.A.

All this choosing up of sides produced terrible tensions. There were even incidents of itchy-fingered Irishmen shooting at each other, though I cannot remember any serious casualties. In March the Republican Military Council, consisting of Rory O'Connor, Mellows, Sean Russell and J. O'Donovan, issued a manifesto signed by over fifty senior officers summoning a "Convention of the Irish Volunteers." This was a straight-out defiance of the Provisional Government, and to dot the i's and cross the t's Rory O'Connor gave an interview to the press in which he said, "Dáil Eireann has done an act it had no moral right to do. The Volunteers are not going into the Empire, they stand for Irish Freedom."

His answers to the reporters' questions made the Volunteers' position clear as crystal. He said that the Army "for which I speak" would not obey the existing G.H.Q. because the Minister for Defense had broken his agreement that the Army should be kept as the Army of the Republic. Asked if it would obey President Griffith, O'Connor answered, "No. He has violated his oath to the Republic."

Asked whether there was any government in Ireland to which the Army would give allegiance, he said, "No," and explained, "We will set up an executive which will issue orders to the I.R.A."

"Are we going to have a military dictatorship then?" he was asked.

"You can take it that way if you like," Rory answered.

The Convention met in the Round Room of the Mansion House on March 26, 1922. Although I was not a delegate Liam Mellows called me back from Germany, where I was keeping up my organization, to give a report on the possibility of the continuance of my activities in gunrunning and the results which could be expected from them. He felt this was necessary to counter the agreement that it would be no use attempting to carry on if the Treaty were rejected by the Irish people and England reacted by declaring war.

As I walked up Dawson Street the airy eighteenth century façade of the Mansion House looked very gay, with red geraniums in boxes by the tall lamp posts and the coat of arms of Dublin City newly painted above the door. But the atmosphere was grim. Parked in the drive was an armored car in which the delegates from the First Southern Division had driven up from Cork for fear they'd be stopped by government troops. The hall and the beautiful reception room, with its great crystal chandelier, delicate English furniture and larger-than-life-size portraits of former Lord Lieutenants, were crowded with somber, excited men. Very few of them wore uniforms, but every one of them was armed. Sam Browne belts buckled over shabby tweed jackets were weighted by one or more .45 caliber service automatics. I remember during the discussions a certain thing was proposed and a delegate objected, "We have no rule for that."

Sean Etchingham spoke softly. "We have the rule of .45!" he said, meaning the rule of the revolver.

That was the spirit of the Convention. Representatives from all areas were present. The vast bulk of them were unknown to me as I was to them. Some of the officers were also members of the Dáil. I did not have the authority or position to make a speech, but I went through the rooms among them and onto the crowded floor of the Round Room, buttonholing individuals I knew and forming little groups to whom I explained that I had had several years now to make contacts in Germany and set up lines of delivery. That if it were to be war again I could guarantee not only that further supplies would keep coming, but they would be in ever larger quantities; that the logistics would be easier because I would not be starting on virgin soil.

The result of the Convention was that the delegates unanimously reaffirmed their allegiance to the Republic and adopted a new constitution placing the Army under the supreme command of an Executive of sixteen officers appointed by the

Convention. Among them were Rory O'Connor, Liam Mellows and Liam Lynch. Our main purpose at this time was that the Army should be kept as a distinct entity and should have something to say in the management of the country.

The next day a goodly number of officers who had been taking orders from Mulcahy announced their adherence to the new Army executive. From that time on, despite the Provisional Government's protests, our troops were called "The Irish Republican Army." The pro-Treaty crowd were known as "Beggars Bush troops," or the "Free State Army," and so I shall hereafter name them.

Action began almost immediately after the Convention closed. On March 29, the high-spirited First Southern raided a British ship at Cobh (Queenstown) and helped themselves to a fine lot of His Majesty's machine guns, rifles and ammunition that were being sent back to England. Shooting incidents became more common and tension tightened fast. On the night of April 13 the Army Council took a long forward step. Acting on their orders the First and Second Dublin Brigades slipped quietly into the Four Courts, chasing the bewigged and bewildered lawyers out. Windows, doors and gates were barricaded and sandbagged; and the I.R.A. announced that this was their new headquarters.

The next day Liam Mellows, Secretary of the Army Council, sent a letter to the Dáil announcing the purposes and position of the Irish Republican Army:

1. *To Maintain the existing Republic.*
2. *That Dáil Eireann . . . be the only Government of the country.*
3. *To maintain the Irish Republican Army under the control of an elected independent Executive. . . .*
6. *No future elections on the issue at present before the country to be held while the threat of war with England exists.*

That manifesto threw the gauntlet right in the face of the Provisional Government. It became clear that this thing could not end without the "fratricidal strife" which de Valera had warned against. In this situation I was brought to an agonizing state of indecision.

For the first time in my life I felt like a stranger in my beloved country. As between Ireland and any other nation there was never a doubt of my allegiance; but in this dispute and looming violence between Irishmen I wondered if I should choose sides. My heart urged me on, but the question was whether as a Jew I had the right to do so. This was the only time in my whole life that I did think as a Jew in connection with my country.

You see these men who were about to settle the fate of the nation by a war between brothers were so closely tied to the land. As I did not, they had a long native ancestry stretching back to the Firbolgs in the dusky druidical dawn of our history. For the Irish are a very homogeneous people bound and kept so by their island habitation. Sure, invaders have come again and again through the centuries, each wave in the ships of their particular genius — in the armor-plated battleships of England, in ships-of-the-line, in caravels and carracks, galleys and dragon ships, and for all I know in rafts with a bull's-hide sail. But they never came in such numbers as to greatly dilute the native strain.

Now it seemed to me that these people being bred and raised with the very soil and substance of Ireland in their bodies, and with their racial memories stretching so far backward into her history, that perhaps these men alone could decide her destiny; and that an alien had no right to choose between them.

Yet my whole life was closely tied up with the men, my true friends, who had taken their stand in the Four Courts; my loyalty was deeply involved; and my solemn oath to defend the Republic bound me to them. I believed ardently in the justice of their cause.

Alone I could not come to a decision. Lily was in Germany; but I must have counsel. So I went out to "Marino," my mother's little house in Monkstown, to ask her advice.

The Choice

As I have said before, my mother was a woman who was both wise and intelligent and a person of sympathetic understanding. For many hours that night she talked with me, listening intently to my problem; discussing it in all its complexity and debating thoughtfully my possible courses of action. In the end she could only counsel me to retire from the political scene. This she knew was what Pappa would have said; for he was a man of peace. And though it was one thing to take arms in defense of one's country, it was quite another to fight over the form of its government.

Before I took my final decision I sent word to Liam Mellows, who had always been my friend and adviser, and who had originally brought me into the movement for independence. He sent word back, "I am coming to see you."

Liam came to Marino in the late afternoon. He and I and my mother sat in the little cluttered parlor while the night came down and sped half its course. For five hours we sat while Mellows did most of the talking. Never was he so brilliant, so ardent and so emotional. I knew that this great effort he was making and the intensity of his feeling was not to save one poor soldier for Ireland. It was because of his love for me. He was wrestling for my soul with the devil of doubt.

There was no denying his logic. To my question of my right to choose, he said that I had earned the right more fully than many another by risking my life for Ireland's freedom; that furthermore it was not a right but an obligation, for had I not played a role in saving the nation from tyranny? And just as one who saves another's life has a sort of moral responsibility toward that man ever after, so I had the same responsibility toward Ireland. Then he added that even though I had not acquired this obligation, I was bound by a still higher one to choose, because this was an ethical question and every human being by virtue of his divine humanity is obligated to make his choice between right and wrong.

Finally, in answer to my qualms about maybe having to shed the blood of Irishmen, he said, "This I will solemnly promise you; that never will the Irish Republican Army make the first move to start a civil war."

When he had done speaking and the night deep around us, even my mother was convinced. "Liam is right, Bob," she said. "You must choose."

There was, of course, no question of what my choice would be. The next morning I went to the Four Courts and enlisted in the garrison.

CHAPTER XIV

The Four Courts

Now is the time to tell you something of the magnificent group of buildings which became the stronghold of the Irish Republican Army and was the place where bloody civil war began. The Four Courts is so named because it is the center of justice in Ireland. Here meet the courts of the four provinces which had been the ancient kingdoms and later the dukedoms of Ireland — Munster, Leinster, Connaught and Ulster.

After Dublin Castle, which is a walled medieval fortress in the heart of the city, the Four Courts is the most defensible position in Dublin. Looking across the Liffey River from the north bank, it consists of a massive stone building surmounted by a huge dome with a fine portico supported by fluted Corinthian columns. Wings stretch out on either side, and behind it are low barracks-like buildings which were used for just that purpose by the garrison, as was the east wing of the main structure. The whole complex of buildings and courtyards is surrounded by a high, wrought-iron fence — almost a military *chevaux-de-frise* with twelve-foot-high spearpoints. Great double gates higher than the palisade give entrance to it on all sides. At the time of the siege they were still surmounted by the royal arms of England.

Massive oak doors lead from the portico directly into the rotunda, which is a huge circular hall under the airy height of the great dome. On its four walls and set in the pavement as well were the shields of the Irish provinces — the three castellated towers which are the arms of Munster, the upraised arm holding the sword and eagle of Connaught; the green harp of Leinster, and the blood-red hand of Ulster.

When I went to the Four Courts to enlist — or re-enlist — in the Irish Republican Army, the rotunda looked like an armed camp. The tall front doors were barricaded by sandbags, as were the windows, through which pointed machine guns. The small windows high up at the base of the dome were constantly manned by sharpshooters. The gates were permanently barricaded, sealed and armed; the only one open for use being the east gate, through which machine guns were trained.

The magazine, in which a great supply of ammunition was kept, was in the cellar under the rotunda. When the realization came to me that almost all the arms and ammunition which defended the Four Courts were the cargo I had brought to Ireland in the *Frieda*, I was both proud and sadly troubled.

Rory O'Connor commanded the garrison with Liam Mellows, who was also Quartermaster General of the I.R.A., as his second in command. Other dedicated young officers who were either members of the garrison or in and out included Earnán O'Malley, Sean MacBride — Maud Gonne's son, and Andy MacDonnell. From the time they established themselves in the Four Courts these men, particularly O'Connor and Mellows, had more influence over the Army than its titular commanders, Chief of Staff Liam Lynch and Deputy Chief of Staff Joseph McKelvey. Cathal Brugha, now no longer Minister of Defense, was temporarily without power or even much influence, as indeed were all the civilian leaders including de Valera himself. Rory O'Connor had announced that the Army was not associated with any political organization. But he added, "I am safe in saying that if the Army were ever to follow a political leader, de Valera is the man!"

I reported to Liam Mellows and was under his direct command. My principal mission was to maintain the supply of arms for the Republican Army. For this purpose I was kept on the move between Germany and Ireland. However, I also was given a few odd jobs to do around Dublin, some of them very odd indeed.

As a result I was constantly in and out of the Four Courts

during those two months of uneasy peace. I had a pass which enabled me to enter the east gate at all hours. The boys soon got so used to me that they never even looked at it. In this connection I had a little trouble one day.

The Barracks Commander of the east wing was Sean Lemass, who is now our Minister for Industry and Finance. At that time he was a very energetic, very pugnacious young cock, short and stocky, with a ruddy skin and black hair. On this occasion he saw me strolling nonchalantly through the courtyard and hailed me sharply. "How did you get in here, Briscoe?"

"Over the wall," I answered flippantly, though it was not true at all.

Lemass ordered out the guard and arrested me. Of course, I told him the truth and showed my pass; but this did not mollify him whatever — they were fiercely touchy of their dignity were these desperate young men. Lemass said, "True or not, your answer was disrespectful to an officer. Ye'll stand a court-martial."

He clapped me in the clink, and it took all Mellows's influence to get me out.

On May 2, 1922, a couple of weeks after I joined the garrison, Mellows gave me one of those odd jobs — delicate, too, it was. He called me into his office in the low building back of the Courts. Here he sat surrounded by ordinary wastebaskets, all of them chock-a-block full of brand-new Irish bank notes. Seeing the amazement on my face, Mellows pulled open the door of a wardrobe, and that also was nearly filled with money. It was the first time I had ever seen new currency with the stubbs attached to the notes as you'd find on a check in a checkbook. Liam told me that there were forty thousand pounds' worth of these new notes and about ten thousand pounds of older money. I gaped like a countryman.

After astonishing me Liam explained that the Army had gone broke. The Dáil had promised to pay all their bills up to March 26, the time of their declaration of independence, but had not done so. As a result tradesmen who had supplied us were being done out of their money and we had none to carry on with.

It seemed only proper, Mellows said, for the Army to make a "levy," as he called it, on the government bank. The day before, armed men of the I.R.A. had held up various branches of the Bank of Ireland. This pile of money was the result of their efforts — a small contribution from the government for the defense of the Republic and to enable the Army to pay its just debts.

"These notes, being brand-new, can easily be stopped by the government," Mellows said. "Now I want you to take as many of them as you think you can possibly manage and change them into used notes of any denomination."

"Give me time to make a plan," I said.

"Surely," said Liam. "You can have ten minutes."

Within that time I had my plan. I stuffed ten thousand pounds' worth of notes in an ordinary handbag, and accompanied by Dick Barrett took a cab to the Land Bank where I had a small personal account. As I walked into the bank between the mahogany counters and the brass grills of the tellers' cages, I was hoping nobody would notice the bulge of my automatic in a shoulder holster under my sober business suit. Being well known there, I asked casually if the manager, Mr. Smith-Gordon, could see me on an important business matter. Word came down from his upstairs office that the manager would see me at once.

We found him alone, sitting behind his flat-top desk. We took chairs facing him. Dick Barrett, being a Cork man, was somewhat blunt in his manner. He took out his revolver and resting it on the desk said, "Now, Mr. Smith-Gordon, ye'll take that telephone and call the teller downstairs. Ye'll tell him that Mr. Briscoe here will be down with some bank notes he wants changed into other denominations, and that he is to be accommodated without delay."

Smith-Gordon merely raised his eyebrow slightly as he reached for the telephone. In a quiet voice he repeated the instructions almost verbatim. I immediately rose and started for the door.

"How much time will you be needing, Bob?" Barrett asked, never taking his gun off the manager.

"Ten minutes should be ample," I answered.

"I'll just stay here chatting with Mr. Smith-Gordon then," he answered.

Mellows was delighted when I brought this nice old money in; but there was still thirty thousand pounds to be changed. I took another load out to Mr. Andrew Woods at Donnybrook. "I've a little cash money with me I'd like to be rid of," I told him.

Mr. Woods grinned — he'd been reading the papers. "What do you want me to do?" he asked.

"Give me bearer checks for five thousand pounds," I answered, "and I'll give you the cash."

"Right you are," he said, and did so.

"Now I have some more money," I said, turning to Mrs. Woods. "It's a fine day and the racing is on at the Curragh. Would not you gather a few friends and enjoy a day at the races? The bookmakers there have plenty of cash and would be able to change a large number of notes."

"Never did I hear of so agreeable a way of serving my country," Mary Woods remarked.

While she organized a racing party, I went on to see Uncle David Cherrick. Though he took no part in politics, he was loyal to his family. I easily persuaded him to give me a series of checks in return for cash. All these little transactions came off perfectly. The people who helped me knew well the risks they were taking; they were willing to accept them for love of country and true friendship's sake. I am happy to say no harm came to them. The only one who had any trouble was Mr. Woods, who delayed a little in lodging the money in his bank. By that time the numbers of the bank notes had been circulated. An inspector of police came to call on him, and asked how he had come by the notes. Woods told him the truth, "A man came to me with them," he said, "and he complained that he was worried at having so much loose money on him in these troubled times.

He asked if I would give him bearer checks for it, and I obliged him."

"Can you describe him?"

Woods responded with a true, if flattering, description of me, "A tall, dark man he was, good-looking, well dressed. You'd have no suspicion of such a one; he could have been a businessman or a big cattle dealer."

Apparently they did not ask my name, most likely assuming it would be a false one anyway, and Mr. Woods was very happy not to have to tell a lie. But he told me he had many uncertain hours as a result of this interrogation.

That is how the Irish Republican Army was financed. As for me, there were certain delayed repercussions. Many years later when I first rose to speak in the Dáil after I had been elected as a member of Mr. de Valera's Fianna Fail Party, shouts of "Bank robber!" came from the government benches. I have to admit they were not entirely unjustified.

Never a time went by without a bit of fun. Such an occasion was the degrading of Darrell Figgis. The Provisional Government had given Figgis the job of drawing up the Free State Constitution, which was to accord with the Treaty and was, in fact, largely dictated by Winston Churchill, who had taken charge of the British Department of Irish Affairs. Figgis was a clever but unstable lawyer and writer, who had a great opinion of himself and the vanity of appearance. You should see him strolling dapperly down O'Connell Street in smartly cut clothes, with his red hair gleaming like newly polished boots and a fine, red, square-cut beard that was his special pride.

Now Figgis began making some very detrimental remarks about the I.R.A. We did not consider him a menace, he was too much the lightweight, but he annoyed us with his waspish stings. It seemed proper to close his mouth.

On a certain day a group of armed men stormed into his office. Some of us held him tipped back in his swivel chair while one man produced a glittering razor. Figgis squealed like a pig with its throat cut, but no one intended him any harm. We shaved off half his beard, and escorted him out to the middle of O'Connell Street, where he liked to promenade so proudly. There we turned him loose. I think he would have been happier had we just cut his throat.

All these little transactions, and some others such as my trip to Arklow on a stolen motor car to bring the boys of Fianna Eireann under the I.R.A., brought me to the attention of the new Civil Guards, which the Provisional Government had organized to replace the Royal Irish Constabulary in maintaining order and suppressing civil liberty.

It was about this time that these gentlemen paid a call on me at my place of business at 9 Aston Quay and marched my guest, Doctor Schuler, and me off to the police station, as I have described earlier.

While Lily was wringing her hands and little Jamie was vowing vengeance, Doctor Schuler and I were questioned in separate rooms. I was taken before Dave Nelligan, a famous detective. He shot embarrassing questions at me, a dozen to the minute, which I think I was pretty canny about answering. One thing he kept pounding at was, "When did you last see Sean MacBride?" Since MacBride had connections in Germany and Doctor Schuler was a German, I guessed that Nelligan thought the three of us were cooking up another deal in arms.

All the time I was talking I kept my hands flat on a broad desk-like table in front of me, and behind me stood a detective holding a revolver by the muzzle. I knew that if I made a false move he'd crack my skull with it. Finally I said to Nelligan, "Can I have a cigarette?"

"For sure," he answered amicably.

I knew if I reached for one my friend in the rear would hit me, so I said, "Will you give me one?"

Nelligan smiled and stuck a cigarette in my mouth.

"Well now, will you give me a light?"

The detective's smile was a broad grin as he complied.

"Well now, you're a smart one!" he said.

I was that, for they got no information from me. However, I was alarmed by a series of screeches from Doctor Schuler. Just what was happening to him in the next room I was not then sure. Later he told me that a detective had come in with a suitably knotted rope and said, "If you don't tell us everything we'll hang you right here!"

Fortunately he did not know anything much.

After several hours of intensive questioning the Civil Guards released us both. I took it more or less as a matter of course, but Schuler was not having any more. When I asked him where he'd like to dine, he said, "All I want you to do is to put me on the night mail boat to Holyhead!"

After all this I went back to Germany with Lily and worked for a little while at my business and getting ready to send in more arms. But the politicians were very busy, so I must tell you what they were doing, and of the great betrayal that brought on the catastrophic civil war. With these things I had no connection, but they are a matter of history.

After the I.R.A. established itself in the Four Courts and other buildings in Dublin, feeling ran so high it almost erupted into war right then. At night in O'Connell Street and along the quays of the Liffey sudden random bursts of machine gun fire sent people ducking into doorways; and there were a few casualties on both sides.

While these skirmishes were going on, men of good will in both parties, in the Dáil and in the sundered Army, were trying to find a basis on which Irishmen could reunite, or at the least stop shooting at each other. These efforts first resulted in an informal truce between the two factions of the Army, beginning on May 4.

Politically the great anxiety of the Republicans was the coming election on the Treaty. They feared that the Irish people would be stampeded by England's threat of war into approving it against their real desires. The Free Staters were for a quick election.

Now a compromise was put forward. There would be an election on June 16, 1922, but the people would not be asked to vote on the Treaty. Instead the whole of Sinn Fein, pro- and anti-Treaty would get together to put forward a panel of coalition candidates. These would be nominated in the same relative strength that the two parties now held in the Dáil. After the election a coalition cabinet would be formed, based on this relative strength.

Though it left his party in a minority, de Valera accepted this proposal for the sake of peace and to avoid the finality of a popular acceptance of the Treaty. Arthur Griffith and Michael Collins solemnly promised to observe "the Pact." The plan came to be known as "a Pact Election." It was ratified at a great *Ard Fheis* of Sinn Fein on May 23, with only one negative vote.

Naturally the agreement did not prevent other parties, such as Labor, from putting up candidates. Nor could individual pro-Treaty or anti-Treaty candidates be prevented from running. This loophole eventually broke the Pact.

Meanwhile, comparative peace fell over the South of Ireland. De Valera and Michael Collins actually appeared on the same platform together speaking for the electon of the National Sinn Fein Panel candidates; and to further the Pact an Army Coalition Conference was called.

This unexpected display of national unity was strengthened to a considerable extent by the extraordinary atrocities committed against Catholics in the six counties of the North.

There had been surprisingly little religious prejudice or persecution of Protestants in the Catholic South of Ireland. Indeed, some of our bravest leaders including Erskine Childers and Bob Barton, who had rejoined the Republicans, were Protestants. De Valera had tremendous influence in preventing persecutions. When some Protestants were killed in County Cork he spoke out for tolerance saying, "The German Palatines, the French Huguenots, the English Protestants . . . later the Wesleyans and the Jews, flying from persecution, in this land of ours have always found safe asylum. That glorious record must not be tarnished by acts against a helpless minority."

Just the contrary was the case in Ulster. Catholics living on mainly Protestant streets were driven out of their homes and took refuge in what became virtually Catholic ghettos like Ballymacarett. They were not permitted to carry arms, while virtually every Orangeman had a revolver. As Joseph Devlin of the British House of Commons said, "If Catholics have no revolvers to protect themselves they are murdered. If they have revolvers they are flogged and sentenced to death."

British Field Marshall Sir Henry Wilson, military adviser to the Belfast Government, was considered largely responsible for the severity of the repressive measures against northern nationalists, and Catholics in general. Certainly he did nothing to stop the flow of blood. The Ulster Special Constabulary, paid by the British Government, were as brutal as the Black and Tans, without even the latter's excuse of fighting a nation in revolt. By the end of May over twenty-three thousand Catholics had been driven from their homes and several hundred had been murdered.

Then things got worse. The shooting of two Special Constabularies in Belfast on May 31, 1922, brought savage reprisals. Specials in armored cars roared through the streets sweeping them with machine guns; breaking into houses and setting them on fire; murdering their inhabitants, men and women alike. A few days later a Belfast mob surrounded the Catholic Misericordia Hospital, shooting through the windows while patients rolled under their beds and fifty children already wounded in the anti-Catholic pogroms lay screaming in their cots.

A tremendous wave of indignation brought both factions in the South of Ireland closer together. The leaders of the Free State Army and the I.R.A. conferred on the possibility of joining together to end these atrocities by an attack on the North, which was garrisoned by sixty-thousand British troops. Though the attempt to reunify the Army failed, the conference did reach a very secret agreement in the matter of arms for fighting against Ulster. Five commandants of northern divisions, who had not yet declared against the Provisional Government, were formed into a committee headed by General Frank Aiken of the Fourth Northern, who is now Minister for External Affairs of the Irish Republic. General Mulcahy himself ordered them to assist Nationalist Volunteers in the six counties. Since rifles supplied by the British must not appear in this campaign the Free State Army and the I.R.A. arranged an exchange of arms. Liam Lynch sent guns — some of them mine — to the North and in return was given rifles which the British had supplied to the Free State Army. During the second and third weeks of June there was a tremendous traffic in arms and ammunition between Beggars Bush Barracks and the Four Courts.

The British were not at all pleased by this sudden spirit of unity in Ireland. The Caesars' principle of "divide and rule," was the policy of the Empire. Sir Henry Wilson was furious. British troops still holding Phoenix Park were alerted. British politicians denounced the Pact as a violation of the Treaty.

Meanwhile Arthur Griffith had taken a draft of the new Free State constitution to England. It was too democratic to suit Lloyd George and Churchill, who altered it drastically. On June 12, four days before the polling, Michael Collins was summoned to England. Once again Lloyd George put the screws on him and once again Collins cracked.

Two days later, while de Valera was speaking in Kildare urging the people to support the Panel candidates, Michael Collins broke the Pact. Speaking in Cork he said, "I am not hampered now by being on a platform where there are coalitionists. I can make a straight appeal to you . . . to vote for the candidates you think best of . . . You understand fully what you have to do, and I depend on you to do it."

With that all pretense of keeping the Pact was thrown away. Handbills were printed to frighten the Irish people, saying:

> *You can get the Republic for all Ireland through the safe and sane method of the Treaty or you can try another round through the alphabet of miseries.*
>
> *A . . . Auxiliaries*
> *B . . . Black and Tans*
> *C . . . Commandeering*
> *E . . . Executions*

So it went through the whole dismal list down to:

> *XYZ . . . the final horrors which words cannot describe.*
> *To get (perhaps) Document No. 2.*
> *VOTE FOR THE TREATY*

These statements were bloody lies.

While breaking the Pact the members of the Provisional Government also brought back the new constitution of the Free State which gave the King of England, and through him the British Government, extraordinary powers. The executive power of the Free State was vested in the King of England. He had the power to veto legislation passed by the *Oireachtas*, as the new two-chamber parliament was to be called. Not only that but the British Governor General of the Free State might withold or reserve a bill passed by both houses of the new Parliament for the King's assent; and Parliament could vote no money for any purpose not recommended by him. This was not anywhere near dominion status.

It had always been agreed and promised that the new Constitution would be published before the election. But so craven was this document that Griffith and Collins dared not give Irishmen a chance to study it. So they broke their word again, in effect if not in the letter. The new Constitution was published in the morning papers on election day. Two-thirds of the voters went to the polls not having seen it. None had time to study it.

The result might have been foreseen. Double dealing, broken promises, stark terror of another war befuddled and weakened an electorate already suffering from battle fatigue. When the votes were counted it was found that although the pro-

Treaty Party had been reduced from sixty-six seats in the Dáil to fifty-eight in the *Oireachtas*, the Republicans had suffered an even worse loss from fifty-eight to thirty-six. Labor, Farmers, Independents, and others made up the rest of the one hundred twenty-eight members. However, three-quarters of the deputies elected were pledged to the Pact. It was a clear mandate for a coalition government, but Griffith and Collins did not choose to recognize it. Since with their allies they had a working majority, they proclaimed the results to be a victory for the Treaty. No coalition government was ever formed.

Now the tentative tendrils of reunification were torn finally apart. The widening breach was blasted further by an unfortunate event in England. On June 22, Sir Henry Wilson, returning from a military ceremony in the brilliant bemedaled splendor of a British field marshal was shot dead on the doorstep of his home. The young men who killed him were captured in the street. They were Joseph O'Sullivan and Reginald Dunne, both former Irish soldiers in the British Army — O'Sullivan had lost a leg at the Battle of Ypres.

To this day no one is sure whether the killing of Sir Henry was their personal protest against the outrages he had sanctioned in Belfast, as they themselves testified, or if it was instigated from Ireland. They may have been acting on the orders of the Irish Republican Brotherhood. That they were *not* acting on the orders of the Four Courts garrison was proved by the definite statement issued by Rory O'Connor: "The shooting of Sir Henry Wilson was not done at the instance of the Irish Republican Army." Rory O'Connor was a man of truth.

The English were wild with rage. This violence in their own sacred capital came near to being the final straw that would overturn Lloyd George's government. The House of Commons "was hungry with Anti-Irish fury." The British Cabinet claimed that they had evidence, which they never produced, connecting the "Irish Irregulars" with the action. General Macready was called from Ireland and asked if the British troops in Phoenix Park could take the Four Courts. He violently protested against an action which was sure to reunite Ireland. Lloyd George and Winston Churchill decided to put pressure on the Provisional Government to do the job for them. In effect they ordered Griffith and Collins to capture the Four Courts or consider the Treaty broken and war declared.

These unhappy men were trapped in their own web of intrigue. They either had to fight against their fellow countrymen; or with them in a cause they considered hopeless. At this point O'Connor and Mellows unwittingly gave them the excuse they needed to make war on their former comrades.

The Army Council in the Four Courts were more worried about repercussions in Belfast than their own situation. They feared terrible reprisals there for Wilson's death, and decided to reinforce the Nationalist Volunteers in the North. For such an expedition they needed transport and in their forthright way they took it by seizing sixteen new cars just imported by Ferguson's of Dublin from Belfast. They got the cars, but Lieutenant Leo Henderson was captured by the Free State police.

As a reprisal for this a party from the Four Courts sallied out and captured the Free State's Deputy Chief of Staff, General J. J. O'Connell. They sent word to Mulcahy that his general would be held as a hostage until Henderson was released. That was all Collins needed.

But it was one thing to decide to take the Four Courts and another to do it. It was virtually impregnable against anything except artillery; and the Free State Army had no cannon. This had been foreseen in London. A. W. Cope ordered Macready to lend General Mulcahy two eighteen-pounder field guns. But there was still a difficulty. General Mulcahy doubted if anybody in his Army knew how to fire a cannon. The way this was solved is described by General Macready: "In the end, General [Emmet] Dalton, the one man among Collins's officers who had any knowledge of such things, came up after dark to our artillery park with some motor lorries on the tails of which the guns were hitched and taken into town."

Meanwhile the garrison was alert, but peaceful. Some of the

senior officers were amusing General O'Connell with a game of bridge. After midnight on June 28, the streets around the Four Courts suddenly came alive with Free State troops. Automobiles were crashed against all the gates effectively blocking them. The lookouts in the dome could see men working like ants around two cannon across the Liffey. Rory O'Connor ordered the garrison not to fire unless fired upon.

At 3:40 A.M. a note was passed through the gates addressed to O'Connor demanding that he surrender by 4 A.M. He made no reply.

At 4:07, in a final act of infamy, Irishmen began to fire *British* cannon at their fellows. The civil war had begun.

CHAPTER XV

Black Summer

IT WAS a lovely day at the races in Berlin and I was having a bit of luck. A nag I had bet on came in at three to one in the fourth race. As I gaily went to get my winnings I saw a boy selling the evening papers. I bought one and stood there shocked beyond moving by the German headlines that told me the terrible news from Dublin.

CIVIL WAR IN IRELAND
FOUR COURTS SHELLED

Though we had talked about and feared this thing so long, it was in the eventuality quite unbelievable. I read the scant details and stood there rooted and trembling. I was unable to think at all; I was stupid from shock. Finally I pulled myself together enough to walk out of that place and go straight home to Lily.

We talked for a long while of what I should do; but we both knew. Though Lily was carrying the baby who was born our oldest son, Billy, she was as staunch as ever. She fully agreed that I must go home and put myself at the disposal of the commanders of the I.R.A.

By the time I was able to reach Dublin the Four Courts had fallen. From the railway that brought me from Dun Laoghaire, as Kingstown is now called, I could see the smoke-blackened shell of it with the sky looking through great holes in the dome. When I reached the center of the city my heart was like a cinder. The Gresham Hotel and the whole east side of O'Connell Street was a blackened gutted ruin.

Not knowing what had happened or what to do, I walked

around that dreadful street until I saw the face of a man I knew was safe. Him I asked what to do, and he whispered to me that Sinn Fein still had their headquarters in Suffolk Street. I went to the familiar house and found little Sean T. O'Kelly in charge. He and the others there posted me on what had happened.

The Four Courts had held out through three days of bombardment and assaults. At first things had not been too bad — General Dalton and his men were very clumsy with their borrowed cannon. But they learned to handle the guns by using them. On the second day, Thursday, June 29, their shells began piercing the thick stone walls of the rotunda. Men were killed and wounded. The latter were nursed by valiant Cumann na mBan women who had gone to the Four Courts after the fighting began.

It was early Friday when the main building caught fire. The flames soared upward into the great dome, and crept down to the vaults beneath it. In mid-morning the ammunition — my ammunition — blew up with a terrific explosion that flung the south wall in shards and blocks of stone into the street and the river. The women were sent away under a flag of truce and O'Connor and Mellows with their men retreated to the east wing. They were prepared to die there in the flames, but an order came from Commandant General Oscar Traynor, now commanding the whole Dublin District, to surrender. Throwing their arms into the fire, the small ragged remnant of the garrison surrendered to the Free State Army.

Meanwhile the main headquarters of the Dublin Brigade had been set up in the Gresham Hotel and other buildings on the east side of O'Connell Street. As soon as the fighting began, de Valera, who had kept apart from the Army until then, went there and rejoined his former unit, the Third Battalion, who called themselves "Dev's Own." He was attached to its headquarters staff.

In the Gresham with the soldiers were our great political leaders Austin Stack, Cathal Brugha, Bob Brennan and the indomitable Countess Markievicz. Bob Barton came in and joined up. Archbishop Edward J. Byrne and Lord Mayor Laurence O'Neill of Dublin came to try to effect a truce. Dev's first reaction to the fighting had been "Let's try to stop it!" But Cathal Brugha exclaimed angrily, "What do you mean stop it?"

However it was decided to send a message by the Archbishop to Collins saying the Republican troops would disperse if allowed to keep their arms. "They must surrender their arms!" was Collins's reply.

This the Republicans would never do.

As soon as the Four Courts fell the Staters brought their two guns back across the Liffey and setting them up in the streets debouching on O'Connell Street, opened fire on the hotels. Gradually they were shattered and set on fire. The Gresham was the first to go, and the Republican band retreated to the back of the Hamman Hotel.

On Tuesday, July 4, exactly a year after the joyful Truce meeting at the Mansion House, the position in the Hamman became hopeless. De Valera, Stack and Traynor escaped by a back door and somehow slipped through the encircling Free State lines to go on the run. Cathal Brugha and seventeen men remained for a last stand. Two very brave medical people insisted on staying with them — Doctor J. P. Brennan and Nurse Linda Kearns.

The end came on Wednesday. With the whole east side of O'Connell Street roaring with flames and the old brick walls ready to tumble in on them, even Brugha could ask no more of his men. He ordered the garrison to surrender. They went out the back door with their hands up; and the Free State troops lined them up in a wretched little group. But their commander remained in the fiery building.

Of all our great political leaders Cathal Brugha was the most uncompromising — he was an all-or-nothing man. The Republic was the only object of his love and his life. I think that he realized, there in the blazing hotel, that its cause was already lost, and he decided that he would not live to see his great dream crumble bit by tragic bit.

His men in the street were waiting for him, guarded by the handsomely uniformed Free State troops with their bright bayonets fixed. Firemen on the pumpers, which were keeping the flames from spreading, waited, too, as did the curious Dublin crowd that no danger could keep away. The Free State officers asked "Where's Brugha?" And his men could only point at the burning building.

Suddenly they saw him standing in the doorway, very small and black and fierce against the flames. "Surrender!" the Staters shouted. "Surrender," pleaded his own men.

Instead the figure in the doorway brought up both hands with revolvers shooting from them and charged the line of troops. There was a quick volley in the dusk and he fell head toward them in the street. "*With his enemies howling around him and their bayonets raised ready to plunge them into his body, Cathal Brugha said, 'No, I will not!'*"

They told me these things in the house on Suffolk Street. I asked them to get word to General Traynor that I was here at his command. O'Kelly told me to go to the Standard Hotel and wait for orders. I was also told to be careful; that the Staters had put me on their roll of honor; they wanted me — dead.

The problem that now confronted me was more serious than any I had ever faced before. Until the Truce I had been unknown to the British and able to move about freely. But now my enemies were my former friends and comrades who knew me intimately; knew all my hideouts and my way of operating. They knew Captain Swift as well as Briscoe. And they were more merciless even than our former foes.

I went to the Standard, a decent sort of hotel on Harcourt Street, and taking a room, tried to disguise myself a little. I wore a cap and powdered the sides of my hair so it would look gray. I wore eyeglasses, which I had never done before. It was a feeble disguise; anyone who knew me well would penetrate it. But I thought I would not be known instantly. I felt that I could recognize these people before they knew me and make the necessary move.

After I had waited a day or so at the Standard a lady came to me who belonged to Cumann na mBan. She brought me an order to proceed to the Dublin Mountains and join the Wicklow Brigade under Andy MacDonnell. This was very satisfactory to me.

However, I needed money, so I decided to risk a visit to that same Land Bank where I had changed the Bank of Ireland notes, for they were still friendly with me and I had an account there. It turned out to be more foolhardly than wise.

The first part was easy. I just walked into the bank like anyone else and presented a check at the cashier's window. He cashed it without question. I took the crisp crinkly notes, and confidently started out the door. Coming up the street I saw a splendid and horrible sight.

It was no less than my old friend the "Fighting Blacksmith of Ballinalee," now styled General Sean McKeon of the Free State Army. A grand burly figure of a man he was, magnificently attired in a new green uniform with red and white service stripes, gold stars on his shoulders, and a shiny Sam Browne belt in the holster of which was a great, ugly .45 revolver with a bright green lanyard.

We met right at the bank's entrance. McKeon's eyes blazed with triumphant recognition. He grabbed for his gun shouting, "I've gotcha, Bob Briscoe!"

There was a fractured second between me and death, and in that time I figured my one chance. Though he'd turned Stater I knew McKeon was as chivalrous as though he sat at the Round Table. So I just turned my back on him and walked away.

He stood there foolish for a moment, gaping at me. Then he bellowed down the street, "Briscoe, you bastard, you know I wouldn't shoot a man in the back!"

Whenever we meet, as we often do now, I politely say to

him, "Thank you, Sean!" And he shakes his great black head and roars, "The greatest mistake I ever made."

From the bank I rode in a bus out to Tallaght under the Dublin Mountains. I recall how lovely was that summer morning, and me with my life brand new in my hands after so close a call. The hills were the bright emerald green which gives our island its nickname. There were purple cloud shadows flying across the fields and up the slopes and ravines. Perched on the top against the bluest sky there ever was I could see the little stone ruin of the Hellfire Club, where the Regency dandies went to raise the devil, and according to legend once actually did so.

Some call these hills the Featherbed Mountains because the turf on them is so deep and soft. In our courting days Lily and I would sometimes walk up them and lie on our backs on that springy turf looking over Dublin City and the wide blue bay to the far off misty mound of Howth Head on the edge of the Irish Sea.

I got off the bus opposite the little pub in Tallaght, and stood for a bit in the sunshine warming my soul in the unchanging quiet of a country village. With the children playing on the sidewalks and a grand old sow rolling in the dust you could not think that there was anything wrong with the world at all.

Then I remembered that life was earnest even if it did not seem real these days; and set out to find Andy. His brigade was supposed to be quartered either here or over at Crooksling, so I decided to make some cautious inquiries. I went into the cold oak-dark bar of the pub and ordered a pint of Guiness.

Now I was alert again, for you could trust no man. Luckily a young priest came in — you could usually trust a priest. So I got into talk with him and found that the Staters had come out in strength and driven Andy far south into the Wicklow Hills, which are as wild and lonely as any Scottish moor. Indeed, the galloping disintegration of our forces that soon left us with nothing but forlorn little guerrilla bands hiding out in the back country had already begun.

Since the Free State Army was between me and Andy, and his whereabouts unknown, I took the next bus back to Dublin, grateful for one last quiet sight of the Irish country.

Back at the Standard Hotel I got new orders from Michael Cremin, the man who had administered to me the oath to defend the Republic. I was to go to London, and await further orders. First thing I must proceed to Cork and report to the MacSwineys there with a view to being smuggled aboard a ship for England.

I have already told you something of my misadventures on that voyage; how the Staters under the command of busy General Dalton got to Cork before me; and of my attempt to go up the River Lee in a rowing boat and being shot at by both sides. I forgot to say that on my way back downriver I found trouble going on aboard my old ship the *City of Dortmund*. The Staters had lost some men in the skirmish I had seen take place at Passage, and they demanded the *Dortmund's* tricolor flag for the purpose of draping their dead. From the rowing boat I saw an attempt at resistance by the crew; so I pulled alongside and boarded her. I ordered her crew to hand the flag over. After all these dead were also Irishmen.

It was after this that I went back to Cobh and was taken by the Free State troopers and released because they did not think that a dangerous character like Briscoe could be a Jewman.

When the trooper booted me downstairs I ran right into the chemist shop with the Cumann na mBan girl. I was badly frightened, for the Staters were swarming through the streets, and every house and every spot in Cobh was now being searched. I knew that I would not get away again.

I gasped out my story to the young lady. She was a brave girl and sensible. She said to me, "If you go up the hill near the church, you will find the cottage where my mother lives. You will be safe there, for it was raided a few hours ago and my brother taken. Wait there and I will get word to our people who will tell you what to do."

Then she gave me directions as to how to know the cottage.

I went up the hill, walking slowly like a man at peace with the world, which I surely was not, and found this cottage just as it had been described. I knocked gently on the door, which was opened a crack by a very old lady with tear marks on her cheeks, but courage still in her heart. I told her my story, and though she had never seen me, she believed me and understood that I was on the run. She opened her door wide, and said, "Come in. I'll put a kettle on, for it's a cup of tea ye'll be needing most."

We sat in her small little parlor, drinking tea and making polite conversation until two or three men dressed like farm laborers came in. They were, of course, members of the I.R.A.

"We know who you are," their leader said. "The orders are to get you out of here. By the grace of God, there's a ship coming in this evening and sailing early in the morning. She'll be taking on cattle. You are to be one of the drovers and help put the beasts aboard. Then you will stay there. Nobody counts drovers."

I saw that it was a good plan, though I hated to stay overnight in the cottage because of the risk it put on the old lady and her lovely daughter. When I told her so, she said, "If danger had troubled us my son would be here with me. It means less than ever now."

And the men said, "Those are the orders. You will obey them."

Then they gave me a very filthy raincoat and told me whatever I did not to shave or clean myself. "We'll be calling for you early," they said, and went away.

At first dawn light they came back and took me with them to the cattle pens. There were half a hundred bullocks to be put aboard the ship. We drove them out of the pen and down a steep narrow street which they filled like a bawling, tossing river in a flood. I kept close on their heels in the concealing cloud of dust, waving my long stick like nobody's business, and my eyes shifting under the pulled-down peek of my cap looking for my enemies. We got to the dock and had the divil's own time herding those beasts up the gangway. I went aboard with the first lot right among their tossing horns and great hairy bodies, which would have frightened the life out of me if it had not been so much safer than standing alone.

Down in the hold of the ship, which smelled like the Augean Stables just before spring cleaning day, there were long lines of stalls in which we tied the bullocks. When the job was finished, the other men went ashore, and I went behind some bales of hay. There I crouched listening to the departure noises — the long whistles and the rattle of winches, and finally the lovely clanking sound of her engines turning over. I made myself wait there a full hour until the engines stopped and started up again, showing we'd dropped the pilot and were clear at sea.

Then I went up and found the purser. He was surprised but not pleased to see me. "What are you doing here?" he demanded angrily.

"I got carried off accidentally," I told him.

"Accidentally on purpose," he said. "I'm tired of you stupid drovers getting carried off for a nice free trip to England. Well, you won't get away with it."

"It suits me to go to England," I said, "but I'm willing to pay me passage."

That so astonished him he forgot to be suspicious. He took my money and gave me a place to clean up.

When I was fairly respectable again, I took a stroll around the ship, and who should I see sitting very miserably on the deck but two very great ladies of the Revolution. One of them was Muriel MacSwiney, widow of the martyred Lord Mayor of Cork, and the other was Linda Kearns, who had stayed with Cathal Brugha to the last. They told me that they were on their way to America to try to arouse sympathy for the Republican cause.

They were indeed in an unhappy condition, half dazed from shock and sorrow. They had no accommodations on this ship nor any place to stay in London while they waited for passage to America.

Well, there was something I could do about this at least. I found the steward and gave him a pound which made him very sympathetic indeed. He gave the ladies a vacant cabin, where they could rest and be at peace.

We landed at Cardiff in Wales and I rode with the ladies on the train to London. They told me that they hated the thought of going to a hotel. They wanted a place where they could be private and secluded. I told them that I might be able to help them in that also.

Leaving them sitting in the waiting room of the Euston Station, I went straight to the place of business of my schoolmate, Joseph Arbib. He had been a friend indeed, for he had sheltered me and helped me many times in the arms-running business. Once again he proved his loyalty. When I told him of the situation of Mrs. MacSwiney and Linda Kearns, he said that they could have his flat in Holborn — he would go to a hotel. He handed me the key, then and there. I hurried back to the station and gave the key to the ladies. I did not see them again until after I finally reached America.

Through my brothers I had arranged to rent a small ground-floor flat in Kensington from a business friend of theirs, an Armenian named Papillon. Lily came over from Germany with Joan to join me there. It may seem madness to have brought her over when I was in so dangerous a situation, but I was most anxious to have her, for I did not know when I could have a chance to be with her again. It turned out that it *was* madness.

Michael Cremin, who had full charge of the operation, had ordered me not to mix with any other persons. I was to wait at my flat until a messenger brought instructions.

Meanwhile, I was in a very uneasy position, moving about Kensington, getting conflicting instructions and awaiting final orders. I made it a point to visit several people I knew on business matters so as to establish a reason for my being in London. I started out one evening to see Joseph Arbib when I had a great impulse to turn back. I kept thinking of Lily alone with Joanie and needing something. I told myself it was foolishness, but went back anyway.

There I found Lily walking up and down the sidewalk holding Joanie's hand and looking very disconsolate. "What's wrong?" I asked.

She blushed and said, "I did a silly thing. I came out for a walk without my key, and can't get back in."

This was more serious than it sounds. We had only one key and to break in would surely attract embarrassing attention. How to get in unobserved? When in doubt you have to act boldly. I knocked at the door of the next house. The neighbor, whom I did not know at all, opened it and I said, "My foolish wife left her key inside our flat. Will you not let me go through your house and scale the garden wall? Perhaps I can find an unlatched window at the back."

The man agreed courteously — bless these honest, innocent English — and I was able to get in by breaking a back window quite unobserved. I do not know what Lily would have done, if I had not come back. She had no money and we were in no position to get mixed up with the police, who certainly would have thought it strange to see a lady and a two-year-old girl promenading around the streets at midnight.

I need not tell you that this was the second time that Lily in her innocence and simplicity nearly walked me into what I would call a very dangerous situation. It made me realize that she would have to be kept as unaware as possible of what I was doing, because by accident she could bring about a catastrophe. Consequently, when certain things subsequently happened and the house she was living in was raided, she fortunately did not know anything of what was going on.

While we were still in London the note of tragedy deepened in Ireland. It became a sort of Götterdämmerung, with the great figures on both sides falling in the rush to catastrophe. On July 30, 1922, Harry Boland was killed. He had been out in the Easter Rising of 1916 and later represented us ably in America. He was a close friend both of de Valera and Michael Collins, and his good offices had helped to bring about the Pact. During the dreadful first week of civil war he was constantly moving between de Valera and Collins trying to patch up a truce.

But when the die was cast there was no doubt where Boland stood. He went to help reorganize the Republican Army in Leinster. On the night of July 30, he was sleeping in the room with Commandant Joseph Griffin at the Grand Hotel in Skerries. At two in the morning a large body of Free State troops with an armored car raided the hotel. Leaving guards at all the doors six soldiers in battle dress burst into the room where Boland and Griffin were sleeping. Boland jumped out of bed; made a grab for his gun; failed to get it, and ran into the corridor where a shot brought him down.

There are those who say it was done purposely, but this I do not believe. I have been told by men who were close to Michael Collins that the death of Harry Boland, his very best friend, caused him great sadness in the last few days of *his* life. Rather, I think, it was due to the influx into the Free State Army of new soldiers who were nervous and untrained. The single sentence in which Dorothy Macardle in "The Irish Republic" sums up the business is, I think, the tragic truth and typical of many sad things that happened: "The soldiers who shot him seemed unaccustomed to firearms and distressed by what they had done."

The next great figure to fall was Arthur Griffith, who was still technically president of Dáil Eireann. No bullet felled him but the strain and tension of a struggle he had sought with all his power to avoid. Poor, gentle Arthur Griffith, who hated the idea of fighting even foreign foes, let alone fellow Irishmen, was distraught and undone by the events of that black summer. On August 12, as he was leaving to go to his office, he fell unconscious of a heart attack and died a few hours later.

Then, on August 18, daring Michael Collins, who had pulled more whiskers from the British lion's chin than any man, and dusted death a thousand times, was shot in a silly little skirmish on a road in Cork.

Collins, who was now commander-in-chief of the Free State Army and in plain fact the ruler of Ireland, was between Macroom and Bandon with a convoy consisting of a motorcycle scout, two automobiles, a Crossley tender with a machine gun, and an armored car. An ambush had been arranged and then called off, but six I.R.A. men had failed to receive the recall order. They attacked Collins's convoy. The commander-in-chief, true to his fighting instinct, jumped out of his car and with his staff officers and troopers began shooting back. The armored car opened up with its machine gun. The Republicans fought on against tremendous odds. After a few moments a bullet pierced Michael Collins's head and he fell, spattering General Dalton with his blood.

That is the official story of Michael Collins's death as I heard it in London. But there has always been a mystery about it. He had a very formal lying-in-state and the great pomp and ceremonial sorrow of his funeral. But underlying it all there was a certain reticence by the Provisional Government, but nevertheless an encouragement by them of the belief that Collins had been deliberately murdered; that the men who lay there in ambush were waiting for *him*.

This is definitely not true. Had it been, we surely would have sent more than six men to do the job when Collins had at least fifteen or twenty with him.

No. Those men were there by accident and the killing of Michael Collins was an accident of war. Had they known whom they were shooting, I am sure they would have held their fire. Indeed there is quite an area of doubt that it was a Republican shot which killed Collins at all.

The story which I now believe to be the truth is that the man on the armored car was swinging his machine gun around this way and that to snap shoot the retreating Republicans, so few in number and spread out over a field a considerable distance off, that in one of those wild swings the gun training mechanism jammed, and a bullet from it went through Collins's head as he ran shooting after his attackers.

This is born out by two pieces of circumstantial evidence. One is the manner in which Collins was laid out in state, which appeared to be deliberately done to hide the fact that the bullet actually entered the *back* of his head rather than the forehead.

The other is that the gunner of the armored car was subsequently arrested and held in prison for a considerable period of time. This would show there was a suspicion that this man was either negligent or, with the largest stretch of the imagination, had deliberately killed his commander. I do not believe the latter theory. Whoever fired the bullet that killed Michael Collins, it was, as I have said, an accident of war.

When I read of Collins's death in the English papers, it was certainly a shock, but I cannot in honesty say that I was greatly saddened. At the time we were all numbed. The whole civil war was an unnecessary, a horrible thing. We knew we were suffering casualties on our side and the bitterness which all this engendered and our sense of betrayal, first when Collins signed the Treaty and then when he attacked the Four Courts, prevented you from thinking or feeling normally.

What did strike me was a great fear that there might be wild reprisals; that innocent people would be dragged into this thing and that leading Republicans might be arrested and destroyed in the anger of the moment.

However, looking back, I am, in truth, saddened now by Michael Collins's death. Sure it is that he had fought mightily for Ireland and no man ever was more brave. If he had not the moral or mental fiber to withstand Lloyd George's blandishments and bluff of war, if bluff it was, that was a weakness he could not, perhaps, help. Furthermore, I believe that had he lived he would have done everything possible to stop the civil war. It is quite likely that he died while trying to do just that.

I am convinced from what I knew of him personally, which is confirmed to me by those who knew him very intimately, that the civil war did cause Collins to change completely; to regret that he had been so largely responsible for the split between Irishmen. Nobody knows exactly what mission Collins was on during that fatal trip. It has been stated that it was his own wish to go to his native part of the country — to West Cork; there was no official business on which he was going. It is my belief that he hoped that down there he would be able to contact our chief of staff, Liam Lynch, or men of his caliber, to try to come to some understanding with them to stop the war that he, and all of us, abhorred.

However, there in London, I had no time to think these things out. We all had to continue. You cannot stop to contemplate on one thing and all its reasons and effects. You must carry on the work you are engaged in yourself until either the whole thing stops or you are ordered to stop by the authorities it is your duty to obey.

CHAPTER XVI

The Twilight Deepens

LATE in August further orders came from Michael Cremin. I was to return to Germany and wait there until someone arrived to take over for me. There would be other instructions after that.

Since I was entirely uncertain of my future, and Lily was expecting her child very soon, it did not seem sensible for her to come back to Germany with me. In Dublin, I thought, my mother and her own family would take good care of her; and perhaps I would be able to rejoin her, or at least see her for a fleeting moment. In both these ideas I was completely wrong. I did not see Lily again until my eldest son was more than six months old. And it turned out not to be sensible at all for her to be in Ireland.

Soon after I reached Germany, Michael Cremin himself joined me there. He was one of the few of the Four Courts garrison who had escaped, and was now director of purchases of the Irish Republican Army. He brought orders that astonished me. After handing over the stuff I had in Germany, I was to proceed to America, where further instructions would be given me. In my opinion it was the intention of the Army Council that I was to organize a new source of arms in the United States; though this never actually came about. As it happened the jobs I was given to do there were even odder than those I had performed during my brief, hectic association with the Four Courts garrison.

For some men there might have been a question of ethics in making over to Cremin the very large quantities of money and the goods that stood in my name in Germany. I held them in trust for the Irish Republic. Had I then the right to hand them over to the Army? Of that I had no doubt at all. For the I.R.A. was the only body of men left in Ireland who were true to their oath to defend the Republic; therefore to my mind they were its legitimate successors. Oddly enough a similar question as to whether the Free State or the Republicans were the rightful successors to the Republic of Dáil Eireann was eventually decided by the Supreme Court of New York State as I had decided it. Only I was several years ahead of them.

Cremin and I made a very careful inventory of all my stocks. There was money on deposit in my name in various banks and cash in a safety deposit box. There were goods in warehouses and goods which had been paid for that various firms were holding to my order. Not all of them were lethal; many of them were ordinary trade goods which I had acquired in the course of the business I had used to cover my military activities. I made everything over to Cremin. He gave me a receipt and his blessing.

Subsequent to my departure from Cherbourg for New York, I understand that Cremin handed all these things over to Sean MacBride, who attempted to carry on in my place. Incidentally, MacBride is a very strange sort of man. He was then an ardent patriot, as a son of Maud Gonne must surely be, but a man warped by ambition. During the civil war he rose rapidly in the Republican Army. When so many of our leaders — nearly half the generals and commandants — were dead or had been locked up by the Free State in Mountjoy Gaol, those who were still outside had to take command. They had little or no forces, but nevertheless they had to assume the authority; and for authority you need rank. It was not until much later, as I shall tell, that MacBride's ambition led him into strange places and curious alliances.

During my last days in Germany I was joined by Mother, who had not been well and came over to take a cure. On the last day of all I received a cable from Lily telling me the news that we had a son. You may imagine how joyfully my mother and I toasted Lily and young Bill in champagne that night!

I later found that it was not a very joyful time for Lily, despite her happiness in the new baby. On her return to Ireland she had moved into a small brick house with a little garden which my mother owned on suburban Leeson Park Avenue. From that moment she was harried by the Free State Central Intelligence Department. They raided the house at odd hours looking for me and caring nothing about Lily's condition.

In addition there was still sporadic fighting going on in the Dublin area. On one occasion shortly before Bill was born, Lily went to a nursing home to engage a nurse for him. On her way home she noticed a poor woman with a very heavy basket on one arm and an infant on the other. So near her own time, Lily felt great compassion for the woman, who looked beseechingly at her. She crossed the street to speak with her and gave the woman a little money. At that moment there was the loud frightening bang of a bomb in the street, and then wagons pulled by horses galloping madly past and motor cars scudding in all directions. Lily wrote me what happened next:

"Even in that moment of terror, I remembered my mother saying to me, 'If at any time you get a shock when you are carrying a baby never put your hand to your face — touch any other part of your body but *not* your face, for it may mark the baby.'

"Strange as it may seem I remembered these words and checked my hand to clasp it around my waist. The woman I had befriended helped me into a little grocer's shop where I sat until the street seemed safe again. Then I went back to the nursing home to reassure the nurse who I thought would be worried about me.

"Now, Bob, I know you think my mother is superstitious, but when our baby was born there was a red mark of a hand on his left side."

I, Bob Briscoe, know that this belief is an old midwife's tale, and yet to this day my son Bill has the mark on his side, as anyone who knows him that well can attest.

Even when she went to the hospital and had her baby, Lily was not safe. I will let her tell about that, too:

"When I got to the nursing home a woman was there whom I had not seen in years, and she had one child and I had one. Hers was a boy and mine a girl, so she said, 'I hope you have a boy and I have a girl.' That is the way it was.

"The shooting outside the hospital was pretty bad. I remember after our babies were born this lady coming up to my room to see me, and the shooting was so bad on that occason that she got behind the bed in case any stray bullets should come through the window.

"After Bill was born I went back to the little house that my husband's mother had lent me. I was not sure whether Bob had reached America or not. I remember getting a lovely letter from his mother telling me about toasting the baby in champagne and how happy they were; and yet how sad it was that at a time like this they could not be with me. Then she added, hopeful as always, that perhaps when all these things were behind us we would have a chance of living a happy life together. She was a very sweet and understanding woman. . . ."

The last raid on the house in Leeson Park Avenue was one of those uproariously funny things that kept us laughing. Lily had received my cable from America saying that she could come and join me, and had moved out.

Now, oddly enough, my mother and brothers were on quite friendly terms with some Free Staters. She rented her house to the Fitzgerald family, who were related by marriage to Sean MacMahon, quartermaster general of the Free State Army. On the very night that Lily moved out and the Fitzgeralds moved in, the C.I.D. raided the house — they had read my cable and thought it was a code that I was coming back.

They caught young Leo Fitzgerald and, with the usual yell of "We've gotcha, Briscoe!" they dragged him out in the alley and beat the divil out of him. Meanwhile old Fitzgerald jumped over the back garden wall and hared off for Portobello Barracks to his son-in-law General MacMahon.

Quick like a wink MacMahon sent a company of troops rushing to the rescue of the Fitzgeralds. And the fun of it was that the Free State C.I.D. and the Free State Army had a brisk little skirmish in Leeson Park Avenue each thinking that the other was those beastly Republicans.

This, of course, neither Lily nor I witnessed. It was told me much later by Leo Fitzgerald who sadly showed me his mouth with all the front teeth kicked out. I am happy that I was not in the premises at the time, because it would not have ended with a beating on the street.

I arrived in New York in September, 1922. I had no money at all, but plenty of contacts with Irish Republicans in exile, most of whom had little more than I. There were also a great number of Irish-Americans who were devoted to the cause of Irish freedom; though not to each other.

I was startled and depressed to find that even in a far-off free country the bickerings and personal jealousies that so often had destroyed our plans at home were rampant. Even during de Valera's triumphant tour of the United States during our Revolution, there had been a violent schism between American friends of Ireland. Now that schism was still present, and in addition our own party was divided into factions and factions of factions.

I was immediately pitched into the middle of it. There was a lady named Mrs. Sheehy Skeffington, though it may seem improbable to you. This lady had in truth played a considerable part in the Irish Revolution, and had been very staunch. She had also acquired a great opinion of herself, which was not completely reciprocated by the Irish-Americans. In short her nose seemed a little out of joint. The main cause of her misery was a gentleman named John Finerty who was national president of the American Association for the Recognition of the Irish Republic. She did all in her power to make me believe that Finerty was unfaithful

to our cause, and that he was a bad influence on Muriel Mac-
Swiney.

Now you must understand that Lord Mayor Terence Mac-
Swiney of Cork was one of the really great authentic heroes of
our Revolution, whom both the Staters and the Republicans
revered. He it was who went on the hunger strike in prison that
lasted seventy-four days, and died of it rather than give in to the
British. Therefore his widow was most important to us.

"John Finerty should be shot," said Mrs. Skeffington. "Will
you go to Washington, Bob Briscoe?"

I answered, "I'll go and see what he's up to."

I took the train to Washington and Linda Kearns went with me.
She was a true heroine, but not the sort of girl who looked right
for the part. Tall and bony she was, with a long face and awkward
ways. On the other hand Muriel MacSwiney was the prettiest
thing you ever saw. She was small and round and rosy. Her hair
was a sort of golden brown, and her eyes under black lashes
were the deep blue-gray that made Irish eyes famous.

Linda and I went to Finerty's office in Washington; it was
very handsome, for he was a great big lawyer. He was not there
so we waited for him. Soon he came in, and I must say he did not
look like my preconception of him. He was tall and very thin
with an elegant way to him that made you say, "This is a gent."

I introduced myself and Linda, and he greeted us most courteously. Then I said, "It's not really you I came to see but Mrs.
Terence MacSwiney. Where would she be now?"

Finerty said straight off, "Of course you can see her. She has
been quite ill, you know, after all her trouble; so she is staying
with my wife at our country house in Virginia. We'd be happy
to have you come out to dinner with us tonight."

Right then I knew that this was not what I had thought it. I
said, "Mr. Finerty, I think we had better have a serious talk."

We went into his private office and I told him what Mrs.
Skeffington had said. The upshot was that we took the Congres-
sional Limited back to New York. Mrs. Skeffington and all her
crowd, including Dynamite Mike Kelly, were waiting in her

apartment in the old Park Avenue Hotel for me to bring back word of what had happened to Finerty. You should have seen their faces when I walked in with the corpse on my arm.

"Why John, how wonderful to see you," says Mrs. Skeffington.

But John was not having it. He spoke his piece; and we cleared that little matter up in a hurry.

No American has done more for Ireland than John Finerty; not only as National President of the A.A.R.I.R., which was a national organization with branches all over America, but later when he and Martin Conboy represented de Valera in the famous case of the Irish Republican bonds. The Free State Government claimed the balance from these bonds still on deposit in the United States, which amounted to nearly two million five hundred thousand dollars. Finerty at his own expense and considerable personal risk came to Ireland to take depositions from the Republican leaders in gaol and on the run. He fought the case in the Supreme Court of New York State, and obtained a favorable decision there. Some of the money from the bonds was used to help found the *Irish Press*, which paper is de Valera's main supporter in Dublin, by transfer of bond holders' rights.

Besides John Finerty there were some other good people working for us in America. Perhaps my dearest and most loyal friend among them was Jeremiah A. O'Leary. He was a criminal lawyer who risked his fortune, and reputation and prison for Ireland in her darkest days. O'Leary had been heavily involved in the so-called German Plot by which Irish patriots had tried to enlist German military aid in their struggle for freedom. Since the United States was in alliance with England during World War I, the authorities naturally took a very jaundiced view of her residents conspiring with her enemy. Poor Jerry was much vilified, and sent to prison.

However, nothing daunted his spirit or shook his loyalty to the Irish Republic. When I got to New York he was up to his neck in the Movement to free Ireland from her own tyrants now. And he was wonderfully helpful to me, as I shall relate.

Another man I met soon after reaching America was Major

Michael Kelly, the president of the New York Chapter of the American Association for the Recognition of the Irish Republic. He was an extraordinary character more widely and accurately known as "Dynamite Mike." He had won his nickname by a very brave action in World War I when with an armful of dynamite sticks he had attacked some German trenches. Hurling the dynamite ahead of him, he shattered the nerves and bodies of the defenders and captured them single-handed.

Kelly was a great friend of Ireland and a very active supporter of the Association's operations. But I did not like him. Apparently the reason Mike and I did not get along together was because I was not prepared to take orders or instructions from him. I knew what his organization was supposed to do, and also that it had no authority over the I.R.A.

There was a meeting called at the Park Avenue Hotel which was attended by John Finerty, the national president, Kathleen Boland, the sister of Harry Boland; Linda Kearns, Muriel Mac-Swiney, Mrs. Sheehy Skeffington, Michael O'Brien, Paddy Codiert, and, of course, Dynamite Mike. A diagreement developed between Kelly and myself. It was hopeless to argue with this man so I finally said to him, "Could I ask you to stand up, Major Kelly?"

He stood up, and having stood, said to me, "What am I doing this for?"

"Oh, Major Kelly," I answered politely, "I was hoping by your standing up you would give your brains a chance."

You can well understand that this did not improve the relationship between the president of the New York State Association and me.

The Park Avenue Hotel, an ancient, musty second-rate hostelry was the gathering place of Irish Republicans. I wanted to live there if possible, though I had very little if any money. So I went to talk to the manager. He told me their prices, which were moderate enough, goodness knows, but far too much for my purse. I said to him, "Have you not some little cubbyhole of a room that I could rent very cheap. I don't care about comforts."

"There is one up on the top floor," he answered, "but it's really for the staff."

"How much is it, then?"

"I could let you have it for a dollar and fifty cents a day."

"That will do me fine," I answered, without even seeing it.

So I was installed at the hotel waiting for orders. Presently a courier arrived from Frank Aiken, who was now second in command of the I.R.A., but all it brought me was instructions to wait for orders from our plenipotentiary.

This time of waiting was a dark one. For in Ireland the twilight of the gods was deepening and the Free State Government was behaving with such barbarity as the British had never dared.

First it was Erskine Childers. This was the man the Staters had sneered at as "an Englishman," and proud England should have been of him. For he was a man with the courage to choose the right and risk everything for it. His father was English, but his mother was Irish, before her marriage she had been Miss Barton of Glendalough House in Annamoe, County Wicklow. Bob Barton, who had signed the Treaty against his will, was Childers' first cousin. Though the Bartons were of the Protestant ascendancy class, they had supported the Republic from the first. Childers and his brave American wife, Mary Osgood of Boston, had used their yacht to smuggle the first shipment of arms to the Irish Volunteers back in 1914. He had then served in the British Navy in the war; but had resigned to return and fight for Ireland. Though he had been secretary to the Irish delegation which signed the Treaty, he had never faltered in his opposition to it. Indeed, his last letter from the prison where he was executed, beautifully expressed his resolution: "I was bound in honor, conscience and principle to oppose the Treaty by speech, writing and action both in peace and, when it came to the disastrous point, in war. For we hold that a nation has no right to surrender its declared and established independence, and that even a minority has a right to resist that surrender in arms . . .

"That is the faith of my comrades, my leaders and myself. Some day we shall be justified when the nation forgets its weakness and reverts to its ancient and holy tradition which we are preserving in our struggle. And may God hasten the day of re-union among us all under the honored flag of the Republic!"

In November, 1922, de Valera sent for him to become secretary of the Underground Republican Government. Childers, making his way secretly up from the South to Dublin, stopped for a night with his cousin Bob Barton and Mrs. Childers at Glendalough House. Early the next morning the Staters raided the huge rambling Elizabethan mansion. They took Childers in the long corridor outside his wife's bedroom with a Colt automatic in his hand, which he dared not fire for fear the women present might be injured if shooting began.

The Free State people took him to Beggars Bush Barrack. There he was tried by a drumhead court-martial under a new law passed by the Free State Parliament making the possession of firearms punishable by death. On Friday, November 24, he was executed. Mrs. Childers was not even allowed to reclaim his body or his personal possessions. Such was the justice of the Free State.

Worse was to follow. On December 8, 1922, I was sitting in the lounge of the Park Avenue Hotel with Muriel MacSwiney, Linda Kearns and Kathleen Boland. I can still see that big tawdry, gloomy, red plush room with its heavy uncomfortable furniture. To us there came a man carrying an evening paper with great red headlines that shook me more than any news I have ever received. My comrades of the Four Courts, Rory O'Connor, Liam Mellows, Joseph McKelvey and Richard Barrett, had been shot at Mountjoy Gaol. They had not been tried or accused of anything. They had been summarily executed as a reprisal for the killing of Tom Hale and for wounding Padraic O'Maille, a Free State brigadier who had voted in Parliament for the law under which Childers and seven other men had been executed.

When I read this news I could not even speak to the ladies who were with me. I bolted from that place and went up to my little attic room, not going out of it for twenty-four hours. I just lay there on my bed trying to realize the incredible; trying to reconcile myself to the unacceptable. I thought of those beloved friends of mine; of Rory O'Connor so gay and gallant and handsome, the very ideal of the fearless fighting devil-may-care Irishmen who in fact, cared too deeply; of Liam Mellows, Liam my friend and counselor, so steadfast and sturdy. Joe McKelvey and Dick Barrett I had not known so well, though they, too, had a place in my heart and I smiled achingly as I thought of Dick pointing his pistol at Smith-Gordon in his office in the Land Bank.

Through that sleepless night a thousand pictures of O'Connor and Mellows flashed in my brain — Rory in trench coat and slouch hat fighting against the British; Rory speaking in the Army Council, thin and vibrant, his eyes brilliant with the pure passion of his love for Ireland; Rory, the last time I had seen him, taking the salute of the garrison in the Four Courts.

And Liam Mellows; he who had been my inspiration in joining our fight for freedom and who had become my most loved friend. Torturing myself, I called to mind the first time I had met him here in New York. I lived again the nights we lay in the Woods's double bed talking of great plans for Ireland; and saw him do that funny little jig-step with my breakfast tray the morning he remembered so thoughtfully that I did not eat bacon with my eggs.

I pictured him the day of the Treaty debate, when he had seemed in that somber chamber like a bright golden flame of conscience and courage. And then I thought again of the fatal Four Courts and Liam's strong, freckled hand clasping mine as he sent me off to Germany and the safety I would not have chosen.

At last I wept.

CHAPTER XVII

We Strike a Blow for Freedom in New York

FORTUNATELY for my morale there soon came a chance for me to resolve sorrow in action. It was only a day or two later that out of the blue appeared Laurence Ginnell, newly appointed envoy extraordinary and plenipotentiary to America from the Irish Republic, or what was left of it. Right away he sent for me and I called on him at his hotel.

Larry Ginnell had a long tradition in the Irish Movement extending all the way back to the time of Parnell. In those days he had been an Irish member of the British Parliament. Later he had been de Valera's envoy to the Argentine. He came home during the Truce and was elected to the Third Dáil — the one which never met. He was the only Republican deputy to attend the opening session of the Provisional Parliament which finally met in September, 1922. At the opening session he kept loudly demanding to know if this were the Dáil, and if it were not, what was it then? He made himself so obnoxious that the Speaker ordered him thrown out. Two guards carried him out of Leinster House and deposited him on the sidewalk. Undoubtedly he was in America to stir things up.

When I met Ginnell I found he was a short little man with a beard and a nervous jerky manner. As I entered his hotel room he was leaning over the wash basin with his shirtsleeves rolled up washing his face and hands. He turned around and gave me one look. Then he continued his toilet while he said to me, "You are a member of the I.R.A.?"

"I am."

"I am Larry Ginnell and I have authority here as envoy extraordinary and plenipotentiary. Are you prepared to take orders from me?"

"I am."

"Will you agree to carry out these orders until I myself personally cancel them?"

"I will."

"Have you any friends you can enlist to help you in a certain matter?"

"I have a few."

"Very well."

At this point Mr. Ginnell stopped combing his beard and turned around to face me. "I want you to go down to Nassau Street and take possession of the Irish Republican consular offices now in the hands of the Free State Government, and to hold them for the Republic until I cancel," he said. "You can report to me here by messenger or by phone. Of course I'll know where to get in touch with you."

"Yes, sir," I said.

Then I left him. This was the first time I had ever spoken with Larry Ginnell. He certainly was an unusual envoy and the mission he had assigned me was in truth extraordinary. At the time I could see no sense in it at all. It turned out later that there was an excellent reason for it, and it would have been better had Mr. Ginnell taken me into his confidence from the first. However, I was not about to ask for reasons why, especially in my mood of anger and bitterness against the Staters. Nor did the fact that I would probably have to fracture a number of the laws of the land deter me in the least. The one thing on my mind was how best to carry out my orders.

To this end I sent for my friend Michael O'Brien. His sister was married to Stephen O'Mara of the famous O'Mara Brothers,

James and Stephen, who had come to America with de Valera organizing the bond drive. Indeed, James O'Mara, along with de Valera and Bishop Michael Fogarty, was one of the three trustees of the funds so raised, and O'Brien was now secretary of Fordham University in New York City.

I also sent for Paddy Codiert, who had left Ireland on the run when the civil war started. Before that he had been courier for Art O'Brien, the secret Irish Republican envoy in England all through the Black and Tan days and the Treaty negotiations. Paddy was a midget of a man, no more than five feet two inches high, but he was full of fight and very desirous of action on behalf of the Republic. There were several more whose names do not come to mind who were friendly disposed.

The meeting was a success. O'Brien, with his eyes sparkling, said I could count on him. "I've two weeks' vacation coming to me from Fordham," he announced. "I'll take it and join you in this escapade." The others were equally spoiling for a fight.

The next day I went alone to reconnoiter the consular offices in an old building on Nassau Street. There was a great crowd of angry Irishwomen from various organizations picketing the place in protest against the executions. I pushed through them, getting some booing, and pretended I had business with the Free State consul general, Joseph Connolly. When I got to his office I found that Connolly had resigned over the executions and gone home, leaving in charge the assistant consul, a Dublin solicitor named Hughes. In the American language I cased the joint, and decided it would be injudicious to make a frontal attack. There might be a fracas and the police be called in; and then, of course, we would lose out. So I developed a stratagem.

I found out where Mr. Hughes lived. That night Mike O'Brien, Paddy Codiert and I paid him a visit. We just rang the bell of his flat and walked in, to his amazement and our satisfaction.

Mr. Hughes and his wife were both present. I said to him, "Mr. Hughes, we are members of the Irish Republican Army, and we have orders to take possession of the Irish Republican consular offices, which as you well know are not offices belonging to the

Free State Government, and never did. Will you be kind enough to hand over the keys?"

"I'll do nothing of the sort," said Hughes.

"Well, now," I said peaceably, "if you keep on refusing we'll have to take them from you by force. This is something we do not want to do, as we are anxious to avoid an incident."

Mrs. Hughes was very frightened, not without cause I must admit, for Paddy and Michael were looking quite fierce and I am a pretty big fellow myself. She begged her husband to give us the keys. I also reasoned with him, "We'll get them in any event, but if you give them to us without too much resistance, I promise to be witness to the fact that you were overpowered and it was impossible for you to lick the three of us."

Mr. Hughes was a sensible man. He produced the keys.

I then instructed O'Brien and Codiert to go down to the consular offices, and ring me from there at the Hughes's. I would then join them. In the meanwhile I sat chatting with Mr. and Mrs. Hughes with the telephone under my control and a careful eye to see that they did not slip out the door. It was not long before the telephone rang and Michael said, "We're in!"

I immediately rose and made a somewhat pompous but effective speech to Mr. Hughes. "Now look you," I said, "you can call the police now if you like, but we'll be in and my advice to you is to leave matters alone or consult somebody before you take any steps; because if you get involved with the New York Police, you might be confronted by an ugly situation. The New York Irish won't be pleased, and there are a lot of us knocking around. So think it over! I'm not going to cut your telephone wire. I'll just leave it to your good judgment."

I took a taxi down to the offices and walked up fourteen flights of stairs — the lifts were not running that late. I knocked on the door, and O'Brien and Codiert opened it circumspectly, with a paperweight handy to knock me on the head if I was the wrong person. I immediately telephoned Larry Ginnell to report mission accomplished. Ginnell said, "Good! Now look around for the list of subscribers to the bond drive."

Next I telephoned Jerry O'Leary and asked him to send along some additional troops. They soon began arriving, led by a Carlow man named Mooney who was an ex-boxer and tough enough to frighten a goat. Others kept coming until there were at least twenty of us there — a boiling broth of boys longing for a scrimmage.

Nothing more happened that night, but bright and early came a surprising development. A slim elegant gentleman came in the door. Assuming I was the vice-consul he introduced himself as Mr. Lindsay Crawford, and told me that he was the Free State consul general in Ottawa and had received orders to replace Joe Connolly in New York. I said to him, "You are welcome here, Mr. Crawford; but the Free State Government is not. This is the Irish Republican Consulate."

Crawford looked a bit fish-faced at that, and said, "But I am the legal representative of the Irish Government."

"Legality is nine points possession," I pointed out. "We are in possession. You can stay with us if you like, or you can go out. But if you go, you will not get back."

Crawford elected to stay. He was really a good fellow. We had the office open for business that day. Crawford kept in the background while I assumed the duties of consul, signing various documents and stamping them with the official seal. Needless to say neither of us went out for lunch. My boys brought food in for us. When night came we were not about to leave either. Again the boys brought provisions; and we sat around uncomfortably in that empty building. Finally Mr. Crawford and I piled some leather cushions on a huge big desk. We lay down on it and slept companionably back to back.

In the morning Ginnell called up saying, "Court proceedings are being taken by the Free State Government to eject you from the consulate. Obey no instructions except those I give you."

However, Ginnell was mistaken as to the nature of the proceedings. The eviction order served on us was from the landlord claiming that we were not lawful tenants. As this was an American suit, I thought we had better obey it. My mistake.

I called Ginnell from outside and he was furious. "You had no right to move without my orders," he almost squeaked. "Did you get the list of bond holders?"

"No," I said. "We looked but could not find it."

"Then you've failed completely. Get back in there, I don't care how!"

Now I saw the sense of this thing. I had been stupid not to realize that the list of bond holders was the key. It was needed in the proceedings as to who owned the two million five hundred thousand dollars in the Chase Bank, the Republic or the Free State. I had searched for it rather casually.

Ginnell also said, "If you get arrested, so much the better. I want it settled in the courts as to who is the rightful tenant."

Now I had to get back in. But this was not so easy, for there was a patrolman on guard day and night. I went over to pay a call on Jerry O'Leary. As usual Jerry was both helpful and ready to stick his neck out. He had a friend with an office on the twelfth floor of the same old building as the consulate, which was on the fourteenth floor. This fact became the basis of his plan.

After calling his friend, who was happy to co-operate, Jerry proceeded to disguise me. He powdered my hair gray and put glasses on me. Then he lent me a gray overcoat and a rather broad-brimmed black hat. After looking me over, he did other little titivatings and declared, "Your mother wouldn't know you, let alone a New York cop."

Then he sent out for a thin strong rope with an iron hook on it. This I wound around me under the overcoat. He also provided a brief case containing a padlock, a screwdriver and a saucepan with a little candle business under it for heating food. "In case you have to stand a siege," he said.

At the height of the afternoon rush hour, we went back to the building and up to his friend's office without any trouble. At five o'clock they both left me alone in the office.

Then my vigil began, a very lonely and tiresome one. As soon as the building was empty, I pulled a chair up close to the door and opened it slightly. It was near the stone stairs, which anyone would have to use after the lifts stopped working. The essence of the plan was that at some point the cop on the fourteenth floor would get bored and leave his post.

I got bored long before he did, but I never moved from my seat. I could hear my friend upstairs moving around occasionally. Apparently he had a chair which he either sat in or walked about. Most of the night went by. One of the hardest things I have done for Ireland was to stay awake.

It was about four o'clock in the morning, I would say, when my friend decided to go downstairs. The clump-clump of his great boots brought me wide awake. He went very slowly down the two flights to my floor, and then on down. When I figured him to be two floors below I dashed out and ran up the stairs in my stocking feet. The door of the consulate had a flimsy old-fashioned lock. I inserted my screw driver where the tongue met the socket and levered and levered. It gave and I was in. Easier than I thought!

My next move was to brace a chair against the door. Then I telephoned O'Brien, Codiert and Mooney to be hanging around next morning. I heard the patrolman come back to his post, but he did not check the door. At eight o'clock his relief came on; and they exchanged greetings and "All's well."

At nine I heard Mr. Crawford explaining to the policeman who he was, and showing his credentials. I politely opened the door. Few people ever really look aghast — Lindsay Crawford did. "However did *you* get in?" he asked weakly.

There were quite a few people behind him on the landing and among them I saw the shining happy faces of O'Brien, Codiert and Mooney. As I talked with Crawford I made them a signal and they brushed past the cop and came in. I pushed Mr. Lindsay Crawford gently but firmly back to the landing into the arms of his patrolman, and closed the door.

We now began to barricade, shoving everything movable against the door. We had desks and tables end to end, with chairs piled up on them. We telephoned O'Leary's friend below and asked him to notify Jerry and others to send supplies. We were in and we meant to stay in.

Then we sat down to await developments. It was not long before the gentleman below telephoned us. "Lower your rope and hook," he said.

We did, and hauled up a bucket full like Christmas. There were sandwiches and cigarettes, bottles of coffee and a variety of items, including fresh fruit. We had not a worry in the world as we merrily ate and drank.

An exhaustive search failed to turn up the bond list. We afterward learned that it was kept at the Chase Bank. However, our efforts were not in vain. The papers had a carnival of headlines over the siege which made the Staters look foolish and brought the Republic to attention. For three days we held the fort. They cut off our telephone so we did not know what was developing in the outside world.

On the third day there was an authoritative knock on the door and a peremptory voice announced, "I am Lieutenant Geoghan! I am Lieutenant Geoghan of the New York Bomb Squad. I have court orders to get in and eject you."

I had learned my lesson. "We're not letting you in," I said.

"You can have ten minutes to make up your mind," he said. "Then we come in. We don't want to hurt anybody, but the law is the law."

Well that was a question. Another question was, what was the bomb squad? Did they disarm bombs or throw them? We were not sure. After a bit things began to crash against the door. The panels were cracking like an egg crate. We could see it would not hold much longer anyway, and maybe the bomb squad had tear gas. So we opened the door.

Immediately we had company — a lot of company. In came Lieutenant Geoghan with half a dozen big policemen — the New York cops are very stalwart, but also very Irish. You could see by their grins that they were really on our side. Next came Lindsay Crawford, followed by Professor Whelan, who was the Free State

minister to Washington. Last of all came the big surprise —
Muriel MacSwiney and Linda Kearns. They said, "We decided to
join you. We are going to stay." Mr. Crawford and Professor
Whelan said nothing.

Lieutenant Geoghan produced a very official-looking document
and read it impressively. In plain English, without the legal
blarney, it ordered us to get out. Geoghan then ceremoniously
asked us to leave. We replied, "We'll not!"

There was not much more conversation after that. A pair of
policemen said to O'Brien, "Are you prepared to leave?"

"No!"

They picked him up and carried him to the landing, where
they handed him to another pair. He was passed along down from
landing to landing, not in the lift. Each of the others was taken in
turn. When they came to Paddy Codiert he said, "Just a minute!
Professor Whelan owes me a pound."

The professor was astonished.

"I do?" he said. "What for?"

"For the taxi the Irish delegates took to the station after they
signed the Treaty in London."

Professor Whelan produced a five-dollar bill and handed it to
Paddy, who in turn looked amazed. The two policemen picked
him up and carried him off. His head was about level with
their shoulders and his little feet were kicking eighteen inches off
the ground.

Next came Muriel MacSwiney's turn. She was sitting in a chair
with her cheeks bright red and her eyes blazing blue. After the
rhetorical question, would she leave, Geoghan nodded to four policemen who each picked up a leg of the chair she was sitting in
and carried her to the lift without laying a finger on her. They
brought her down to the lobby where she sat enthroned like a
queen.

They had left me to the last and I thought I would be arrested.
But no, they carried me downstairs like the others. Somehow on
the way my nose got a slight bump. Ever since that footballer
kicked it, it has bled easily. Now it began to gush blood. The

crimson went all over my face, drenched my shirt and suit; I looked as though I had been massacred. And there outside the building was a great angry crowd of New York Irish. When they saw my condition they began howling and roaring with rage. It was no good trying to tell them it was an accident. They wanted to believe that the police were acting like Cossacks instead of doing their duty as politely as possible.

The crowd picked me up on their shoulders and rushed me all the way up to Columbus Circle. Part of the way I was carried, and sometimes I was hustled along with odd pauses of standing on street corners. When I got there I was a horrid mess of blood and dirt, with a three days' beard on my face and my one suit in rags. Fuel I was for incendiary violence.

They stood me up on a soapbox, and I made a speech. I never could remember what I said, but it must have been bitter and violent. For the thought of my dead friends was a scar on my brain; and the events of the last few days had not left me in a reasonable frame of mind.

The newsreels were there taking our pictures. I saw the films a day or two later, and I must admit that O'Brien, Codiert and I looked like gangsters. We were no credit to the Irish Republican Movement.

These newsreels were the means of conveying to the authorities of Fordham the news of where their Mr. O'Brien was spending his holidays. When he went back to work, he was handed a check in lieu of notice and informed that he was no longer secretary of Fordham University. Michael O'Brien should be grateful to me for this. Shortly afterward he got a job with the Irving Trust Company and today he is one of the senior vice-presidents with a remarkably luxurious office in the Empire State Building.

Instead of things ending with the siege, we found ourselves at the beginning of our effort. Notice had been taken of me. Many newspapers damned me, but the article I treasured most was written by an old Fenian named John Devoy, who was editor of a paper called the *Gaelic American*. He paid me a grand tribute. He warned the United States Government in Washington that there had arrived in America "one of de Valera's leading gunmen. He is such a desperate character that he has his own private graveyard to bury his dead in." The article said I should be deported, because if allowed to remain I would surely cause the death of people in America.

The saying that any publicity is good publicity seemed justified in my case. I was invited to many places to make speeches, and I began to get around. I went to Washington to meet that allegedly great liberal, Senator Walsh of Montana, to see if something could not be done to stop the illegal executions in Ireland. It was wasted effort. The senator listened to me, all the time twisting his heavy gold watch chain, but he did not give me the time of day.

From him I went to see grand old Senator Robert La Follette. He was horrified. Some effort must be made to stop these barbarities. But through no fault of his, no effort was made.

Another good man I met was Judge Robert Wagner, later Senator from New York. I admired him greatly for his friendliness, his warm sympathy and his genuine humanitarian spirit. It was one of my great pleasures to meet Mayor Bob Wagner, Jr., when I came to New York as Lord Mayor of Dublin.

The largest and most enthusiastic meeting I addressed took place in Faneuil Hall in Boston. The chairman of the meeting, a wonderfully charming gentleman named John T. Hughes, told me that there was a prospect of trouble as the Boston Irish were just as divided as the Irish Irish. "It is possible they may heckle you for being a Jew and not even an Irishman," he told me. I decided to confront this prejudice at the start.

Now just at that time an article had appeared in the *Atlantic Monthly* violently attacking the Irish Republican leaders. It referred to Gerry Boland, who later was Minister for Justice for some sixteen years in de Valera's Cabinet, as a convicted thief. On de Valera it went the limit, saying that he came from "the lowest stratum," and adding, "de Valera's father was a Maltese horseboy and his mother was in domestic service." By implication it asked by what right such a man aspired to lead the Irish people.

We Strike a Blow for Freedom in New York

I carried this magazine onto the platform in Faneuil Hall. Facing the great turbulent crowd stretching up to the dusk of the furthest corners, I opened my address by saying, "I have a question to answer."

Then I read the question about de Valera's right to lead Ireland. Rolling up the magazine I pointed it at the crowd and said, "I am not of your faith. I am, as you well know, of a particular faith of which I am probably the only member of this great hall. But I would like to say to you good Christians that if it was right for you to accept as your Savior a man born in a stable, surely we Irish have the same right to accept as our leader a great man, no matter how lowly his birth, although it certainly was not as described in this article."

At this point a riot burst loose in the audience. Thinking that the poor fellow I had accidentally pointed at was to blame for the attack on de Valera, the crowd assailed him tooth and nail. Luckily for him and for my conscience, the fire department was on hand and ready for trouble. Pointing the long brass nozzles at the boiling knot of people they yelled that unless the fight stopped they'd hose out the hall.

Evidently the Boston Irish were familiar with this procedure. The fighting stopped. There were no further interruptions. In fact, I was very enthusiastically received.

Now I would like to tell you something more about Mr. Hughes. He was a man with great knowledge of our Irish culture, owning what was said to be the finest private library of Irish books in the world. He was a great friend of de Valera and, indeed, of all of us in the movement.

After my talk in Faneuil Hall Mr. Hughes invited me for a meal in his house. During it I saw him looking at my suit, which was the same I had worn during the battle of the consulate, and now in sad shape indeed. After dinner, he asked a series of questions about my means in so kind a manner that I could take no offense. Indeed, I was completely disarmed, and confessed that I had not a sixpence or a dime.

The way I managed to live at all was that Mrs. Ginnell, the wife of our envoy, had opened a secretarial office in New York, and had given Paddy Codiert, Michael O'Brien and me jobs addressing envelopes at two dollars a thousand. We had managed to save up ten dollars and decided to use it to buy a new suit. But for whom? We tossed for it. Michael won. We were all interested in the suit, even though Michael was going to wear it, so we accompanied him down to a shop on Canal Street. Michael acquired an olive green suit, the color of which I shall never forget; the fit of which I shall never forget. Nevertheless, Michael felt that he was a great toff now.

Mr. Hughes must have recognized that there was not much fat in such a job as I had. He asked where he could reach me when he came to New York. In a matter of days, Hughes called me and invited me to dinner with him there. I still recall the grand porterhouse steak I ate. My kind host was making sure that this meal would last me for a few days. When I got back to my closet room in the Park Avenue Hotel I found an order on a clothing store which permitted me to select anything I wished and charge it to Mr. Hughes's account.

From that time on Mr. Hughes kept coming back and forth to New York, watching over us. However, we were very independent, and much more concerned with our work for the movement than for our appearance or our stomachs. We were getting news from home — all of it bad. More and more of our leaders were being killed in the field or executed in prison. Of the rank and file there were now eleven thousand men and women in Free State jails — the British had never used such inhumanity! It was evident that the Republic could not long survive. Yet being stubborn, as only we supposedly volatile Irish can be, we refused to admit the possibility of failure, as long as those brave, ragged, starving men, hunted and harried through the wild southwestern hills of Ireland which were all that was left of the Republic, would not surrender. All we really cared about was trying to drum up as much interest, support and good will as possible for the cause we would not admit was lost.

Gradually, in spite of our lack of interest in them, the personal prospects of we three sea-green musketeers improved. Paddy got a job in a wholesale grocery firm at a reasonable wage. Michael acquired the position — this seems a properly dignified way of putting it — with the Irving Trust Co., which eventually rocketed him to the ionosphere of finance; and I worked a small shenanigan which gave me enough capital to start a little business.

As you recall I had once before been in the electric light business in America. I knew my way around. I also knew that my brothers, Bert and Wolfe, had an importing firm through which they could send me cheap foreign light bulbs that I might be able to dispose of in New York. So I started calling on prospects in my spare time.

One of the first wholesalers I saw, said, "No soap here. Look in the cellar. I've cases of bulbs I can't get rid of. And what burns me up is that my competitor around the corner needs bulbs badly, but won't buy from me because he hates my guts, as I do his."

"Perhaps we could work a deal," I suggested. "If I were to sell twenty cases of bulbs to him what would be my commission?"

"Fifteen per cent," he answered.

I had on my new suit and the nerve that went with it.

"Thirty," I tried.

"Robber," he howled.

We settled for twenty-two; and I put the deal through.

With this first little piece of capital, I sent for Lily. I also wrote my brothers about sending me bulbs. Bert arrived before Lily and tried to persuade me to go back to Europe. He promised to set me up with an agency of his import-export business in Switzerland. But my work was not yet done here, so I refused. However, he agreed to send me bulbs.

Then Lily came, bringing Joanie, and the son I had never seen. Bill was a puny baby, weakened I think by the hardships and terror Lily had experienced. But he looked beautiful to me.

Now I had to settle down somewhere besides a room in a hotel.

I found a tiny walk-up flat on Kingsbridge Road in the Bronx. Then I had to furnish it. I went to blessed Jerry O'Leary, who lent me a considerable sum of money. It was Jerry's love of Ireland that made him help as many people as he could in this way. He was astonished when before leaving for home in 1924, I went to his office to repay him what I owed him — money which he never expected back, and money he never wanted back. In fact, the only way I could make him take it was by telling him to put it in the safe to be lent to the next Irish Republican who came to him for help.

With Jerry's loan I went to a place on Seventh Avenue that sold furniture on the hire-purchase plan. Two days later Lily and I with our two children moved into our new home.

We were happy there, though we had no easy time of it. The small uncertain money I made as a little entrepreneur of imported light bulbs just about kept us fed, and poorly at that. We had plenty of porridge and potatoes — luckily I happen to like porridge. But I remember one time when I had made a small deal I celebrated by buying some sugar rolls. Lily looked at them with glistening eyes, and said with an unconscious pathos that twisted your heart, "My they're beautiful, Bob. May I have one?"

I continued now in the business of making a meager living, for my principal reason for existence had come to a dismal end. In January, 1923, Liam Deasy, deputy chief of staff of the Irish Republican Army, was taken with arms in his hands and sentenced to death; though this was not carried out. In February Austin Stack was captured and imprisoned. Finally on April 10, 1923, Chief of Staff Liam Lynch was brought down by a rifle shot on the slopes of Crohan West in the Knockmealdown Mountains.

Speaking sadly to the Army, de Valera eulogized Lynch as "the lion heart who with exalted soul and tenacious will, backed by his loyal Allies, the hills . . . baffled the forces of an Empire and brought them to terms . . . It is better to die nobly as your chief did, then to live a slave . . ."

The death of Liam Lynch broke the back of the I.R.A. He was

the last of the great irreconcilables. Frank Aiken, the new chief of staff, was a moderate and reasonable man. For the first time since Rory O'Connor had repudiated the Dáil after the approval of the Treaty, de Valera, still hiding out in the houses of his friends in Dublin, re-established civilian control over the Army.

For many months de Valera had realized the hopelessness of the Republican cause in arms. On April 30, 1923, he ordered the Irish Republican Army to "suspend aggressive action." It was the seventh anniversary of his surrender of Boland Mills that ended the Easter Rising of 1916.

However, the Free State Government were not satisfied. Their Army kept right on fighting and Cosgrave announced they would do so until the Republicans surrendered their arms. This they felt they could not in honor do. However, on May 24, Chief of Staff Aiken ordered the Army to "cease fire" and "dump arms," a very different thing. Accompanying this order was de Valera's farewell address to the Irish Republican Army:

SOLDIERS OF THE REPUBLIC, LEGION OF THE REARGUARD:
The Republic can no longer be defended successfully in arms. Further sacrifice of life would now be vain . . . Military victory must be allowed to rest for the moment with those who have destroyed the Republic. . . .
Do not let sorrow overwhelm you. Your efforts and the sacrifices of your dead comrades will surely bear fruit. They have even already borne fruit . . . You have saved the nation's honor, preserved a sacred national tradition and kept open the road of independence. . . .
Seven years of intense effort have exhausted our people. Their sacrifices and sorrows have been many. If they have turned aside and not given you the active support which alone could give you Victory . . . it is because they saw overwhelming forces arrayed against them, and they are weary and need a rest. A little time and you will see them recover and rally again to the standard . . . when they are ready, you will be, and your place will be again, as of old, with the Vanguard. . . .
May God guard every one of you and give to our country in all times of need sons who will love her as dearly and devotedly as you.

EAMON DE VALERA

So ended the fight to save the Republic.

But if the battle was over reprisals were not. The arrest and imprisonment of Republican leaders continued. A general election was called for August 27, 1923. De Valera announced his candidacy for his old constituency of Clare. He came out of hiding to address an election meeting there on August 15, and was arrested by Free State Troopers firing volleys over the heads of the wildly cheering crowds who shouted, "Up Dev!" While imprisoned in Arbour Hill Gaol, he was elected for Clare, receiving twice as many votes as his opponent, Free State Minister for Education Eóin MacNeill.

It was not until nearly a year later that William Cosgrave's Free State Government decided to call off its unilateral war on the Republicans. In July, 1924, de Valera was freed and the jails were emptied of Republican prisoners. A general amnesty bill was introduced in the Dáil, as the Free State Parliament was still called.

These actions brought serious considerations to Lily and me. We were making our way in America and happy enough. Our circle of friends was growing. I had re-established contact with the Arbibs, and we saw a great deal of the O'Learys and Michael O'Brien. Paddy Codiert was always welcome, and not only for the fact that he usually managed to bring some very necessary tidbits from the grocery where he worked.

In addition Lily and I well knew that despite any act of amnesty the position of a former member of the I.R.A. in Ireland would not be a happy one. We expected persecution and difficulties both political and economic. There were thus many reasons for staying in this great free land which had twice welcomed me when I was unwelcome in my own.

And yet so greatly did the love of our country possess us, so strongly did the ties that bound us to Ireland tug at our hearts, that our decision was never in doubt. Even before the Act of Amnesty was passed we sailed for home.

CHAPTER XVIII

Return

Our ship, the *Carmania*, stopped at Cherbourg, where I disembarked; for until the governor general signed the Amnesty Bill it was not safe for me to set foot in Ireland. Lily and the two children went on to London and thence home. I went to Merano in Italy to stay with my brother Bert.

As you remember he had generously offered to set me up in Switzerland as a means of getting me out of my Republican activities. Now he told me that he and Wolfe were thinking of partly retiring and that I could have their Briscoe Importing Company in Dublin while they concerned themselves with the foreign business they had established. This was a tremendous thing for them to do and a great relief to me. For it meant that I could give Lily and the children a decent home instead of grubbing a livelihood with the Free State stacking the cards against me. Not that I was greatly surprised, for it was in keeping with their generous natures.

As soon as the Act of Amnesty was signed I went home. Just to be back made me happy, but it was a troubled land I found. There were still some Republicans who would not accept the cease fire. They had been fighting all their young lives and knew not how to stop. They called themselves the I.R.A., but they were not authorized by the Army of which I had been a member nor by Sinn Fein. Nevertheless, there continued to be isolated bombings and other incidents. The government naturally reacted vigorously, even violently, with continued searches and seizures. There was almost as much tension as during the Troubled Times.

For my part I was determined to have no more to do with politics. I would leave knight errantry to others and settle down to make a living and perhaps a little fortune to leave to Lily and my children. Symbolic of this resolve seemed the name of the small brick house I rented in the suburb of Rathfarnham — "Snugboro."

Now it is one thing for a man of my nature to resolve to avoid trouble and quite another to be able to do so. Like any good suburbanite I rode a bus each morning to the company office; worked hard at business all day long, and at night went home to supper and cultivating our little garden. But certain circumstances conspired against me. These were the economic state of the country; the vengeful nature of Cosgrave's government and the loyalty I found I could not disown toward my former comrades.

When the cease fire had emptied the Free State jails nearly twelve thousand young men had been turned loose on an economy already suffering from unemployment. Add to these perhaps an equal number who laid down their arms. Most of these men had no means of livelihood and not much hope of getting one. No civil service appointment was open to them, for the government gave preference to men who had served in the Free State Army, which was partially demobilizing. They had no capital to set themselves up in business, and it was difficult for them to get any sort of normal employment, since most businessmen had been unsympathetic toward the I.R.A. Even if they were not, few firms liked to have raids on their premises and investigations conducted in connection with these ex-prisoners, which was apt to happen every time the illegal I.R.A. shot off another bomb.

Finally, the Briscoe Importing Company was located in my old brick building at 9 Aston's Quay where Fianna Headquarters had been. On the street in front of it were the terminal points of the bus lines that ran to all parts of the city and suburbs. As the big green buses discharged their passengers many a discouraged lad instinctively came in to seek help or at least friendliness. Could I, sitting in my office looking up the thin blue Liffey to the melancholy ruin of the Four Courts, refuse them?

Therefore without design I found myself gradually associating

with many old friends and ex-jailbirds. There was Andy Mac-
Donnell, the brigadier of Wicklow. There was Sean Nolan who
had been at my side in the Dáil the day of the Treaty vote. And
there was Andy Woods! There were many others. As time went
on I took into my employment the best of our people who were
not able to find other work. In fact Briscoe Importing became almost exclusively staffed by former members of the I.R.A. It is no
wonder the government regarded us with a malevolent eye.

Perhaps the most notorious character who ever worked for us
was Ned Kelleher. In the days of the Black and Tans, Kelleher
had been one of Michael Collins's dreaded "Twelve Apostles" —
the Special Active Service Unit was its official title. This group
under the command of "Holy Joe" O'Connor — also known as
"Rasputin" — had the job of fighting the worst of the Black and
Tans and dealing with British spies and Irish informers. Their
name was terror. Ned Kelleher was the only one of them who
did not follow Collins into the Free State. He came to the Four
Courts with his brother Sean. After the surrender Ned had been
the ringleader in many attempted jail-breaks.

You may imagine what chance he had of finding work when he
was finally released. For Ned was a fearful man who brought the
suspicion of the government down upon any person with whom
he associated. Somehow he scraped up enough money to buy a
Model T Ford truck secondhand and started a little carting business. People like myself gave him jobs delivering parcels or collecting goods from the docks. He did so well that one day I con-
gratulated him.

"My luck won't last," he answered cheerfully. "Something's
bound to happen, for misfortune tracks me like a hound."

Just before Christmas, 1924, I sent for Ned to cart some parcels.
He had completed loading his truck, when he came into my office
and said, "What did I tell you?"

"What's happened, Ned?"

"The engine just fell out of my truck."

I went out the front door, and there, right enough, the whole
engine in scattered parts and pieces was lying in the street. There

was only one thing I could say. "Ned, the best thing you can do is to come in and join the staff of Briscoe Importing."

Ned could not stop being a soldier. I remember coming in a few mornings later to find the whole staff lined up against the wall, some with brooms and some with other sticks, and Ned drilling them.

When Ned came to work for me our troubles started. Detective Mark Byrne, formerly of the I.R.A. and now, regarded by us as a renegade, a member of the Central Intelligence Department, came nosing around, jaunty as you please in a new bowler hat. He told us he was taking a course in "anatomy."

"What do you mean anatomy?" asked Ned.

"Well," said Byrne, "it will make me so that when I look into your eyes and I ask you questions, I can tell what you're thinking in spite of what you're saying."

A light dawned on me and I said, "God help us, Ned, and God help the country! He means psychology."

Whereupon Ned picked up the flap of the counter and brought it down on Mark's new hat, roaring, "Go mind your own anatomy and leave us alone!"

After that incident, the C.I.D. detailed three men to follow me. They were Inspector Ennis, "Mouthy" Hughes and a man called Mooney. If I went into Gallagher's Shaving Parlor to get a shave, these three gentlemen sat in chairs waiting. If I dropped into Bewley's for my cup of tea, they sat at the next table. When their working day ended another man followed me home.

This went on for some months. Kelleher was getting even angrier than I was, and I remember him telling me he would not put up with this much longer. Then our place was raided. The police searched it from top to bottom looking for ammunition or anything else that might incriminate me or some member of the staff.

These raids became fairly regular after that and we realized that the game was to put us out of business. Our customers, who had nothing to do with politics, did not like being stood up against a wall with their hands behind their heads and searched.

Timid people decided it would be better to buy their goods elsewhere. We noticed our business falling off.

"Now this must stop," Ned said angrily. "Will you come with me to the College Green Police Station?"

"I will that," I answered.

We strode into the place, black-browed with fury. Ned was a huge big man over six feet tall and well did they know his reputation. I had some small notoriety of my own. The blue-uniformed sergeant at the desk asked us our business a little nervously. Without a word Ned pointed at Ennis, Hughes and Mooney sitting on a bench in the barracks room. We almost broke out laughing at their antics. Ennis shot into a telephone booth like a rabbit to its burrow. Hughes backed toward the inspector's office, and Mooney sidled like a crab for the door.

Kelleher said, "I want to talk to you gentlemen," and they stood like waxworks.

"I'm here to warn you," Ned continued. "Leave us alone at 9 Aston's Quay. You mind your business; we're minding ours. If I have to come here again about this matter it will be with a gun in one hand and a bomb in the other. Good-by!"

For months thereafter all was quiet at 9 Aston's Quay.

Despite his ferocious reputation, Kelleher was an excellent employee, completely trustworthy, absolutely honest and kindly. He finally became my manager and general factotum, and he kept the rest of the staff right up to the mark. He continued in the business until I sold it in 1928. Then I managed to get him a job with the Irish Sweep. When we took over the government in 1932, and de Valera became Prime Minister, I asked Ned to become the Chief's personal bodyguard. I had a lot of trouble persuading him to take on the job, for he hated policemen and did not want to be one. However, once he accepted, I was sure of the Chief's safety.

Kelleher served de Valera loyally for six years. He organized the Prime Minister's security detail himself, selecting the men who guarded the entrances of the government buildings. Day or night Ned personally accompanied the Chief wherever he went. Ned knew the right men to trust. The security guard became known as "The Broy Harriers." A man named Broy was the head of the police department. They were not men you would care to cross, what with their stalwart appearance and the machine guns caressingly cradled in the hollows of their arms.

Ned is now employed by the National Coal Board. He has grown somewhat stout and a little stodgy. I have not seen him for some years, but I know that if I, or any member of my family, were to ask his help in any matter either within or without the law, Ned Kelleher would be there quicker than you could say, *Dia linn!*

Other old I.R.A. men whom I tried to help ended up with a pyrotechnically spectacular failure. They were Liam Deasy, who was Deputy Chief of Staff of the I.R.A. and who was under sentence of death when the civil war ended, and Tom Crofts. In 1924 they started an agency business in Cork. Deasy, who looked more like a portly, prosperous farmer than a desperate rebel, came to Dublin with his partner and asked me to give them the agency for some of my imported articles. Of course I obliged them with liberal credit terms. They went back to Cork with a fine assortment of electrical appliances and a new English fire extinguisher that particularly pleased them. This gadget looked like a pistol. You were supposed to aim it at the fire, pull the trigger and your worries were over.

Back in Cork Deasy and Crofts got permission from the fire department to stage a demonstration of the extinguisher. They put up a cock of hay in back of a building, poured paraffin over it, and invited Cork's leading businessmen in. Then they set it on fire and said, "Now watch!"

Liam aimed the pistol at the blaze and pulled the trigger. A white frothy mass of stuff streamed out of it. There was a roar and what had been a fire became a conflagration. People ran for their lives and only the fact that the fire brigade was alerted saved the building.

After that I was on the run from Deasy and Crofts for a long time. And from Cork to Donegal the joke ran around Ireland about the "Jewish fire extinguisher" that added fuel to the flames.

Meanwhile my family was growing. When our third child, Joseph, was born, Snugboro became a little too snug for us and we moved to a larger house on Garville Avenue. People told me it was a house of misfortune; everyone who lived in it had bad luck; but I laughed at them. Lily laughed at them too. We moved in. What happened?

My mother died. Lily's father died. Lily fell down the stairs and broke her ankle — a Pott's fracture that caused her months of misery and cost a deal to repair. Our baby son Joseph developed a mysterious disease and almost died. Billy got scarlet fever. The maid got diphtheria and I had to take her suddenly to a hospital. Things got so bad we decided to flee from that house.

That is how we came to the place called Ballure at Ballybrack in Killiney. From the moment we entered that house, with the nurse carrying little Joe, bad luck stopped at its threshold. Joe mended miraculously. Lily became a new woman, and the two older children had room to play and grow. Never were we so happy.

Ballure was a big old house with four acres of land surrounded by one of those high stone walls that enclose so much of the beauty of Ireland. The house was distinctly dilapidated, so I got it very reasonably on a repairing lease. But however down at the heel it might be, there was welcome on its wide front door and serenity under the big trees on the lawn. And there was nothing wrong that a little paint and work would not restore. Renovating it gave me a chance to employ some more of the young relics of the wars. This was good business for me, since I got the job done cheaply if not efficiently, and it was very good for them to be started back on the road to self-sufficiency.

Once the house was fixed there was plenty to do in the grounds. The whole time we were there the place was a hive of activity. We had a fine vegetable garden and an orchard of fruit trees. There were cows in the barn and we made our own butter and buttermilk, while our hens were laying the eggs we ate and supplying us with fowl for our pot. In almost everything except beef, which is very cheap in Ireland, we were self-contained. It gave us a glorious feeling of accomplishment.

As a result of living in Ballure with its four acres of ground, never having had so much as half an acre before, I got a hunger for land that led me after some years, to an adventure in agriculture that was my economic undoing.

I am getting a little ahead of my story, for these events took place in the 1930's; but they were a sequel to our lovely life at Ballure. Having sold the Briscoe Importing Company for ethical reasons which I shall presently relate, I had a little capital and a lot more time; and the craving for land was strong in me. So I took a place, Somerset in Blackrock, which was in the suburbs, but still open country, with nine acres of lush land. Here I thought I would turn farmer, an amateur farmer if you will, for of course I was by then a member of the Dáil and of the Dublin City Council, so you could say that in spite of good resolutions my real profession was politics. However, in my innocence I expected to make farming pay.

I branched out in all directions. We had a big greenhouse in which we grew, I think, the greatest number of tomatoes of anybody in County Dublin. After paying the bill for heating the greenhouse and all Lily's work in nurturing those tomatoes, plucking them and packaging them in fancy style we got four pence a pound for them. We also grew cucumbers, corn and experimented with tobacco. Disastrous! Our lettuce won prizes at the agricultural shows, but at what a price!

Then we turned to horticulture. The greenhouse blossomed and burgeoned with magnificent, exotic chrysanthemums. We sent a hundred bunches of them to the Dublin market one day and Lily asked the salesmaster to deliver one bunch to a friend in the hospital. We got the following statement of the transaction.

CREDIT. Sale of 100 bu chrysanthemums 18/9
DEBIT. One bunch delivered at nursing home 18/9

Return

Every time I attempted something it came back to the story of the bullocks. I bought four yearlings for twenty pounds each, planning to fatten them on my land and sell them again. It was a foolproof scheme. After a year of care and feeding the bullocks prospered and grew twice their original size. I sent them to market where they brought — *twenty pounds each.*

I have often said we Irish are a stubborn race. Quite undaunted, I rented some land in Wicklow and went into partnership with a young farmer to experiment with sheep. I planned it very carefully. I would buy twenty ewes and a ram. The ewes would have lambs. I would sell or exchange the males and buy more ewes. After a few years I would have an enormous flock of sheep.

One Sunday morning a knock came at my door. My sheep partner was there with his brother.

"I have bad news for you, sir," he said.

"What bad news have you?"

"Well, some dogs raided the field in which we had our sheep."

"And then?" I asked.

"The sheep were destroyed, sir."

"All of them?"

"All of *yours*, sir."

"Well," I said, "I must compliment the Wicklow dogs on their intelligence in killing my sheep and leaving yours alone."

Lily still says I was the biggest sheep.

My final foray into agriculture was raising race horses and hunters. I have always been fond of the turf and flatter myself I can pick a winner as well as the next man. Once I sat in the lounge of the Shelbourne Hotel and played a three-horse parlay — all outsiders. Believe it or not they all came in and I won nine hundred ninety pounds for an investment of fourteen pounds. We will not talk about the parlays that went wrong.

Now horses were something about which I had knowledge — not like sheep or cows or chrysanthemums. I saw a lovely colt which would make a fine hunter and bought him. He was by Battleaxe so I named him after a Dublin pub — Tubs of Blood. Lily and I used to go out regularly to look at our Grand National winner. But the blood was on my head. He was injured in training and I sold him for eight pounds. I never told Lily what I paid for him and will not even now.

On another occasion I went down to Wicklow to look at a horse I thought of buying. At that time, being closely identified with de Valera's government, I was decidedly unpopular with certain elements who were "agin the government." I was warned that there might be an attempt on my life. Nevertheless I went, and inspected the animal in a field far out in the country. His owner and I bargained for an hour and finally agreed on a price provided the horse went well. A friend mounted, and after cantering around a bit, leaped him over a high hedge into the next field. I, following, landed right in the midst of five or six men with guns. To my amazement they did not fire. This seemed a good omen and I bought the horse.

Some years later I recognized one of these men on a street in Dublin. "Good morning to you," I said.

"Good morning, sir," he replied, grinning.

"There is something I've wanted to ask you," I continued. "Was that gathering of you and your friends in that field in Wicklow for the purpose of shooting me?"

"It was, sir," he answered.

"Why did you not do it then?"

"Well, sir," he replied, "we heard you make the bargain with that fellow in the next field, and it seemed a pity to spoil a deal that was so good for him and bad for you."

All these financial disasters troubled Lily and me very little. Those were years of great happiness for us. Our family grew and grew. After Joe came two more boys, Brian and Benjamin. Then to complete the tally two more girls, our daughters Ida and Elise. So I had seven children as my father did. We were particularly blessed. All of them grew up strong, intelligent and affectionate.

Those were years of accomplishment as well. For it was during this time that the Irish people rallied again to the standard of the Republic; and we, who had been the young revolutionaries and irreconcilables, metamorphosed and matured into responsible politicians to whom was entrusted the precious destiny of Ireland.

CHAPTER XIX

Army of Destiny

Now I must tell you a little of what had been happening in Ireland since my return. The Free State Constitution had gone into effect while I was still in America. This provided that the government of Ireland should consist of:

(1) The Governor General, appointed by the King of England with a salary of ten thousand pounds paid by the *Irish people*. Timothy Healy, a clever barrister, who had been an Irish member of the British Parliament, was designated the first Governor General and moved into the long, white, classic Viceregal Lodge in Phoenix Park from which a long succession of haughty Lord Lieutenants had ruled Ireland.

(2) The Executive Council of Ministers appointed by the Dáil, but acceptable to the Governor General.

(3) The *Oireachtas* or Parliament, a mongrelized combination of the British Parliament and American Congress, consisting of an upper and lower house. The former, which had little political power was called the *Seanad Eireann* (Senate). It consisted of sixty members who were supposed to be Very Important People. In the first Free State Parliament, thirty members of the Senate were nominated by the Executive Council and thirty by the Dáil. Needless to say the Cosgrave government failed to detect any Very Important People in the Republican ranks. The lower house consisting of one hundred fifty-seven members, still called itself Dáil Eireann, though by what right? It was elected directly by the people. The Executive Council was responsible to it just as the British Cabinet is responsible to the House of Commons. Wil-

liam Cosgrave was the first President of the Executive Council, in effect, Prime Minister.

The Constitution further provided that every member of the government and of Parliament must take the oath of allegiance to the King of England. This the Republicans swore they would never do. During the period between 1923 and 1927 there were an average of over forty elected Republican deputies who refused to take their seats. As a result Cosgrave's party, which called itself Cumann na nGaedhael had an absolutely free hand in the government with no more than sixty-three seats in the Dáil. Their only real opposition was the Labor Party with fourteen votes. The splinter groups were Farmers (fifteen) and Independents (seventeen). Trinity University (four). What did Cosgrave do with his power?

Apart from the many illegal and ruthless acts of suppression which I have described, Cosgrave's government betrayed the Irish people by two more unjustifiable treaties with England. One was an agreement, kept secret for nine years, by which Ireland agreed to pay England five million pounds every year for fifty years in compensation for the land repurchased by Irish farmers from British subjects, who had stolen it from its Irish owners after the conquests of Elizabethan and Cromwellian days. These payments were called Land Purchase Annuities.

The second was even worse. We had all been told by Griffith and Collins and Cosgrave that the Boundary Commission set up by the Treaty would rectify the border between Northern Ireland and the Free State to give places with a nationalist majority to the South. On December 3, 1925, Cosgrave signed an agreement with England perpetuating the original Lloyd Georgian boundaries. The pro-Nationalist counties of Tyrone and Fermanagh and the large Catholic city of Derry were forever denied their right to be Irish. In return England agreed to cancel Ireland's share of the British war debt, but not the Land Purchase Annuities. By this deal the northern Nationalists, who had suffered so greatly for their loyalty to Ireland, were sold into British bondage for the remittance of a debt that was of dubious legality and in any event uncollectable by England. Colonel Maurice Moore, no Republican, hit the nail when he said, "We have been burgled and we have bribed the burglar."

And what was de Valera doing about these actions? Of the Land Annuities deal he knew nothing. Against the partition agreement he could only protest ineffectually, since though he was an elected member of the Dáil, he felt he could not conscientiously take his seat. At this time he began to think that he must put himself in a position to represent the wishes of his constituents, help to realize the ideals of Irishmen and curb the power of Cumann na nGaedhael.

There were two possible courses of action. One was to resume the struggle in arms. The skeleton organization that remained of the Irish Republican Army favored this. They even sent Sean Russell and Gerald Boland to Moscow to investigate the possibility of obtaining Russian help and Russian guns. But de Valera, who had reappraised and regretted the policy which had led to the civil war, rejected this with the words, "Are you going to have the same sort of thing started again?"

The second alternative was to compromise with principle for the sake of real political power. De Valera was still President of the Irish Republic, a shadow government which governed nothing. He was President of Sinn Fein, a shadow political party which took no part in practical politics. He decided that this situation must end.

This was where I came into the picture. In the last days of 1925, Eamon Martin, Seamus Robinson and other Republicans with whom I was on friendly terms came to the conclusion that the Free State would go on for all time if no way could be found of breaking this impasse. I remember saying to them, "By our own acts we are supporting this illegal government. For example we use the Free State postal and wire services. Let us give up our telephones and send no more telegrams or letters. Instead why not get old Fianna boys, or young ones for that matter, and let them carry our messages as they did in the days of the Black and Tans? Let us take away from this government even the few pence we pay in postage!"

This was of course a very elementary way of thinking, but I was trying to show that by our contributions to the ordinary civil services we were in fact strengthening the Free State. What I had in mind was a sort of strike against them, which I admit was the typically visionary conception of an Irish mind.

However it did bring Robinson, Martin and me an invitation to confer with de Valera. We went to the offices on Suffolk Street which he occupied as President of Sinn Fein. It was a very simple place — just two rooms. The larger of them was divided by a green curtain behind which the Chief sat at his battered desk. Though the furniture was cheap and worn, the space cramped and gloomy, and de Valera at the nadir of his political power, there was a sense of greatness about him that filled me with wonder. As I passed behind that dingy curtain into his presence I moved into a close association and friendship with him that directed and inspired the rest of my life.

Martin, who knew the Chief best, was our spokesman. He explained our despair of getting rid of the Free State and enlarged upon my plan of passive resistance. De Valera listened intently. Then with that wonderful warm smile which dissolves the sternness of his features he said, "You are not the only ones who have been thinking about this wretched situation and our impotence to alter it. I also have been thinking and I have reached a difficult decision. I am about to make an announcement which I hope will meet with your approval and support, though I do not know how it will be taken in the country."

In January, 1926, de Valera announced an about-face in his political attitude. Provided the oath to the King was not required, he would enter the Free State Parliament. He then attempted to rally Sinn Fein behind him. His first move was to summon an *Ard Fheis* of Sinn Fein. Four hundred and thirty-eight members responded to his call. Speaking with all the power and gravity of which he was capable, he told them that he now believed that physical force was no longer possible or desirable because it would again involve fighting between Irishmen. He had come to the definite conclusion that Irish independence could be achieved by constitutional means. As a step in this direction he made a motion that, if the oath to the King were not required, entering the Free State Parliament should be regarded by Sinn Fein "not as a question of principle but as a question of policy."

This mild move toward participation in the government caused what Countess Markievicz described as "an unholy row." Austin Stack, gaunt and shadowy as a ghost from the past, denounced it. Mary MacSwiney, sister of the martyred Lord Mayor, vehemently called it the first step toward the descent into hell. Sinn Fein's vice-president, Father Flanagan, obdurately proposed that the motion be amended to read, "It is incompatible with Sinn Fein principles to send representatives into a usurping legislature." In a wildly tumultuous scene the vote was taken. De Valera and the moderates lost by two hundred twenty-three to two hundred eighteen — five votes in more than four hundred.

So another unfortunate split had broken the ranks of Irishmen; a split which resulted in the disintegration of Sinn Fein. For de Valera was determined that he would no longer remain a helpless spectator of Ireland's ruin. Having wrestled with his own conscience and come to a decision, he would abide by it. He resigned as President of Sinn Fein, and a few days later, as President of the Irish Republic. So he was free to enter the arena of action.

But he knew he could not successfully fight alone; he must found a new constitutional political party. For this purpose he called on those Republicans who were still willing to follow his leadership. Among them were Sean T. O'Kelly, Sean Lemass, Gerry Boland, Sean MacEntee, Frank Aiken, Patrick J. Ruttledge, Doctor James Ryan of County Wexford and Countess Markievicz. I was one of those he sent for, and I became a founder and member of the Executive Committee of the new party which we named Fianna Fail — Army of Destiny.

Now began one of the busiest times of my life — there were so few of us to organize a national party throughout the whole of Ireland. We had only about a year to do it before the general election of 1927. The irreconcilables of Sinn Fein would not join us — in fact they jeered at us for renegades to the Republican faith.

Since his office on Suffolk Street belonged to Sinn Fein, the Chief had to move out. We rented a couple of rooms over Jameson's Jewelry Shop on O'Connell Street and opened the first offices of Fianna Fail. Funds we had none, and the office was as bare as a boneless cupboard — no typewriters, no desks, not even a chair to sit on. Money for all these things as well as the rent and a small staff had to be found. We, the founder members, rushed around collecting donations from our friends and personally pledging what we could. I was one of the few able to make a commitment. I remember saying, "My contribution toward the office will be at least ten shillings a week." It was not much that we could afford in those days.

However, collecting funds was easier than we expected. A great number of Republicans who had not been active since the surrender, found new hope in our party, and gave with reckless generosity.

The founder members were divided up into committees. I worked on one of these under the chairmanship of Sean Mac-Entee. Once a week we all met as the Executive Committee, and I was in almost daily contact with the Chief. Every one of us had to do the work of a dozen men. Instead of running my business I was continually chasing around Dublin holding organization meetings or even just acting as a messenger boy.

All of us had to become public speakers. Sean MacEntee taught me how to handle the excitable crowds who gathered around the automobiles we used as platforms in the squares and streets of Dublin. The bitterness of civil war lingered like thunder in the air, and every crowd was charged with potential lightning. The Free State Government still had great fears of us and at every meeting would draw a cordon of Civic Guards between us and the people.

MacEntee advised me how to discomfit these blue-uniformed gentlemen. "Pick out a particular Guarda," he said, "and stare at one particular part of him, say his belt, while you're speaking. Soon he'll begin to wonder what you are looking at. He will nervously feel his belt and other parts of his uniform. Other people will begin to wonder and stare at him, too. Pretty soon, he will be a nervous wreck, and you will be in command of the situation."

I tried it, and it worked so well, I could hardly keep from laughing out loud.

By November 26, 1926, we were ready for the first convention of Fianna Fail. It was held in the La Scala Theatre, which is now a cinema house. Five hundred old Republicans were jammed into it. Looking across the footlights from the stage you could see them crowded up the steep heights of the balcony and standing packed like the five o'clock bus in the ornate proscenium boxes. Many a fond familiar face I saw among them, faces that had once had the radiance of courage and the joy of fighting for ideals, and now looked gray and beaten. The wonderful thing was to see hope light them up again when the Chief began to speak.

De Valera was dressed as always like a preacher in a dead black suit, but his somber clothes did nothing to conceal the fierce light of his leadership. This speech he made was a hard thing to pull off, for it was in some measure a recantation of the principles he had held so long. But by the transparent integrity of the man, even more than by the carefully brilliant logic of his words, he won his audience and led them from doubt to triumphant enthusiasm for his new policy of political action. In truth, de Valera's speech that day formulated the philosophy and creed by which Fianna Fail has lived and governed Ireland.

What was the purpose he outlined? That I will tell you in fewer, less moving words than his for the sake of brevity.

If elected to office we first would remove the oath of allegiance

and abolish the Governor General. De Valera rightly believed
that England would not fight us again if this were done constitutionally. Fortunately, the British had left a loophole in the Constitution they had forced upon us — it could be amended by a very
simple process.

After these first things were done, Fianna Fail proposed to
stop paying the Land Annuities to England. We believed they
were an illegal debt, since England had officially renounced them
in 1920, and then taken back her much advertised "gift to Ireland." De Valera felt that Ireland should owe no money to the
British. Whatever just local debts were due England, whether
from cities or counties or public institutions, should be taken over
by the Irish Government and paid at once.

We also had a policy of making Ireland self-sufficient, to curb
the adverse external trade balance and free her from dependence
on foreign countries. We were buying eggs in tins from China,
bacon and wheat from Canada, sugar from Cuba, and food from
many other countries. Virtually every manufactured article we
used, except textiles, came from abroad. If there were another
world conflict we would be dependent on some foreign country
to whom we would have to sell our freedom and our souls for
bread.

To redress this condition we proposed to buy from the great
landowners the grasslands which were only used for grazing
bullocks and give them back to the landless people for tillage
farming. We also wanted to protect and encourage the development of Irish industry. For this we needed power. The Shannon
River was partly harnessed, we wanted to complete the job.

The flight from the farms to the cities and to countries abroad,
de Valera believed, was partly due to the lack of all amenities on
our farms. We wanted to bring about rural electrification, and to
provide a proper water supply to end this business of village people going to the town pump or the nearest well every time they
needed a pail of water.

Finally there would be an attempt to get the people of the
North to understand that their well-being, and the well-being of

the country as a whole, depended on the elimination of the border. We would try to end partition *without a resort to arms*.

After the La Scala meeting we went on to organize the country. Meetings were held in all parts of the land. Groups of speakers would be sent to the county towns and villages to explain Fianna Fail and arouse enthusiasm. Then one of us would be left behind to organize a Fianna Cumann — a political club. In less than a year we organized seven or eight hundred of these — there are now about fifteen hundred. You may imagine what work we all had to do. There were then only about twenty or twenty-five regular speakers among us and we covered the whole country from Bantry Bay to Malin Head.

I had acquired my first motor car and I remember every Sunday and sometimes on a Saturday evening leaving home with four or five speakers in my car bound for Kerry or Carlow, down to Limerick and west across the Shannon, where some of our supporters would have arranged public meetings. At other times we would just try to catch the crowd coming out of church after Mass.

One time we went to Ballyseedy in Kerry, which had become famous in the civil war as the place where a number of Republicans were chained to the gate of a farmyard and a mine was then exploded killing them all. For many years tempers flared in Ballyseedy, and still to this day the most insulting thing you can say to an opponent is to accuse him of being one of the murderers of Ballyseedy.

In this touchy area our local leader was Willie O'Leary, ex-commandant of the I.R.A. This Sunday I went with O'Leary and some of his friends to the church. They all went into Mass, while I remained with the car from which we would speak when it was over. O'Leary turned back and said to me, "Will you not go in to Mass?"

"I don't go to Mass," I replied.

"Everybody goes to Mass here, you'll have to do likewise."

I began to explain the difference in our faiths, when O'Leary interrupted me. Speaking between clenched teeth he said,

"Haven't we enough bloody trouble explaining Fianna Fail without having to explain you as well? At least go to the door and *pretend* you're going to Mass!"

I complied.

After the meeting we adjourned to Mr. O'Leary's stone farmhouse where breakfast was being prepared for us in his ample kitchen with its enormous stove and a wide ancient hearth still supplied with the wrought-iron crane and primitive utensils of an earlier age. He sat me at the head of a long deal table around which gathered some of the local Republicans. I was confronted immediately with cabbage and *bacon*. How should I deal with this problem?

While I sat indecisive, O'Leary asked with a twinkle, "Are you not hungry?"

"Indeed I am," I answered, "but I think I will be hungrier when I leave here."

"You need not fear," he answered. "I have some boiled eggs for you."

Thanks to O'Leary's courteous recognition of my faith, I had a sumptuous breakfast of eggs and great glasses of foamy milk with home-made bread and farmer's butter. I am glad to say this was only the beginning of our friendship, for O'Leary was subsequently elected to the Dáil, and we served together there for many years.

Early in 1927, de Valera made a quick trip to America — legally this time. What a howl the irreconcilables raised when he applied for a Free State passport! His reason was that the bond case was coming up. At the trial in New York the Supreme Court refused the Free State's claim for the cash in the Chase Bank and ordered it returned to the subscribers to the bonds. Many of these generously gave the money right back to Dev. These funds gave Fianna Fail's treasury a much-needed injection and enabled us to move to more spacious offices on Middle Abbey Street.

They also made possible the founding of the *Irish Press* some years later. Until that time there was no big paper in all Ireland which expressed our principles. Frank Gallagher and Bob Brennan were the new paper's leading spirits. In the last dark days of the civil war, Brennan and his pretty young wife, Una Brennan, had published the little one-sheet paper which was the only voice of the Republic. They hid the printing press in a horse-drawn delivery wagon which they kept moving from street to street and suburb to suburb, while the C.I.D. vainly chased a newspaper published on the run. The respectability of a genuine, legal, daily paper like the *Irish Press* fortunately did not dull Brennan's fiery wit.

The general election was held in June, 1927. Our opponents plastered the countryside with posters crying that if Fianna Fail got into office with such a policy the British would be back. It was a ghost of the past; a terror they were striking at the hearts of the people. And it did them small good.

I ran for a seat in the Dáil and was soundly trounced. But my own misfortune hardly mattered. In spite of the disadvantages of newness, the split in the Republican ranks and the terror tactics of Cosgrave's crew, Fianna Fail won forty-four seats in the Dáil. Cosgrave's party fell to forty-six. The rest were Labor and the splinter parties.

However, when de Valera led the Fianna Fail delegates to the Dáil, they were turned away because they would not take the oath of allegiance to the King of England. Cosgrave jeered that Dev was using the oath to evade the responsibilities of office.

At this moment of uncertainty and confusion in our councils, two tragic events further darkened the political scene. That great lady of the Revolution, Countess Markievicz, died. And in the same week Kevin O'Higgins, Vice-President of the Executive Council and also Cosgrave's Minister of Justice and Minister of External Affairs was shot and killed as he walked to Mass on a Sunday morning.

I remember that sunny July day better than day before yesterday. Seamus Robinson and I went swimming in the Irish Sea at Seapoint near Dun Laoghaire. I remember the tingling shock of the cold blue water, and the brief serenity of spirit as we lay on the sun-warm rocks after our bath and talked of frivolous foolish things. At last we started back for Dublin.

As we reached the close-built suburbs we saw bodies of soldiers and police marching out and forming a cordon around the city. Every vehicle and every person walking in the streets was being stopped and questioned.

Our turn soon came. The Guarda who stopped us was a fresh-faced lad who knew little of Irish politics. He asked our names and they luckily meant nothing to him at all. Besides, we were still in our wet bathing suits, which was a sort of proof of innocence. He was about to let us go when Seamus asked, "What's up? What's happened to cause all this stir?"

"Oh," he said quite casually, "Mr. Kevin O'Higgins, the Minister of Justice, has been murdered."

Then he waved us on into the city.

Seamus and I drove on white-faced. Well did we know what this would mean — reprisals! Though we suspected that it was the work of the Irregulars, the government saw small difference between them and us. They would surely believe that this was done by Fianna Fail or the I.R.A. It took Seamus and me no more than the blink of an eye to realize this. Our first thought was of the Chief.

I swung the car in the direction of Sandymount where de Valera was living in a house that stood alone in its own small grounds surrounded by the usual stone wall. We came to this house and drove through the open gates up the little drive. To our enormous relief everything seemed quiet. I knocked on the door and Mrs. de Valera herself opened it. She knew us well, and gave us welcome.

"Have you heard what's happened?" Seamus asked.

"I have," she answered sadly.

"Where's the Chief?"

"He is on his way home from Clare," she replied.

"Holy God, I hope nothing happens to him on the road!" I exclaimed.

Then I added, "In any event, we are staying here until he arrives, and we will stay with him until we can make other arrangements. We'll see about means and methods of defense later."

Mrs. de Valera looked at both of us, and she said in a very beautiful, gentle manner, "You go home and stay with your wives and families. Surely one widow would be sufficient instead of three."

Nevertheless we stayed. After a while I walked out into the road and saw that a uniformed policeman had taken station there. He was a man I knew, and I knew that he was absolutely nonpolitical.

"What are you doing here?" I asked.

"I am here to see that no unauthorized person tries to enter Mr. de Valera's house," he answered.

I concluded that the government was taking precautions not only to see that de Valera was safe, but also that he would be certainly available if and when they decided to arrest him. Somewhat reassured I went home.

Later I learned that the Chief had heard the news on his way home from County Clare and issued a statement denying that he or any member of our party had done this act.

However we were all suspect. People were continually being arrested and released, including our next door neighbors, the Carrols. The Bridewell Prison was full and could not contain them all. My house was raided and I was told "When you go to bed, sleep in your clothes. We will be back! When we come we will take care of you as we did Noel Lemass."

That was unpleasant news. For Noel Lemass, the brother of Sean Lemass, had disappeared some years before, and his mutilated body was found months later in the Featherbed Mountains.

The deaths of Kevin O'Higgins and Countess Markievicz had left two vacant seats in the Dáil. Bob Brennan and I were assigned to contest them for Fianna Fail, he in County Dublin for O'Higgins's seat and I in South Dublin for that of Countess Markievicz. We ran a joint campaign and our election slogan was

234

"Give it to Bob!" That was a boomerang for when we were both beaten our opponents wrote on our election posters, "We gave it to Bob — in the neck!"

When the Dáil reconvened in August, Cosgrave's government introduced fresh repressive measures, including a law which forced every candidate for the Dáil to declare in advance that he would take the oath to the King if elected. Dev instantly realized that this would be the end of Fianna Fail, for no candidate with our outlook could ever run for office. With the courage of his conviction that in so doing he would be serving Ireland best, he publicly declared that he and the Fianna Fail members would enter the Dáil. He stated that signing the oath would be "an empty formula," and that Fianna deputies would push the Bible aside, and announce that in signing they were not accepting any obligation or taking any oath.

The officials accepted this arrangement, and de Valera led the Republican deputies into the Chamber amid the jeers of Cumann na nGaedhael. The Labor Party supporting Fianna Fail immediately proposed a vote of no confidence in the government. It was a tie, broken in Cosgrave's favor by the deciding vote of the *Cean Comhairle* — the Speaker of the House.

No government could function on such a narrow margin. Cosgrave immediately dissolved the Dáil and called another general election. For the third time in three months I ran for office. This time I was elected, representing South City with Sean Lemass.

So in September, 1927, I went with the other Republican deputies to take my seat in the Dáil. That is another day I remember in its least detail. I came through the high wrought-iron gates of Leinster House, which had been the huge Palladian residence of the Dukes of Leinster and is now the permanent home of the Parliament. In the courtyard was a massive statue of Queen Victoria, which was so ugly that it was known to Irish and English alike as "Ireland's Revenge."

Trying to walk with nonchalant dignity in spite of my strong emotion, I moved toward the enormously long, gray stone façade

For the Life of Me

of Leinster House and into the marble lobby. Ushers showed the way to a side room where the clerk was swearing in the new members. Frank Aiken, bulking huge and dark and solemn, stood beside him to witness that in signing the oath each Fianna deputy repeated de Valera's formula.

When it came to my turn I varied the procedure slightly. I pointed to the New Testament lying on the table and said, "Even if I swore on that Book, I would not be bound, for it is not my Testament."

Then pushing it aside as the others did, I repeated the words prescribed for us: "I am not taking any oath. I am signing this document merely to gain admission to the Dáil."

Then with my colleagues I climbed the long broad flight of marble steps and entered the double glass doors of the Chamber. It was an ornate oval room almost as deep as a well. The benches for the members climbed up three sides of it. On the fourth was a high dais where the Speaker sat. On either side of him were the swinging doors of the Yes and No lobbies through which the members passed to record their votes.

Cumann na nGaedheal sat to the right of the Speaker — Cosgrave, Mulcahy, Desmond Fitzgerald, Earnest Blythe and the rest of the Cabinet.

On the front bench to the Speaker's left was the tall, black-clad figure of de Valera, his pale strong face as stern and otherworldly as one of the great prophets of my people. Close beside him sat Sean T. O'Kelly seeming even smaller and more vibrantly pugnacious by contrast. The other members of Dev's shadow cabinet were there too, Sean Lemass, Frank Aiken, James Ryan MacEntee and the rest.

These things I noted as I stood for a moment in the gallery looking down into that cockpit of politics or well of destiny, whichever you have a mind to call it. Then I walked down the steep, red-carpeted stairs and took my place on a back bench behind my Chief where I have sat for thirty-one years.

CHAPTER XX

Respectability

FIANNA FAIL had gained thirteen seats in the election of 1927, giving us fifty-seven. But Cumann na nGaedhael had gained fifteen, giving them sixty-one. These gains were made at the expense of the smaller parties. This crystallization of the voters around the two major parties was a good sign for the stability of parliamentary government in Ireland, since nothing so disrupts it as numerous splinter parties combining and recombining so that each shift of the political wind blows down the government. Although Labor, under the leadership of Deputy Tom Johnson, stuck with Fianna Fail, the independents for the most part voted with Cumann na nGaedhael. This gave Cosgrave a comfortable working majority.

De Valera appeared quite happy to lead the Opposition for the time being. He realized that we, who had so long been outside the law, needed training in the science of government before we accepted its responsibilities. Like the schoolmaster he once had been he set us hard at work learning our trade with himself as our headmaster.

Each of us was assigned to a conscientious study of different aspects of the state. There were those who knew about agriculture or finance, and others like myself who had engaged in industry and commerce. Professional men among us had knowledge of health, sociology and the law. But none of us had any experience in the application of this knowledge to government. We were formed into various committees dealing specifically with the matters in which we were most interested and could make the greatest contributions in debate and the betterment of legislation. At the same time we were preparing ourselves for the time when by the inevitable process of democracy we would be entrusted with the government.

De Valera kept in close touch with all our studies and activities. The Fianna Fail deputies met regularly once a week when the Dáil was in session, and at these meetings anyone could criticize proposed legislation, or even the policy of the party, and make recommendations. The Executive Committee of which I was a member met even more often.

De Valera has frequently been described by his enemies as a dictator. This is the exact opposite of the truth; in fact on many occasions I wished he were. In the debates at the party meetings and even in the Executive Committee, he would not exercise his authority to speed things up. Even though no more than one or two people opposed the will of the majority, the Chief always insisted that they be heard in all their voluminous verbosity. It was his hope that they might eventually see sense and agree with the majority, or alternatively convince the majority that *they* were wrong. Remember he was the author of the much-criticized remark, "A majority never has the right to do wrong." In my opinion this far-seeing man, whose wisdom and patriotism enabled him to oppose the tyranny of the mob while insisting on the right of the people to rule, is a true democrat.

You would think, now that we were respectable members of society and part of the machinery of government, that our persecution by the police would end. Not at all. The alarm caused by Kevin O'Higgins's murder was compounded by other incidents of bombing and violence. The authorities were inclined to lay every happening of this sort like a dead cat on our doorsill.

The bitterness of civil strife was carried into the Parliament, and our opponents were forever digging up the corpse of the past and flourishing it under our noses. One of our angriest and wittiest opponents was Senator Oliver St. John Gogarty. Doctor Gogarty was a square, powerful man of great attainments. He was Dublin's leading eye, ear, nose and throat surgeon; and his poetry formed a soaring Gothic arch of Irish literature. Unfortunately he was as stubbornly wrong-headed as only an Irishman can be. Cumann na nGaedhael had made him a senator — they loved to bedeck their party with literary lights. In the Senate he used his mastery of words to hurl invective at de Valera, whom he hated. He once referred to the Chief's economic theories as "a voice from a mathematical madhouse," and on another occasion said that anyone who aspired to lead Fianna Fail evidently had to "dress like the manager of a home for cats."

Even I was not unnoticed by Senator Gogarty and got my share of biting quips. One day I was caught in the Dáil by one of the fiendish migraine headaches to which I was subject at that time. I staggered into the members' bar; had a quick brandy and then lay down on a settee in the back of the room. Into the bar with his arrogant bump and walk came St. John Gogarty with several friends. Some reference was made to me and he said, "Briscoe must go to Moscow. That's where he belongs!"

Miss McKeon, the barmaid, an old Cumann na nBahn girl, said, "Senator Gogarty, I don't think it's at all nice of you to attack poor Deputy Briscoe, and him so sick and suffering one of his horrible headaches!"

"Is he now?" said Gogarty, and walked over to where I lay. "What's wrong with you?" he asked.

I told him, and he questioned me about my symptoms and how often I had these attacks. When I had answered he said to Miss McKeon, "Get a taxi and have it come to the door here under the arch."

When it arrived, Senator Gogarty slung all six feet, fourteen stone of me over his shoulder in the fireman's lift and carried me out the door and put me gently in the cab. He took me to his surgery where he propped me up in a chair and went to work on my sinuses while I yelled with pain.

When it was over he told me to go home and take it easy. "You'll be sore for a day or two," he said. "But you're cured."

So I was! Never since that day have I had a serious migraine headache.

A couple of weeks later, I met Gogarty in Leinster House and thanked him. "Send me your bill," I said. "Whatever it is, it's worth it."

"No bill," said Gogarty irritably. "That was not business or politics; 'twas my Hippocratic oath."

Being a member of the Dáil did not protect us from raids, both authorized and illegal. I became so worried about Lily, that I hired a big, stout fellow from County Carlow to be our gardener, but mostly as a sort of bodyguard for her. Then one day Lily telephoned me at the Dáil and said, "Some people have dropped by. Use your own judgment about coming home."

I knew this meant that a raid was taking place, and I was to stay at the Dáil; or go on the run if I thought it necessary. Meanwhile the C.I.D. were ransacking my house. The big bruiser I had hired to guard Lily was a paper tiger. At the first sign of trouble he went out to the garden and threw up.

Lily did not lose her head. She realized that the C.I.D. might try to plant evidence against me so she followed them from room to room never letting them out of her sight. The searchers did a thorough job, especially in the library. Every book was taken off the shelves, opened and thrown on the floor. My desk was turned inside out. Little Joanie and Billy watched round-eyed. Suddenly a detective turned to them and asked, "Has your father any other papers besides those he keeps in here?"

Joanie said, "Oh yes. My father keeps an awful lot of papers in the little cupboard under the stairs. Oh, we would be in very much trouble if we disturbed those papers."

Fairly whooping, the detectives rushed to the cupboard. And what did they find? Rolls of wallpaper left over after papering the house which the children had been forbidden to play with.

After thinking things over at Leinster House, I decided to go home, but circumspectly. I borrowed Tony Woods's car so that if a trap were set for me I would have time to take action before they recognized me. Nothing happened that night, but the following evening as I was driving home in my own car several shots were fired from behind a stone wall that I had to pass.

The next morning I went to the Police Barracks and complained that I had been fired at — or over — not far from there. I remember the sergeant on duty saying to me with a really whimsical smile, "Ah yes. We were only clay shooting yesterday."

"What do you mean clay shooting?" I asked.

"Shooting clay pigeons."

"Well," I said crossly, "just remember I'm not your pigeon."

After a time these excitements and alarms gradually subsided. We drifted into the routine of opposition. Once, though, this was nearly broken. On a routine vote in the Dáil in 1930, the government was defeated. Cosgrave resigned. Sean T. O'Kelly quickly put de Valera's name up to succeed him, while we of Fianna Fail vehemently demanded of the deputies if they wanted the Crown of England over us and their fleets in our harbors forever. This frightened some of the minority groups, who cared more for peace and prosperity than honor. They rallied to Cosgrave again, and he went back into office. For two more years his government walked the tightrope of a scant majority.

Meanwhile, in 1930, the Corporation of Dublin, which had been abolished by the Free State Government during the civil war, was re-established. In the first election Fianna Fail was represented by a group of well-known Republicans. There was Oscar Traynor who had commanded the Dublin area for the I.R.A. in the civil war; Mrs. Tom Clark, whose husband was executed after the Easter Rising of 1916; and Sean T. O'Kelly. Tom Kelly, who had been a Sinn Fein alderman during the Troubled Times, and I completed the first five Fianna Fail members to be elected to the Dublin Corporation. With the exception of three years when personal problems and government service made it impossible for me to run for re-election, I have been an alderman ever since.

Of course we were then only five members out of forty-five, but we had made a good start. Others elected in 1930 included

James Larkin, the great revolutionary labor leader, and Larry
O'Neill, who had been Lord Mayor all through the Black and Tan
period.

It was in the Council Chamber that my friendship with Sean
T. O'Kelly warmed to intimacy. Of course I had known him for
years. He was a good friend of my father-in-law back in the days
when O'Kelly was a Sinn Fein member of the Corporation and
Mr. Isaacs a Unionist alderman. In spite of their political differences they admired and liked each other. Sean T. told me of his
respect for my father-in-law and Mr. Isaacs said of him, "He's a
man who stands for the well-being of Dublin City. He has this
Sinn Fein point of view, and foolish as it is, he believes in it. He is
an honest man!"

In fact many people on both sides loved little Sean T. O'Kelly
who is now Ireland's President. He was one of the most immacu-
late gentlemen in Dublin. A top hat on Sean T. seemed no strange
thing. Gloves on his hands, patent leather boots, a morning coat
with striped trousers became him well. And yet nobody would
ever have mistaken him for an Englishman. He was always recog-
nizable as one of the most ardent, devoted and pugnacious Irishmen of those violent times.

For several years O'Kelly was Irish Republican envoy in Paris.
When he tried to attend the Versailles Peace Conference he was
physically thrown out, though I imagine the gendarmes must have
felt it was a terrible thing to do to so fine a gentleman.

I remember meeting Sean T. in Berlin. I had a problem about
some of the men Seamus Robinson had sent over to buy arms.
These fellows, named Beaumont, Roddy Connoly and McGrath
went broke and were on the verge of being put out of their lodg-
ings. They asked me, as Irish Republican Consul, to buy them
tickets home. I went to see John T. Ryan about it. Jetter, being
the sort of man he was, said, "These men came here on their own,
they will have to get home on their own."

But Sean T., who happened to be present, overruled him.
"Don't be a fool, Ryan!" he said. "These men are Irishmen, and
we are responsible for all Irishmen. You give them the money

to pay their bills, Bob. Better still, *you* pay the bills, buy them tickets and make sure they get on the train for home."

In the Dublin Corporation we were, of course, allies, and much more than that. I remember one time when Patrick Belton, who was physically powerful, attacked me personally in the Council Chamber pouring ridicule on my gunrunning activities. We had a very hot exchange. Somehow Pax Whelan's words of long ago about my being an Irishman from choice and conviction came to my mind and I shouted at Paddy Belton, "You're only an Irishman by accident."

He took it to be a reflection on his paternity and howled, "I was born in holy wedlock."

I tried to explain, but he kept roaring at me that if I did not withdraw he'd pummel me to smithereens. I shouted across the Council Chamber at him, "You and who else?"

At that he came rushing across the floor and stood within five feet of me. Shaking his fist he asked, "Are you going to withdraw?"

Stubborn as the next man, I said, "No!"

At this stage Sean T. O'Kelly — all five feet, one-half inch of him — stood up between us. With his chest out and his little fists clenched, he said, "Mr. Belton, if you strike down my colleague and friend, Mr. Robert Briscoe, you'll have to deal with me!"

No matter how wise a government may be, people tire of it eventually, like the Greek who voted against Alcibiades because he was tired of hearing him called "the Just." The Cosgrave government was neither wise nor just, and by 1932, the Irish people were very tired of it indeed. When his majority had been reduced to a doubtful two or three, Cosgrave could keep on no longer. He dissolved the Dáil and went to the people.

In the general election of 1932, Fianna Fail won seventy-two seats, while Cumann na nGaedhael was reduced to fifty-seven. Labor voting with us gave us a majority. After the vote which elected Fianna Fail's Frank Fahy Speaker of the Dáil, Cosgrave resigned and de Valera paid a formal call on the new Governor

General, James MacNeill. In the stately reception room of the Vice-regal Lodge he was named President of the Executive Council.

So at last the power over Ireland's destiny was entrusted to our beloved Chief. Surely it was no new thing for the Irish people to elect him to their highest office. But this time he was not the leader of a *de facto* government but the legal head of the Irish Government, recognized as such even by his Britannic Majesty. We of Fianna Fail, who had fought so long and talked so long, now had the opportunity to act. It was up to us to make our long dreams for Ireland's future come true.

CHAPTER XXI

The Pains of Power

THE leaders of Fianna Fail moved smoothly into the positions for which they had trained themselves under the tutelage of de Valera. The Chief himself took charge of External Affairs. Sean T. O'Kelly became Vice-President and Minister for Local Government, MacEntee was given Finance; Aiken, Defense; Lemass, Industry and Commerce — he is back there now; Ryan, Agriculture; Thomas Derrig, Education; and Patrick J. Ruttledge, Lands and Fisheries.

Very soon after taking office in the autumn of 1932, the Chief appeared for the first time on the world stage. It was Ireland's turn to take the Chairmanship of the Council of the League of Nations and as his own Foreign Minister de Valera presided at Geneva. It was an odd experience for those soft-mouthed professional diplomats to listen to a man whose sincerity was too scrupulous for equivocation, who was so naïve that he spoke hard truth in the marble halls of compromise. As Stanley Baldwin once said, "de Valera is as narrow, unbendable and as straight as a gun barrel."

The delegates watched nervously as the great gaunt rebel reared his height above them. Tearing up the speech thoughtfully provided by the Secretariat and speaking with the voice of a prophet he told them that unless they were prepared to pledge the use of force against an aggressor the League of Nations was doomed. The delegates had been prepared to be horrified. They were.

At home we had our program and we pushed it forward. The first order of business was to get rid of the Oath to the King. There was not too much controversy about this in the Dáil —

even Cumann na nGaedhael were not enamored of it. Its abolition was made easier by the fact that in 1931 the British Parliament had passed the Statute of Westminster giving all the Dominions, Ireland included, much more autonomy within the British Commonwealth. This clearly invalidated any restrictive clauses in the Treaty.

Only the Senate opposed it; they seemed to consider opposition their principal business. De Valera went before them in their elegant rectangular chamber, with its classic marble mantelpieces and bas relief medallions, where the Dukes of Leinster had entertained the nobility and gentry. The gentlemen waiting to hear him sitting in blue leather armchairs still considered themselves aristocrats, for Cosgrave's government had valued social eminence quite as much as ability in their appointment of Senators and some of the members were genuine peers like the Earl of Grannard and Lord Glenavy, the Speaker.

Such men were bound to take a prejudged view of any further loosening of our ties with England. Nor were they apt to respond favorably to the tall thin figure in loose-hanging black clothes standing before them, however eloquent or logical he might be. They heard him courteously, for courtesy was their stock in trade; but when the debate began, politeness went out of the window and they relieved their feelings by a series of useless tirades. These were useless because, like the House of Lords, the Senate could only delay legislation not veto it. Their rejection simply meant that we had to wait eighteen months to be rid of that obnoxious oath forever. Indeed, their obstructive action led us to get rid of the Senate too.

If the bill to abolish the Oath had comparatively plain sailing in the Dáil, there were plenty of ructions over other things. I remember one small matter which caused a minor tempest. Someone presented the Dáil with a crucifix to hang in the Chamber, and the question was whether we should accept it. The problem was referred to the Committee of Procedure and Privileges of which I was a member. The discussion, for once, was not on strictly party lines. Many deputies favored accepting it because

Ireland was, in fact, a Catholic country. Others opposed it for the reason that it might seem to give credence to those who accused us of religious prejudice. Because I was the only deputy of the Jewish Faith, I carefully abstained from expressing an opinion.

Pro and con were so evenly divided in the Committee that they finally came to me and directly asked my views. "Gentlemen," I said, "if having the Crucifix in the Dáil will make you any better Christians, I certainly have no objection."

Other matters of real import caused violent arguments. Such was de Valera's determination to get rid of the Governor General, a symbol still of British domination. Also, with his salary and expenses he cost Ireland twenty-eight thousand pounds a year, which he was not worth in our calculations.

We succeeded in passing the bill to abolish him in the Dáil, but again the Senate held it up. During the interim de Valera proposed Donal Buckley for the post. The last Governor General of Ireland was a strange successor to the long line of aristocrats who had represented His Britannic Majesty. Buckley, who owned a small garage at Maynooth in County Kildare, always reminded me a little of my own father. He was an esthetic-looking individual with a short, well-trimmed beard and a very quiet manner that should not have deceived anyone, for he was a great patriot. When he heard of the Easter Rising of 1916, he walked all the way from Maynooth to Dublin to join that desperate endeavor.

At the time Buckley's name was proposed as Governor General, King George V summoned Irish High Commissioner James Dulanty to Buckingham Palace and asked, "Is it true, Mr. Dulanty, that Mr. de Valera is proposing for Governor General a man who makes his living turning the handle of a petrol pump?"

"It is true, Your Majesty," said Dulanty nervously. "Mr. Buckley owns a small garage in Maynooth."

The King smiled genially. "An excellent idea," he said. "Mr. de Valera is quite right."

When he became Governor General, Donal Buckley refused all but two thousand pounds of his ten thousand pound salary, and would not move into the Vice-regal Lodge at all.

The most controversial of all de Valera's moves was withholding the Land Purchase Annuities from England. This he did by executive decree without the consent of the Senate. It caused an uproar that agitated the Halls of Westminster and brought on the economic war.

Difficult as it is to believe, the agreement of 1923 had been kept so secret by the Cosgrave government that when de Valera became President of the Executive Council he did not know the legal basis for Ireland's annual payment for fifty years of five million pounds to England. He could see no sense in it at all, and promptly announced that it would no longer be paid.

British Colonial Secretary J. H. Thomas was equally hurt and puzzled by his refusal to pay. He wrote an indignant letter citing the agreement. The Chief incredulously set everybody searching the dusty back files of the Office of External Affairs, and sure enough they turned up a copy of this strange, secret treaty. De Valera was dumbfounded.

As a result of this, Mr. Thomas paid a visit to Dublin and de Valera returned the call in London. However these negotiations came to nothing. The Chief stoutly refused to recognize the validity of an agreement which not only had never been ratified by the Dáil, but which had been kept secret from the Irish people. Lloyd George from retirement called him, "That pillar of salt who always looks to the past." The payments were withheld and put in a special suspense fund against a possible future settlement. In retaliation the British placed prohibitive tariffs on Irish beef and the other exports by which our economy lived; and we replied by taxing British imports. The economic war was on.

The results were dour for all Irishmen, including myself. Indeed, the downswing of my personal fortunes had begun in 1928. That year in the Dáil I was ardently supporting de Valera's policy of self-sufficiency for Ireland. It occurred to me that it was too inconsistent even for an Irishman to be inveighing against the nation's dependence on foreign countries while I contributed to it by making a handsome living out of imported goods. I'll not say that I did not have to wrestle with my conscience; for the Briscoe Importing Company was keeping Lily and my children in fine style. But in the end my lamentable romanticism allowed conscience to triumph over common sense. Not only did I sell Briscoe Importing, but I persuaded my brothers to give up their lucrative foreign connections.

This left me with a small amount of capital but no way to employ it, which in turn led to the distressing experiments in agriculture which I have recounted.

Meanwhile the economy of the country went downhill like a runaway tram. Ireland had been tied so long to England's economy that the rupture of trade cut off her nourishment. Manufactured articles got scarce and their prices towered. Coal became as precious as diamonds. Meanwhile Irish cattle roamed the fields not worth the killing, and the farmers could not pay their rates. This, of course, forced the government to seize their livestock and sell it at public auction for whatever it would bring. Frequently there were no buyers and mobs attacked the pens where the seized animals were kept. Times had never been so hard since the Famine.

Our opponents played England's game. They bitterly complained against this "foolishness," and cried that the people of Ireland were not only starving but freezing to death for lack of coal. When the Chief observed that a peat fire kept you nice and warm they shouted "Back to the bogs!"

De Valera considered that he had a mandate from the people to refuse payment of the Land Annuities. Nevertheless, he also realized that the voters could not have anticipated the hardships they must now endure. With reckless integrity he dissolved the Dáil in 1933, and gave the people a chance to disavow his policy.

The election of 1933 was fought on that issue, and brisk it was. But however seriously we took our principles, there was never a time in peace or war when we could not have a bit of fun. I remember that during the campaign it was announced that a particularly pompous member of Cumann na nGaedhael was to hold a great meeting in a hall at Naas, about thirty miles from Dublin. "We must break that up," we said to each other.

A few days before the meeting I paid a visit to Miss Phyllis Ryan, sister of our Minister for Agriculture. Miss Ryan is now the First Lady of Ireland, having married President Sean T. O'Kelly some years after his first wife, her sister, died. But at that time she was one of the few lady chemists in Ireland. She was a strapping big fair girl with hair like spun bullion and the ripple of mischief in her blue eyes.

I went to the laboratory she owned, and I said to her, "Miss Ryan, do you think you could concoct a really foul smell?"

"I might," she answered, "but what do you want with a stink bomb?"

I told her, and her eyes lit up with glee. She got out a retort and various liquids and powders. For a bit she worked mixing her noisome brew and then invited me to try it. I gave a tentative sniff, and staggered a little.

"What do you think?" she asked.

"Adequate," I observed.

"It must be more than that," she said. "Here goes!"

She poured some yellow stuff into the retort. There was no need to sniff. "Holy God!" I gasped, and ran for the door and Miss Ryan close after me.

With handkerchiefs over our noses we went back and bottled the stuff and I distributed it to the right parties. The night of the meeting these gentlemen occupied seats in different parts of the hall. As the speaker was being introduced they spilled the contents of their bottles on the floor and quietly went away.

The Cumann na nGaedhael candidate got off to a rousing start amid great enthusiasm. But as his oratory soared he was disturbed to notice people ebbing out the exits. The drift to the doors became a stampede while the speaker exerted himself to hold their attention. Then that fugacious miasma reached the platform. His roaring oration stopped in mid-word as suspicion mingled with olfactory distress. He shouted a very impious description of Fianna Fail, clapped handkerchief to nose and ran.

The Pains of Power

The result of the election showed that the Irish people had regained their courage. They voted for defiance of England — and austerity. We came back to the Dáil with seventy-seven seats, a gain of five, and a clear mandate for our policy. That number seventy-seven had a mystic meaning for us, because seventy-seven was the exact number of Republicans executed by the Free State in the civil war.

Immediately after this the Chief sent me to England with a group of other deputies, including Erskine Childers, Jr., to explain our position to the members of the House of Commons. I must say we were most courteously received.

One afternoon High Commissioner Dulanty took me to the Distinguished Strangers' Gallery of the House to listen to a speech on the Land Annuities by J. H. Thomas. It was not at all like the supposedly true record published in Hansard. The text as printed was pure Oxonian English. What Mr. Thomas really said was, "If Mr. dee Valeera is the kind of man wot thinks as wot he can withhold these annuities and get away with it, 'e 'as another think coming to 'im."

Our job was to buttonhole Members of Parliament whom we happened to know and give them our point of view. Many of them were amazingly ignorant about Irish history and even the current dispute. But they were willing and even eager to listen to us. An example of their sporting attitude occurred as I was sitting in the Distinguished Strangers' Gallery. An usher asked me to step outside for a moment. Waiting for me was Mr. Amory, a former Secretary of State for India. He invited me to have tea with some of his colleagues in the lounge.

"Are you sure they want to meet me?" I asked. "Are you familiar with my record? Possibly my past behavior would make you think I was no fit person to have tea with."

He laughingly said, "We know all about you. What you have done makes no difference. In England we look on these things like a game of cricket. While it's on we play to win; but when it's over, no matter who wins or loses, we think a cup of tea is best to talk it over."

So we went down to the members' lounge. Do not think because I have fought the British that I did not have a sense of honor in being entertained in that House where so many of the great traditions we share were nurtured. And also do not think that I permitted my emotions to silence me. We talked of the Land Annuities and I gave them our point of view straight out.

"To me the matter is quite simple," I said. "You British long ago conquered Ireland by force. Your Queen Elizabeth gave title to the lands to the conquerors as being the rightful, legitimate and honorable owners of the same. Now you have left Ireland; now we want our land back. But you say to us, 'How much will you give us for the land we stole from you?'

"Now you say that possession is nine points of the law and that possession for over three hundred years wiped out the manner in which the land was acquired. But I say, the passage of years since the wrong was done makes no matter. It is as much a wrong now as then, and the time has come when it must be righted."

Due to the reasonable attitude of members of the British Parliament and a change in the British Government when Ramsay MacDonald's party fell from power and Stanley Baldwin became Prime Minister, the economic war eased up somewhat. An agreement was made for lessening the duties on Irish cattle exported to England and their exports of coal to us. However, complete agreement on the Land Annuities had to wait for yet another Prime Minister.

Meanwhile matters moved forward in Ireland. The old Senate was abolished in 1936, though we had in mind the creation of a new consultative upper chamber to be representative of all the aspects of the Irish State. At almost the same time a bill was passed changing our people from British subjects to Irish citizens.

In December 1936, the abdication of King Edward VIII gave us an unexpected break. According to the Statute of Westminster the Dominion Parliaments must assent to the accession of the new king, George VI. The Dáil assented on its own terms, recognizing him as head of the British Commonwealth but *not* as King of Ireland. Thus de Valera, who never gives up, got External Association at last.

All this time the Chief was drafting the new Constitution. In his methodical way he made a minute study of the great legal documents of democratic government from the Magna Charta to the Constitution of the United States, not slighting the great French, German and Italian thinkers on this subject, and even going back to the Romans and the ancient Greeks. From these he endeavored to distill the essence of wisdom and apply it to the particular conditions in Ireland with due regard to our own ancient concepts of liberty. For two years or more he devoted all his free time to the painstaking perfection of this document. It was submitted to the Executive Council of the Fianna Fail government where we went over it intensively line by line, even word by word.

There are those who criticize some of its provisions in regard to censorship of immoral literature as abridging freedom of the press. But you must remember that this Constitution was drawn to suit the Irish people, who are very strict in matters of morals. It is generally considered that the Puritans of America were the most uncompromising moralists of all time and that Roman Catholics are distinctly flexible in this respect. I assure you this only applies to Catholics in Latin countries. The Irish Catholic is as puritanical as any passenger on the *Mayflower* and de Valera is notably straight-laced, even among Irish Catholics. Indeed for purity of mind and rectitude of conduct he would make Elder Brewster seem a libertine by contrast.

There are many in Ireland, the majority by far, who are of Dev's mind about these matters of morality and that is why the censorship provisions in our Constitution are right for them.

As to the rest of it, the safeguards of democracy were as strong as we could make them. The new Consultative Senate chosen on the basis of vocational representation was instituted; and, of course, the Governor General was abolished and replaced by a President elected by the people for seven years, who would have approximately the same nonpolitical function as the President of

France. The real executive power would be exercised by *An Taoiseach* — the Prime Minister. The Roman Catholic Church was expressly named as the faith of the majority, but religious liberty was strictly safeguarded. The name of the country was changed from the Irish Free State to *Eire*, meaning all of Ireland.

This brings us to the question that both our opponents and the Republicans asked, why did not Dev have done with compromise and openly proclaim the Irish Republic? The answer lay in the problem of partition. De Valera was convinced that the six lost counties would find it far harder to reunite with a Republic than with a country which still, however tenuously, acknowledged the Crown. He was tenaciously determined to end partition sometime by the free choice of all Irishmen; and he would put no obstacle in its way. That is the dream — no, dream is not the word — it is the fixed intention which he has never given up. And never will!

The Constitution which we proposed to the Irish people was de Valera's work. No matter how many the sources from which he derived his ideas or how many of us worked on refining a sentence or phrase, it was he who distilled and crystallized it into what I believe is the most perfect instrument for the particular purpose of the government of Ireland that could be devised.

Though the new Constitution was unanimously approved by Fianna Fail, it naturally failed to please a large number of Irishmen. Cosgrave's party, which now called itself Fine Gael, jeered at "The Royal Republic," and the irreconcilable Republicans and the remnants of Sinn Fein would have none of it. In 1937, de Valera dissolved the Dáil and called a general election and a national plebiscite on the Constitution. The document was approved by a vote of 686,042 to 528,196. After seven centuries of oppression Ireland had a form of government chosen by her people in a free election. Fine Gael and all other parties now accept the Constitution.

When the Constitution went into effect in June, 1938, both political parties, with a unanimity unparalleled among Irishmen, nominated Doctor Paul Douglas Hyde as the First President of Eire. Doctor Hyde, who was seventy-eight years old, was the grand old man of the Gaelic League Movement to revive our ancient language and culture. Our first President was a Protestant. His unanimous election may seem strange to those who regard Ireland as a land of bigotry.

In January, 1938, Neville Chamberlain was Prime Minister of England and J. H. Thomas had been replaced as Secretary of State for Dominion Affairs by Malcolm MacDonald, a much more reasonable man. The time seemed opportune to settle once and for all our last differences with England. These included partition, the Land Annuities and trade restrictions, and British naval bases in our ports.

Late in January, de Valera went to London to negotiate these matters. He chose Cabinet Ministers Sean Lemass, Sean MacEntee and Doctor Ryan to go with him. The rest of the Cabinet remained in Dublin. I went along as one of the couriers. This was no sinecure. De Valera was determined to keep the Cabinet members in Dublin informed of every move in the negotiations — he remembered painfully the lack of communications which had resulted in the disastrous Treaty. Since the Chief feared that the mails and the telephone might be tampered with, all these communications went by special courier. I was kept tearing back and forth across the Irish Sea like a racing pigeon.

The Irish Delegation had a whole floor of the Piccadilly Hotel and there we stayed for nearly three months. This was due more to the complexity of our task than to British intransigeance. For Chamberlain, who is known to history as the Great Appeaser, was in truth a flexible diplomat, which made him an easy victim of a fanatic like Hitler, but contributed greatly to the success of sincere negotiations. Furthermore, with England facing the growing military menace of Nazi Germany, she wanted a friend not an enemy in her rear. Thus, once again, England's difficulty was Ireland's opportunity. I like to think that this time we did not take advantage of her.

The negotiations started well. On the first day when de Valera took his place at the conference table in 10 Downing Street, he said to Chamberlain, "You may have heard that I am an intractable man to deal with. This is not true. I am aware of the difficulties you have. I can always see the problems of the men across the table from me. This makes me a poor bargainer."

Chamberlain's face was the picture of amazement. Then he smiled and said, "Tell that to the Marines."

The Chief looked around the room and said with a twinkle, "But I don't see any Marines!"

The roar of laughter was better for harmony than any number of flowery speeches.

The first question was partition. De Valera gave our reasons for opposing it, and Chamberlain unexpectedly agreed that he would like to see the border removed. It could all have been settled then and there except for Lord Craigavon, formerly Sir James Craig, who had changed his name but not his nature. He obdurately refused to consider any means of ending partition. Chamberlain could not force him to, so in this vital matter de Valera failed again.

In all other respects the Conference was a complete success. The Land Annuities matter was settled by a lump sum payment of ten million pounds, which liquidated in full the local loans. Freedom of trade between our countries, so natural and necessary to both, was re-established. Chamberlain also agreed to give up the British naval bases at Cobh, Berehaven and Lough Swilly. When the news came out there was a terrible angry roar from Winston Churchill. But since he was temporarily out of office and out of favor with the British public, the old lion could not prevent the agreement.

So de Valera came home to Dublin in the spring with a new treaty that assured Ireland's freedom, economic and political, excepting only the last injustice of partition. The Dáil quickly approved it. That summer the dockyards were dismantled; the

British garrisons embarked. The gray ships of England weighed their anchors and sailed past the forts at the mouths of our harbors while the cannon saluted, and the Irish Tricolor and the White Ensign were dipped in mutual acknowledgment of friendship between our two nations.

CHAPTER XXII

Zion

I HAVE always tried to be a good member of the Jewish Community in Dublin, supporting the temple and attending it regularly, observing the feasts and fast days of my faith, and doing my share in the charitable activities of my co-religionists. Though I must confess that I do not adhere as strictly as my father to the dietary laws — he would never have eaten a meal in the Shelbourne Hotel, which is my favorite dining place — I have never tasted pork or shellfish and never intend to.

However, until the nineteen thirties I had not thought very deeply about the world position of Jewry or the ambition of my people to regain their homeland — Zion. Ever since the Diaspora — the scattering of the Jews among the nations of earth when the Roman soldiers drove them out of Palestine — we of the orthodox faith had believed that the Messiah would come to lead us home in God's own time. However, in the nineteenth century Theodor Herzl founded Zionism. His basic idea was that since it was God's will that the Jews return to their Holy Land there was no reason why He should not accomplish His purpose through human instruments. Never doubting the coming of a Messiah, he nevertheless felt that Jewish faith and Jewish culture would be strengthened if they had a country they could call their own. Some narrow orthodox Jews denounced this as an impious attempt to hurry God. But a great number of our people hailed it as a new hope for world Jewry.

I regarded Zionism as a magnificent inspiration, but I was not personally very concerned — as you have observed, I was somewhat preoccupied with my activities as an Irishman. Then, too, I was fortunate in living in a country where we Jews were subject to no persecution and very little prejudice, far less even than in the United States of America. The terrible pressures which forced European Jews into compact, self-defensive communities were totally absent in Ireland.

I remember the first time I ever encountered any real anti-Semitism. It was in 1922 when I was in Germany during the Truce. Our new Trade Commissioner Charles Bewley arrived in Berlin and set up offices. I had not known him before but we were soon on friendly terms. Charley McGuiness and I often met him at our favorite coffeehouse. We had a regular table there, and now that the Truce was on we proudly put a little green, white and orange tricolor on it so that any visitor from Ireland would know that he had friends there.

The owner of this cafe was an amiable Jewish gentleman whom Charley and I liked very much. One day he came to our table in great agitation and said that Mr. Bewley had been there the night before making extremely derogatory remarks about Jews in general and himself in particular. He repeated some of these insults to our race. They were the usual sort of thing, but I was totally unaccustomed to such epithets.

Now, as perhaps you have noted, I am not the meek, mild suffer-in-silence sort of person which those Jews who have lived in a ghetto have been forced to become. I was roaring mad that a fellow Irishman should behave in this way. Charley was even madder because of his affection for me. "We'll get this fellow, and bring him around to apologize," he said.

We went to Bewley's office and found it empty. It was all spic and span, neat and new. Charley said, "We'll deal with this bastard the way he deserves."

He took a large inkwell off the desk and jerked it upward so the ink found itself on the ceiling. Then he took the brand new typewriter and threw it on the floor. By the time he had tackled a few more pieces of office equipment I found myself joining in. It was not a thing I would do today. Time and experience have inured me to insults, and the young revolutionary who got fighting mad at the least sign of human intolerance has realized that such things are but a manifestation of human ignorance.

But we had a grand time wrecking the office; tearing up stationery; ripping posters off the walls; making a shambles of the place. Right in the middle of it Bewley came in. At the sight of the wreckage and our ferocious expressions his face turned a lovely lavender shade, and he said shakily, "What's going on here?"

"You know very well," I said. "You have said things no man should say to another about his faith, and particularly not the Representative of the Irish Republic."

"What do you want me to do?" he asked, quivering.

"You'll come with us and make a humble, abject apology," Charley answered.

We marched him around to the cafe, and sent for the proprietor. When he came, Bewly said, "I wish to apologize most humbly for the remarks I made last night. I withdraw them completely."

Frankly I was amazed and disgusted that a man could be so childishly fearful of what might happen to him that he would be so servile.

Since this is the last time Charley McGuiness appears in this book I will finish his story. Charley went to America some years later. In New York he saw an advertisement in a newspaper of the Byrd Antarctic Expedition stating that two mates and a cook were needed. He marched in to see Admiral Byrd and said:

"You advertised for two mates; I am both."

He went with Byrd to Antarctica. Later he returned to Ireland and got command of a small coastal schooner. For perhaps fifteen years he appeared to lead a more or less uneventful life — though this I can hardly believe. At last perhaps he grew unwary of his favorite adversary. In 1948, his little ship was lost in a violent storm. The sea never returned his body to the Irish shore.

In the early nineteen thirties several circumstances combined to arouse me to an ardent interest in Zionism. The most important of these was the rise of Nazism in Germany, which was reflected in growing anti-Semitism throughout the world. The era of the men in colored shirts had begun — Black Shirts in Italy; Brown Shirts in Germany; Blue Shirts in England and Silver Shirts in America. We even had a Fascist organization of Blue Shirts in Ireland, though we soon got rid of them. All these organizations were to some degree anti-Semitic, though only one of them seemed dangerously so — the Nazis. This I saw at first hand.

In the early days of the economic war when we first took office, we were desperate to dispose of Irish cattle barred from England by the high tariff. I invested some of my money in an Irish meat packing company, the Roscrea Meat Company, and also sought markets abroad. I interested a German friend, Hans Fasenfeld, in importing cattle to Germany. He chartered his own vessels and came to Dublin every Wednesday where he bought a shipload of cattle and took them to his own abattoir in Bremen. In the course of these transactions I made several trips to Germany to visit him. Herr Fasenfeld was a Christian, but by no means a Nazi. While staying with him I discovered his friendship for many unfortunate Jewish people whom he helped to escape to Holland from Hitler's insane persecutions which were just getting into high gear. These things he did at considerable personal danger. Even having me in his house was a risk.

However, Herr Fasenfeld went farther than this. I discussed with him the possibility of improving trade between Ireland and Germany. He talked to his close friend, Doctor Hemmin in the German Foreign Office and brought word that these people would receive me officially. I made a quick trip to Ireland to get de Valera's permission to enter into informal negotiations with the German Government.

I remember the day of my meeting with the Germans very well. In our taxi on the way to the Wilhelmstrasse I said to Fasenfeld, "First off you must inform these people that I am a Jew."

"I don't think that's necessary," he said.

"It is very necessary," I answered. "If they don't know it, these men may say something derogatory about Jews which would offend me. I might lose my temper."

He agreed to do what I asked.

We passed through the imposing portals of the Foreign Office guarded by smartly uniformed soldiers with steel helmets and bayoneted rifles, and were shown into a big conference room. Six officials awaited us. Two of them were in civilian clothes; two were brown-shirted Nazis and the other two wore the sinister black uniform of the SS Guards. I began to feel hemmed in.

However the discussions were amiable. Herr Fasenfeld told them that I had insisted that they know I was Jewish. A quick discussion in German followed. The upshot amused me. "The religion of this foreigner is no business of ours," the spokesman said. "As far as we are concerned he is here as an Irishman."

We then got down to business. I pointed out that the balance of trade in favor of Germany was forty to one, and that it should be more equal. I would have settled for bringing it down to ten to one. Instead they offered five to one. I kept elation out of my eyes, and said, "I don't know what Mr. de Valera's reaction might be to such a poor offer, but I should like to telephone him."

They were delighted.

When the call went through I told Dev that I was calling from the Foreign Office to tip him off that there would be people listening in. Then I told him of the German offer, and added, "Five to one is the best I can do."

De Valera quickly said, "Well, we could negotiate. Will the Germans send a delegation to Dublin?"

The result was that a German delegation came to Dublin and negotiated an agreement eventually to reduce the adverse balance of trade to two and a half to one.

As you can see, I would do business with Hitler if it was for Ireland's good. However, when the pact was concluded in Dublin one of the Germans said to me, "I have the honor to bring you the thanks of our Fuehrer for what you have done for our country."

This was too much. I said very stiffly in German, "I am glad to have been of service to my own country, but my conscience would trouble me if I accepted thanks from the government of another country."

The Nazis' politeness to me did not fool me for a moment. I saw how my fellow Jews were being treated there; and I foresaw their situation becoming worse as the Nazi regime consolidated itself and the terrible power of their great military machine grew until they felt strong enough to disregard world opinion. Desperately I begged my Jewish friends to flee at all costs; but they foolishly answered, "Hitler's rantings are really directed at the *Ostjuden* — the Jews of eastern countries. He does not mean us." So they waited for the black trains to Buchenwald.

The second thing which fired my enthusiasm for Zionism was the arrival of Vladimir Jabotinsky in Ireland. Jabotinsky, a Russian Jew, was an extraordinary man. He was a profound thinker who had written brilliant books and many poems, some of which have been put to music and are the war songs of Israel today. He was a man of action as well. In World War I he organized the Zionist Mule Corps which carried supplies to the British Army in Gallipoli and later helped Allenby to drive the Turks from Palestine.

As a result of the Allied victory, Britain was given the League of Nations mandate for Palestine. This seemed at first an admirable arrangement. Jews from all the oppressor countries began to flock to Palestine. As its Jewish population swelled from fifty-five thousand in 1919 to three hundred and seventy-five thousand in 1935, the Arabs took alarm. The surrounding Arab countries controlled the oil England needed. To appease them the British began to shut down on immigration to Palestine. The Jewish homeland became barred to Jews.

It was then that Jabotinsky formed a militant Zionist movement called Irgun, which in Hebrew means scout. Its object was to form a fighting Jewish force to defend themselves against the marauding Arabs, who frequently attacked and murdered Jewish settlers; and to drive the British out of Palestine or force them to liberalize the immigration laws. When he led a force which broke into a British barracks for arms to defend themselves against these Arab murderers he was imprisoned and then exiled from Palestine by the British.

Jabotinsky came to Ireland to learn all he could of the methods we had used in training our young men and boys for the Revolution against England in order to form a physical force movement in Palestine on exactly the same lines as Fianna Eireann and the I.R.A. He could not have come to a better place. Since I was, perhaps, the only Jew in the I.R.A., he was naturally directed to me. Though I say it myself, he could not have come to a better man.

I taught Jabotinsky how we had secretly trained our Fianna Eireann boys in the time of peace; and the methods we had found most effective in the guerrilla war. I explained British military weaknesses and where their strength lay; and how to profit by the first and combat — or evade — the second. In fact, I appointed myself to a full professorship with the Chair of Subversive Activity against England.

Jabotinsky wanted to meet de Valera and I arranged that, too. The Chief received us in his office in the government buildings on Merrion Square. Ever since his chairmanship of the Council of the League of Nations, de Valera had been tremendously interested in the Palestine problem. He had even sent Joe Walshe as his personal envoy to the Arab countries and Palestine to discover the truth of the matter if he could. Though Dev was sympathetic to Jewish aspirations he questioned Jabotinsky like a king's counsel.

"How can the Jews establish a legitimate claim to Palestine?" he asked. "Did they not leave it; and has it not been in the possession of the Arabs for nearly two thousand years?"

"Mr. de Valera," said Jabotinsky, "I have been reading Irish history. As a result of the great famine of 1847 and 1848, I believe the population of Ireland fell from eight million to four million. Now supposing it had been reduced to fifty thousand and the country had been resettled by the Welsh, Scots and English, would you then have given up the claim of Ireland for the Irish?"

"No," said de Valera. "As long as one Irishman remained, Ireland would still rightfully belong to the Irish."

"Now," said Jabotinsky, "we did not leave Palestine. The Romans conquered it and they dispersed our people to all the corners of the earth as was written and prophesied. But there have always been a few Jews left in Palestine. And so we claim it by right of inheritance; and also by right of the declaration made by Lord Balfour for England and President Wilson of the United States."

I am not sure, but I think the Chief was convinced by these arguments. Certain it is that I was.

All these things summed up made it incumbent on me to do something for my co-religionists. Hitler, well in the saddle, no longer made any secret of his intentions toward German citizens of the Jewish faith. The three and a half million Jews in Poland were perhaps in greater danger not only from the Jew-hating dictatorial government of President Moscicki and Field Marshal Smigly-Rydz; but from the frightening possibility that the Nazis might attack Poland. In fact all the eastern European countries were in danger of Nazi conquest. The world was not going to give refuge to all these millions of Jews. Where but in Palestine could they find a haven?

My first move was to sell my interest in the Roscrea Meat Company, which enabled me to pay my debts and have a little cash in hand. I then began to work closely with Jabotinsky in organizing Irgun on the lines of the I.R.A. In the course of this collaboration I made many trips to England.

I remember one of these in particular. Its purpose was to plead for the life of young Dov Joseph, the first member of Irgun to be taken and sentenced to execution by the British for carrying arms. I saw many leading members of Parliament whom I knew, and I endeavored to see my old schoolmate Hore-Belisha who was Britain's Minister of Defense, but he refused even to admit me to his office.

On the night before the execution Jabotinsky and I worked until long after midnight — to no purpose. We returned unhappily to the Piccadilly Hotel and waited in our room for the time set for the execution which was 4 A.M. in London, dawn in Palestine. When we heard Big Ben strike that hour Jabotinsky collapsed weeping on the bed. It was a strange sight to see this strong, stocky man who had proved his own courage on a dozen battlefields crying hysterically and blaming himself for the death of that brave boy in Palestine.

I decided to try to put the essential iron of leadership back into his soul. "You are a fine leader!" I said. "You are the general who wants to command men in battle, yet at the first casualty you want to call the war off.

"If you believe in your mission, if you believe in the things you have preached and the movement you have started, you must be able to accept the inevitable tragic deaths. You must understand that in Ireland we never accomplished anything until we showed that we were willing to shed our blood for our cause. Unless you are willing to do that there will never be any foundation on which you can build a Jewish Nation, or any nation."

Jabotinsky shook himself like a dog coming out of the water. He said, "You're right! I have to face these things. They are a responsibility I must accept."

In 1937 the British Government had proposed a second partition of Palestine between Jews and Arabs — they first split Palestine into Jordan and Palestine in 1922. You may imagine with what anger I heard that solution proposed for yet another country to which I was emotionally attached. Jabotinsky, equally enraged, campaigned violently against it. However, many Jews supported it and the Zionist Congress in Zurich reluctantly accepted the idea.

Professor Selig Brodezky came from England to see de Valera on this subject. He thought that partition was inevitable and that we must try to get the biggest possible slice of Palestine. I arranged an interview with de Valera for him, but begged him not to advocate partition of Palestine, explaining how the Chief would react to that word. After hours of argument, he agreed not to mention it.

The meeting took place. Imagine my horror then, when Brodezky began to urge de Valera to agree to partition when it came before the League of Nations. I remember Mr. de Valera's very wise answer. "Professor," he said, "I read the Old Testament many years ago. I am afraid I have forgotten many things I read; but one passage I recall clearly. It is the story of Solomon's judgment of the two women who claimed the same baby. I remember how when Solomon ruled that the baby be divided the real mother screamed, 'No! No! Give the baby to the other woman!'

"This is my answer to partition. The rightful owners of a country will never agree to partition."

The idea of partition was given up in 1938. By that time the position of the Jews in Germany and eastern Europe had become even more perilous. It was quite obvious to me that war was inevitable, and with the war would come the mass destruction of the Jewish people. Try as I might I could not convince people of the terrible danger. Even after the conference at Munich when Chamberlain threw Czechoslovakia to the Nazi wolves to buy a little more time for England, they would not believe me.

Jabotinsky fully realized the threat hanging over our people. We believed one of the greatest danger spots was Poland, to which Hitler was now turning his attention. At Christmas time, 1938, I went to Warsaw with a plan that might yet save millions of Polish Jews.

There I sought an audience with Colonel Jozef Beck, Polish Minister for Foreign Affairs. We met in a great, cold, gloomy room in the Foreign Office where Beck received me surrounded by the gaudily uniformed colonels of his staff; for this government was basically a military dictatorship. Colonel Beck was a delicate-looking man with a high color and a barking cough that suggested tuberculosis. While he talked he clasped his fingers together and moved them nervously backward and forward. His manner of speech was typically Continental with shoulder shruggings and elaborate gestures. Despite his sickly appearance, he had great charm and the flash of humor in his eyes. While we talked through interpreters he never once took those eyes off me.

I began by saying, "Colonel Beck, you are soon to leave for London to negotiate a treaty of alliance with Britain (it was signed on January 30, 1939). On behalf of the New Zionist Movement, speaking mainly for European Jews, not for those of England or America, speaking for them, I suggest that you ask Britain to turn over the mandate for Palestine to you and make it in effect a Polish colony. You could then move all your unwanted Polish Jews into Palestine. This would bring great relief to your country, and you would have a rich and growing colony to aid your economy."

When this was translated I could see that Beck was both amused and astonished at such a sudden peculiar proposal. Watching his face intently as he thought it over I saw the idea begin to appeal to him.

"I am sure the Jews would never leave Poland," he said thoughtfully.

"The Jews would never leave Poland?" I said. "There is one simple way to find out. Put an advertisement in your papers tomorrow asking all Jews who wish to leave Poland for Palestine to apply to you."

The Polish Minister smiled as he conceded my point. "We have not a sufficient staff to deal with all the applications we would get.

"But supposing we did what you suggest," he went on. "Think of the terrible impact it would have on our economy. Millions of Jews, many of whom have large possessions, properties, shares and bonds, throwing these suddenly on the market to realize cash. There would be so devastating a depression that no one could foresee where it would end. Almost certainly it would bring about the most terrible pogrom in history. Thousands of your people would be slaughtered."

"Do you suppose I have not thought of that?" I answered. "This is no half-baked plan of mine. You can deal with it in a very simple way. Get from the Jews a fair assessment of their property, their possessions. Give them government bonds in exchange for it. Then you can liquidate these assets properly according to your own best judgment. You can make the bonds long term, thus giving yourselves plenty of time. And you will be getting possessions of great value."

We discussed my plan at great length. Beck became more interested, even enthusiastic. However he had one final objection.

"But what is the attitude of the Jews of Poland?" he asked. "That we must find out. You know the system we have had for the representation of your people in our Parliament. Their rabbis represent them. Before we talk further you must go to see the Rabbinical Authorities of Poland and find out their reaction."

I was highly elated by Beck's reasonable attitude. If he gave his approval, my plan had a fair chance of success; for Palestine was nothing but an expensive headache for England and she might well be glad to get rid of her mandate.

My Jewish friends in Warsaw arranged an interview for me with the most authoritative of the rabbis and came with me to interpret since I spoke no Polish. I did understand Yiddish, but that language as spoken in Poland was incomprehensible to me.

My friends took me to the Yeshiva — the House of Learning — where the rabbis sit together, study and teach. It was a large, dismal building in the ghetto of Warsaw. We passed through a gate into a cobblestone courtyard surrounded by tenement houses in which hundreds of families lived crowded together. The pavement was covered with stalls in which were all sorts of goods for sale — boots, clothing, hardware, housing materials and kitchenware. From the courtyard we came into a room in the house which was indescribably bare and cheerless. Its walls were whitewashed plaster, and though it was meticulously clean, there were no decorations or comforts in the place; none of the shelves of books and writing materials which one expects to see in the house of a rabbi. The furnishings consisted of a plain wooden table and some straight chairs. It was cold, severe, ascetic, as perhaps one should expect of the habitation of people who were so devout in their faith that they wanted no material things.

Three men were seated around the table. The chief rabbi was a big man wearing a long black coat and a magnificent black beard. Glossy black side curls hung beneath his flat black hat. The other two rabbis were smaller, but identical in their somber garb.

To these men then I made my plea that they consent to a plan for large-scale emigration to Palestine. I spoke with an ardor and eloquence inspired by the terrible urgency I felt; and my friend translated with equal emotion. The three rabbis sat absolutely still. Even when they spoke to each other in low tones they did not turn their heads. Their rigidity was frightening, their features as frozen and expressionless as the ice-bound Vistula.

When I had exhausted every argument the chief rabbi said, "We must ponder your words. Return tomorrow for our answer."

The next day we went back. The chief rabbi received us alone. Standing like a figure carved in basalt on a Judean tomb, with Europe in flames around him and Azrael soaring on sable wings above his people, he gave this pronouncement, "We must wait for the Messiah to lead us to the Holy Land. All forms of Zionism are to us *traif* (unclean)."

Perhaps nothing could have been done even had those words not been spoken. Perhaps too little time was left. But those words ended the last hope of life for three million Jews.

CHAPTER XXIII

The "Coffin Ships"

In 1939 the British promulgated the White Paper which limited immigration to Palestine to fifteen thousand a year for five years, and then no more, unless the Arab population agreed, which they would never do. Diplomacy had failed. The time had come for action. This suited me better.

The new Zionists' answer to the White Paper was the most useful of all our endeavors and the most bitterly criticized by our fellow Jews. It was the famous illegal emigration which we organized and carried out under the very bowsprits of the British Navy. After World War II, Haganah of the regular Zionist organization did similar work. But we pioneered it.

We raised money from Jews all over the world and with this money we bought ships. Little, rusty, dirty tramp steamers they were, the more inconspicuous the better for our purpose. Meanwhile we gathered Jews who wanted to escape to Palestine. From Poland, Bulgaria and Hungary, we took them down the Danube to Rumanian ports; and from Germany and Austria they went to the Dalmatian coast or the ports of Greece. There they would be packed into our own small steamers, not like cattle who must have stalls and a decent space to live; but like mackerel in a trawler's hold.

Conservative Jews in England and America condemned our efforts. They called our vessels "coffin ships" because many people died in them. They were right in a way. The conditions in our boats were perhaps more dreadful then than those on a Yankee slaver. But these people were carried *out* of slavery; and the sum of lives we saved was infinitely greater than those we lost. Many a family who were bound for Nazi incinerators reached Palestine and safety and a new life.

The Mediterranean was a British lake, ranged by their war-ships which sometimes stopped our ships with their threatening guns and brought them back to Cypress or Malta or other naval bases. But they could not cover all that sea; they could not stop and question every small, trading vessel that sailed across it. Timing themselves for the deepest night, preferably in thick weather, the miserable little steamers came close in to the beaches of Palestine. Our people there were waiting. They would form floating human chains out into the sea, and the refugees, holding their children in their arms, would climb down the sides of the ships and be passed from hand to hand until they stood on the Holy Land. More of our people would hurry them inland to be lost in the anonymity of villages and towns. No one knows how many lives were lost, how many saved; for this was not a business of which you could keep records.

The safe careful people who decried us had no conception of the conditions in Europe whereby a whole race had nothing, not even their chains, to lose.

One of the criticisms was that we charged rich refugees out-rageous prices — several thousand pounds for a passage to Palestine. So we did. In the expressive American phrase we soaked the rich. But for every rich man who paid the price of liberty we were able to rescue five or ten impoverished Jews who had no means to pay at all.

When we had this business well started I asked de Valera for a six months' leave of absence to go to the United States to campaign for an aroused American public opinion which might force President Roosevelt to bring pressure to bear on England to allow large scale immigration to Palestine.

It was a difficult mission. My fare was paid by the New Zionist Organization, but I paid my own expenses in America and my means were very slender. In addition, the Jewish organizations in America looked upon me as anti-British and believed that I was less interested in helping the Jews than in embarrassing

England in her hour of trouble. Of course I had back of me members of the New Zionist Organization and numerous personal friends, but those who listened to me, and understood me, and helped me to get a platform from which to speak, were none other than the Irish friends I had made on my other mission to America.

One of the first Irish-Americans who came to my assistance was the handsome, charming Brooklyn District Attorney, William O'Dwyer, who became Mayor of New York. He appeared with me on the platform at Manhattan Center which I hired in an attempt to reach the public and interest the press. Another American of Irish descent who helped me was James J. Farley.

I once had an interesting discussion with Mr. Farley and Governor Herbert J. Lehman of New York. Governor Lehman pointed out to me that Britain was on the spot with Nazi Germany poised to attack her. Perhaps, he said, it was wrong to embarrass her at this time. Jim Farley spoke up, "Look, Governor, England has been on the spot for the last thousand years, and she is likely to be on the spot for the next thousand. Do you people think you can wait that long for a solution to the Palestine problem?"

Though Lehman was not for me he was not against me. Through these men I was invited to call on Justice Felix Frankfurter in the Supreme Court Building in Washington. I remember walking up the broad impressive steps of that beautiful marble building. Waiting for me inside the great bronze doors was a little cricket of a man in a short black coat and striped trousers, who said, "Do you wish to see Mr. Frankfurter?"

"I do."

"Follow me."

He led me through a corridor to a grand big office all soft carpets and shining furniture. He stopped there and said, "Well?"

"Well," I said. "Well, I want to see Mr. Justice Frankfurter."

Twinkling, he said, "You're seeing him. Sit down."

When I had told him all about my mission, he said, "I think you should see my predecessor here, Justice Brandeis, who has great influence with our people. He is very old and fragile, but I believe he will see you if I ask him to."

So I was received by the famous Justice and his lovely wife in their Washington apartment. Justice Brandeis was as delicate as Frankfurter had said, but his mind had lost none of its penetration. He questioned me acutely on the physical force movement of Irgun, and the illegal shipping of human beings to Palestine. I told him of my fears for European Jewry and my hopes of influencing President Roosevelt to pressure England.

When I had finished, Mr. Brandeis said, "I am sorry but I cannot go along with you. I do not agree with your ideas, nor can I approve of the things you are doing."

It was a great blow to me that I had made no impression on this wonderful old gentleman. He must have seen the distress and sorrow in my face for he said very kindly, "Anyway, let's have a cup of tea."

Mrs. Brandeis brought the tea and we chatted for perhaps half an hour more. He told her some of the things I had said, restating my arguments in a brilliant and accurate summation. When the time came for me to leave, he said, "I am against you because I am an old man and have seen too much of bloodshed and violence, and fair hopes befouled by the fog of war. But if I were a young man like you I would be with you, talking as you have talked, doing exactly what you are trying to do."

"Will you then wish me luck?" I asked.

And he answered emotionally, "I wish you luck."

Ambassador Anthony D. Biddle tried to get me an appointment with President Roosevelt. My way was blocked by the man to whom Roosevelt turned for advice on all matters concerning Zionism. Rabbi Stephen S. Wise was a great and good man, of magnificent appearance and most persuasive oratory. He was a leader of our people and an ornament of our faith. I believed, and still do, that he was mistaken in his policy toward Palestine. Rabbi Wise was an Anglophile. He believed the promises and protestations of the British, and he saw in them the only hope of saving the world from Hitler — about this he was probably right. But it made him regard me as a foolish fanatic.

I had already crossed words with Rabbi Wise. In 1922, when I was in America for the I.R.A. the first partition of Palestine was proposed. Rabbi Wise spoke in favor of it at several meetings. I went to two of them and heckled him, "Will you not ever learn by Ireland's example what happens when a country is partitioned?" I shouted from the floor. I was thrown out of Temple Emanu-El.

Once I sent Wise a telegram saying, "You have chosen the wrong vocation. Mephistopheles as in Faust would suit you better."

It was rude, but I was ardent.

In the end Stephen Wise and I made friends. It was in London after the War. Israel Ziev, a great British businessman, rang me up at my hotel and said, "I have a great surprise for you. I want you to come to dinner at Claridge's Hotel tonight. There will be someone there whom you will be glad to see."

Of course I went, and when I arrived, I asked Israel Ziev who was the friend I would be glad to see. He answered, "Oh, Stephen Wise. He will be along in any minute."

I said, "Stephen Wise is no friend of mine."

Ziev said, "He expressly asked to meet you. He has been very ill and is on his way home to America."

Into the private room at Claridge's came a bent old man and his aged wife — he was so different from the magnificent specimen I had seen in 1922. He rushed up to me and grasped my hand in both of his. To my amazement he asked, "Have I your forgiveness? I must have it!"

I gasped a faint assent, and he rushed on incoherently. "How could any man believe that out of three and a half millions there could remain but thirty or forty thousand? No civilized human being could believe that what you said would happen could have come to pass. I was wrong and you were right. I want your forgiveness."

That was all he said. I was too moved to speak, or do more than press his hand.

My mission to America in 1939 failed completely. This was partly due to the circumstances of the times, and partly my own fault. The American people — Gentile and Jew alike — were wrapping the ragged remnants of their once-splendid isolation around their heads and telling each other that nothing very bad was going to happen to anybody. I was like a man in a nightmare; I saw this monstrous thing approaching but no matter how loud I shouted nobody heard me.

My fault I am afraid was that I was more than a bit tactless. I irritated many fine people who might have been my friends by my angry advocacy of my views. My terrible sense of urgency in those last days of peace made me hot-headed. In a speech I made at the Astor Hotel I said that it was wrong for a British subject to hold the position of World President of the Zionist Organization, because "Jewish and British interests are in conflict, so if he foregoes the rights of Jews in favor of British policy he is letting down his people; and if he stands for the Jews against British interests he is a traitor to England. We should elect an American president."

Chaim Weizmann was the President of World Zionism, a fine and able man who later became the first President of Israel. To Jews he was as sacrosanct as Eisenhower is to Americans. A lady in the audience rose and shouted, "Why are you attacking Chaim Weizmann?"

I replied, "I am not attacking him. I'm attacking any Chaim who puts himself in that position."

Nevertheless it was generally considered that I had made a personal attack on this great Jew, and I was bitterly criticized.

At the end of six months my funds were finished. I kept cashing small checks at the American Express Company which Lily had to meet somehow in Dublin. She exhausted my brothers and all our friends who were willing to help. Finally she cabled me: "Please come home. We have just sold the piano."

I went.

Hardly was I home before my fears were realized. The mechanized Nazi horde poured over the Polish border and conquered that country in three weeks. World War II had begun.

Later I will speak of Ireland's problem of whether to join with England or to maintain a benevolent neutrality, and how I reacted to it. Now I must finish the story of the New Zionists.

Although six million Jews were trapped behind the German lines, there were millions who might yet be saved. Men and women could still escape to Italy and the Mediterranean islands. Late in September, 1939, I received a call from Vladimir Jabotinsky in England. He told me that our work must still go on; but money was desperately needed. In South Africa there were ninety thousand Jews; rich Jews and generous. Would I go to South Africa? With one compassionate look at Lily's face, I said, "I will."

In October, I left Portsmouth, England in an Imperial Airways flying boat. We port-hopped down the length of Africa, stopping every night — Alexandria, Cairo, the Sudan, Kenya, Portuguese East Africa and at last to Durban.

As the flying boat taxied in I saw through the porthole a large crowd on the dock. The hatches clanked up and an emigration officer came in. "Is Robert Briscoe aboard?" he asked.

I said, "I am."

The passengers were milling around uncertainly. "Everybody may leave but Briscoe," the official announced.

The captain of the plane came up angrily. "This is nonsense," he said. "I'm bound for China, and I'm damned if I'll take Briscoe along."

"Well, he can't land," said the official, and marched off.

By now the crowd had forced its way down the dock. It appeared they were there to greet me. There was a large group of

Irish from Durban and a committee of Jews from Johannesburg. Its leader was a Mr. Haskell, an old South African Jew who had fought with the Boers against England and was an intimate friend of such grand old men in the government as General Smuts and Hertzog. Haskell called his friend, Minister of Justice Colin Steyne, on the telephone, and got me permission to stay in Durban under house arrest until the next plane to England.

That gave us a little time. I cabled home and the South African Foreign Office were informed that Ireland expected a member of the Dáil to receive the same courtesy that members of the South African Parliament always received in Ireland. Haskell went to work on his political friends and between Dev and him they convinced the government that it would not endanger the Union of South Africa if I remained there a little longer.

A few days later I lunched with Mr. Steyne in Pretoria. He told me that the Ministry of Justice had received reports from England that I was coming to South Africa to foment a new Boer War, or at least to incite the people against joining England against Germany.

I told him this was the last thing I wanted to do, and how could he think that I would help the Nazis who were slaughtering my people? Then I outlined my real mission; and was given permission to stay as long as I liked.

From Pretoria I went to Johannesburg where a meeting was called for that evening at the Carlton Hotel. As I was in my room preparing my speech someone brought me a copy of the *South African Zionist Review*. Looking at the leading article I found I was in hot water again. It said that Robert Briscoe had come to South Africa to squeeze money out of its Jewry for the dreadful "coffin ships." It enlarged on the inhuman conditions on those vessels, and rang in all the old charges of brutality, indifference and rapacity. It also introduced a new complaint: "These people are dumped into Palestine without regard for their usefulness to the country. No screening or selection is attempted. Some of them are Viennese prostitutes."

That suited me. Here was the text of my speech.

That night as I stood before an audience of Jews and Christians in the great ballroom of the hotel, I began my speech by reading to them the charges made against me. Then I said, "If we were all passengers aboard a sinking vessel and we were ordered to abandon ship; and I was the officer in charge of the gangways, do you think it would be right, if before allowing you into the little boats that would row you to safety, I should ask for a confession of your sins or in what profession you made a living?

"It is none of my business what these people are. If they profess Judaism, and because of that their lives are at stake, then if I can save them I will, no matter how they have sinned."

Then I looked searchingly at the upturned faces and said, "Now may I paraphrase Jesus and say to you, Let him or her who is without sin raise their hand here and now."

Not a hand was raised.

Despite its dubious beginning my mission to South Africa was very successful. I visited every city and town in which there was a Jewish community and went even as far as Rhodesia. Almost daily I was able to cable substantial sums of money to places when it was needed. I was not under the stress of my American trip, for my expenses were paid by our organization; though of course, Lily, the loyal darling, had to fend for herself and the children back in Ireland.

Indeed, I had a very happy time. It was summer and the weather was beautiful. My schedule was not so heavy that I could not take time to enjoy myself, bathing on the golden beaches at Capetown; seeing lovely places in the wilderness that is always so close to civilization in Africa. In preparing for our Revolution I had studied the military history of the Boers. Now I enjoyed following the route of the Great Trek when the Boer population retreated across the veldt in their ox-drawn wagons; and visiting the places of battles and sieges of the Boer War. Best of all, I made many good friends. But I had one horrible experience.

I was back in Durban to make a speech; and a friend lent me his beautiful new motorcar to go sightseeing. I drove to a park outside of the city. It was a wild sort of park, really an enclosed bit of the wilderness itself on the edge of Zululand. There were fine big Zulus at the entrance selling bananas to feed the monkeys of which there were said to be thousands loose in the trees. Remembering the fun I had feeding the animals in Phoenix Park in Black and Tan days, I bought a whole great stalk of bananas weighing perhaps fifty or sixty pounds.

When I got well into the park I cut a big bunch off the end of my stalk and went strolling down a jungle path looking for monkeys. Suddenly I was knocked flat on my face. Monkeys were jumping on me from the trees, jumping from everywhere. They were all over me chattering and screaming. They took my bananas before I had time to present them, and made off fighting among themselves. I picked myself up feeling very inferior, dusted myself off and started back to the car.

When I reached it I was mortified. There was no car to be seen; it was practically hidden under a boiling heap of monkeys. I had left the door open. Little hairy faces and tails were pressed against the windows and the interior was seething with simian life. Not only were the bananas gone but fresh hordes of monkeys kept arriving, and in their disappointment they ripped out everything that was loose or tearable. There were no upholstery or seats left; every piece of leather was gone. So were the metal gadgets. It was stripped like the shell of a car on the assembly line waiting to be upholstered.

I said out loud, "Holy God! what do I do now? This poor man loaned me a new car and I have got to bring it back to him in this condition!"

Sitting on the bare spiral springs of the front seat I drove slowly back to Durban and parked it outside the club. Quick like a wink I telephoned my friend and asked him to come to my hotel; I was afraid if he saw his car before he saw me there would be murder.

When he arrived, I gently told him that I had an accident with his car.

"What happened?" he asked.

"Oh," I answered, "it is destroyed."

"Anybody hurt?" he asked.

"My feelings are deeply hurt," I replied. "I am humiliated."

"Well, that's all right, the car is insured."

"Against monkeys?"

"What???"

"You'd better come and look at it," I said.

We walked around to the club, and I told him what had happened. That man had the grandest sense of humor I ever saw outside of Ireland. He stood there looking at the wreck roaring with laughter.

Then he dragged me into the club with him to start through the length and breadth of Africa the great news of Briscoe's latest war — with the monkeys of Zululand.

After six months in Africa, I flew home. At Portsmouth the old cry went through the flying boat, "Everybody ashore but Briscoe."

Detectives took me to a secluded part of the landing stage and held me for questioning. Finally a higher official arrived. He asked me nothing except where I was going, how long I expected to stay, and my address. I told him I would be at the Piccadilly Hotel in London for a few days. Then they let me go.

As soon as I got to London I went to see friends in the House of Commons. Make no mistake about my attitude. I think the British Parliament is a magnificent institution which accurately reflects the opinion of the English people — whether that opinion is right or wrong is another question. There I met my friend Wilfred Roberts who was Junior Whip for the very small Liberal Party. He took me by the arm and brought me to the lounge where he introduced me to Minister for Air Sir Archibald Sinclair, a Scot. There were other members brought into the room and we laughed; we joked. I remember Sinclair saying as I came through the door, "So this is Briscoe! I expected him to have a machine gun under each arm and a pistol poking through his navel."

I said, "And I expect to be arrested any minute, for I have

broken all your rules, regulations and laws. I am responsible to a considerable extent for thousands of Jewish people smuggled through your blockade into Palestine."

"What is your defense?" asked Sinclair.

"None," I said. "I would love to go to jail, for I would be the first man in the world sent there for saving life instead of taking it."

Very seriously Sinclair said to me, "If I were you I would have done the same thing. I don't think England will molest you."

And right enough, I was in London for a few days and nobody bothered me at all. Then I went back to Dublin. Lily, poor girl, was glad to see me.

Our efforts finally ground to a stop. Jabotinsky died suddenly in America, still trying to get money for the ships. They called it heart disease, but I think his heart was broken. Italy entered the war. France fell, and England was hard beset. Fortress Europe became an impenetrable dungeon for my people, and the rescue work ended. But the effort to regain Palestine was merely postponed.

CHAPTER XXIV

I Remain an Irishman

Eamon de Valera has the precise, logical mind of a mathematician. But he is so high-minded, so essentially *good*, that his heart will sometimes not accept the findings of his head. He is armored in an invulnerable innocence which, though it has enabled him to endure persecution, prison and the abuse of his own people without becoming cynical, also prevents him from assessing accurately the malevolence of certain men. In 1939, Mr. de Valera did not believe that there would be war.

As I have said, my travels back and forth to Germany during the nineteen-thirties convinced me that Germany intended war. I saw the military training of her youth; the elaborate preparations for civil defense — air raid shelters, gas masks, civilian drills. Later, as they grew careless with power, I saw the great heavily armored tanks, the stub-winged Messerschmidt fighter planes and the horrible long mobile cannon. And I heard the troops singing the "Horst Wessel Song" and the thrilling, chilling shouts of *"Sieg Heil!"* that greeted Hitler's guttural, warlike speeches. By 1939 the emotional trend toward war had attained such momentum that it is doubtful if Hitler could have checked it if he had wanted to.

I described all these things to the members of my party and to Mr. de Valera, but they thought me prejudiced. Their attitude was, "Because you are a Jew, and because of the truly dreadful things Hitler is doing to your people, you are anti-Hitler and anti-German. You are wishing for war in the hope that the Nazi regime will be overthrown."

It was difficult for me to convince people that I was objective.

Even after Munich and the beginning of Hitler's move on Danzig and the Polish Corridor there was hardly a man in Ireland who believed that he would really attack Poland. So when they were finally faced with the irrevocable fact of war, the Irish people and their leaders, were stunned. They had to reorganize their thinking very rapidly.

All the Dominion Parliaments of the British Empire were summoned; and all of them except the Dáil voted to stand with England. In the Dáil de Valera laid the matter before the deputies in a speech which showed how deeply shaken and how disillusioned he was. This war, he prophesied, "will ruin victor and vanquished alike, and the settlements it will secure will be short-lived . . . Hardly will the cease fire have sounded when the conquering group will begin their own rivalries and in the new war that is set in train they may well be found on opposite sides . . ."

For once Fianna Fail and Fine Gael, de Valera and Cosgrave, saw eye to eye. The Dáil voted almost unanimously for Ireland's neutrality and to declare a state of national emergency.

In England and America, herself neutral at this time, there was complete lack of comprehension of Ireland's failure to join with the other Dominions in supporting England. To a considerable extent our action was caused by the cancer of partition. Britain to us was still an aggressor nation with her troops on Irish soil. By her policy of divide and conquer, by deception and economic bribery, she had divided us.

We in Ireland believe in democracy. We believe in it for all nations; but we also believe that democracy begins at home. We felt, and still feel, at a disadvantage as a democracy as long as our country is not united. We are still looking for those lost counties, still hoping to find a way to reunite North and South. And we believe that if Britain would remove herself entirely from Irish land then this union of the Irish people would take place. It was on this account politically impossible for Ireland to join England in the war.

Was it desirable? I think not. Before the war I represented the Dáil at a meeting of the Empire Parliamentary Union — incidentally I had the name of these meetings changed to the Inter-Parliamentary Union; I don't like the word empire. At this meeting the point was made that Ireland might be seized by Germany and used as a jumping-off place for the invasion of England. Nobody believed that Ireland would fight to defend herself. I told them that Ireland would fight as hard against Germany as she ever had against England — harder! We proposed to defend our neutrality at any cost, even that of becoming an ally of our ancient enemy.

Furthermore I told them that if Ireland were a united country she would then re-assess her responsibilities toward fighting for the democratic way of life. I proposed that this be accomplished by setting up a Federal Body representing both the North and the South, to which Body Britain should surrender the functions which she exercised in the government of Northern Ireland. I pointed out that under this plan Northern Ireland could still retain the same measure of autonomy that it had from England, and that North and South would then be working together in matters of fundamental common interest such as defense and trade. After a period of years, I told the conference, I had no doubt that suspicions between Irishmen would lessen, feeling would become more fraternal and ultimately the Federal Body would be freely exchanged for a Parliament of a united Ireland. Under such circumstances, I felt, England would have a strong and loyal friend and ally across the Irish Sea.

Now how did I personally feel about Ireland's declaration of neutrality; I who had seen with my own eyes Jewish people hunted and persecuted by the Nazis; who already knew about the plans for the genocide of my race; who had a prevision of that ultimate incredible horror, the crematoria; I who hated Hitler and all he stood for with a fury beyond my power of speech? I thought it was right for Ireland.

As a member of the Dáil, I have never forgotten that I represent an Irish constituency — that no more than four or five out of every hundred people who vote for me are Jews. Therefore when I act in my official capacity I think only of what is best for Irishmen and do not permit my emotions or my loyalty to people of my faith to sway my judgment. But, as I shall relate, in my personal capacity as a Jew I was prepared to fight alongside of England.

Neither in my mind, nor in Mr. de Valera's, nor that of most Irishmen was there ever a doubt as to whom we wanted to see win this war. Therefore Ireland's neutrality was so benevolent toward England as hardly to be neutral at all, which even Winston Churchill now admits. Did a British plane have a forced landing on one of our airports as many did, was it impounded and its crew interned? Not for a moment. It was secretly refueled and sent on its way. No obstacles were put in the way of Irishmen who wanted to go over the border and enlist in the British Army. So many thousands of them did so that the ratio of men from Eire fighting for England was actually higher than from Ulster.

We did deny British warships the use of our ports, for this would have been the end of neutrality. But this was less of a disadvantage for England than you would think, for most of the shipping used the safer northern route which could be protected from Belfast. Also we enormously increased our shipments of food to England. It is true we got a good price for our exports, but we brought fierce threats from Hitler on our heads, to which de Valera answered, "Ireland is neutral and will sell to any nation which sends money and ships to carry the stuff away," knowing full well that German ships could not get through the British blockade.

In 1941, the Chief was awakened one night by a telephone message that Belfast had been badly bombed. He immediately ordered most of the Dublin Fire Brigade north to its assistance. Was this neutrality? Certainly not, but the Chief's attitude was that Irishmen were dying in those flames and he would help them whether Hitler liked it or not.

When Germany began the intensive bombing of England I was there. I immediately returned to Ireland and proposed to Mr. de Valera that we offer sanctuary to as many British women and children as they could send us. The Chief extended the invitation immediately. That the British did not see fit to accept it was another matter. However, many British people came to Ireland to rest and recuperate from the stress of war. British soldiers, and later Americans, stationed in Belfast, constantly came to the South in civilian clothes on leave and were made welcome. Indeed we did everything we could, short of officially entering the war, to preserve democracy. This we would not, could not, do so long as we were denied a share of that democracy.

Now I am forced to admit that there were a few foolish Irishmen who intrigued with the Germans. The extreme irreconcilable element of the I.R.A. did try to profit by England's difficulty. But de Valera clapped these people into jail as fast as he could catch them. This gave rise to ridiculous rumors in England that there was a German division in the Featherbed Mountains waiting to take over. The truth is that two or three Germans parachuted into Ireland and were caught and jailed. Other stories had it that German submarines were refueled off our coast. This is ridiculous. In the first place Ireland had not a drop of the kind of diesel fuel these submarines required. Since we got what limited supply of petrol we used by the courtesy of England they knew very well we had no diesel fuel. And if we had, the Germans would never have gotten it.

Finally, we put our Army on a war footing to the best of our ability. During the later years of the war we had a hundred and seventy-five thousand men under arms — a large percentage for so small a country. They were prepared to die to the last man if the Germans attempted a landing in Ireland.

A general election was due in Ireland in 1943. At this time my finances had reached the lowest possible level. I was heavily in debt, and I found it difficult to meet even the ordinary household expenses, grocer, electric light and telephone bill. I had an interest in some businesses, but I had neglected them to such an extent I did not feel it was right even to draw directors' fees. At the same time the expenses of raising and educating my seven children were at their peak. I lay awake many nights wondering how I would find the means to meet my commitments.

At the time I entered the Dáil my salary as a member was thirty pounds a month. Then it was raised to forty pounds and during the war to fifty-two pounds a month. It is a full-time job. When the Dáil is sitting you have to be in Leinster House at least three days a week, and to be available to your constituents at all times of the day and night. You have to pay for telephone calls, make contributions to charity, and, of course, there is the expense of entertaining and eating out. I felt I could not go on.

I went to see Mr. de Valera in the Taoiseach's Office in Merrion Square. That was a meeting I shall never forget. I told the Chief of my circumstances. "I do not feel that I can stand again for the Dáil," I said.

He looked at me with great understanding, yet there was sorrow you did not often see in his eyes. "Have you burnt your boats?" he asked quietly.

"What do you mean," I asked.

"Have you made any public announcement?"

"No. I would, of course, tell you first."

"I'm glad of that," he said. "Please make no decision now, and come back and see me in a few weeks' time. Mark you, I do not want to press you unduly to do something that may be hurtful or impossible for you."

Then he rose from behind his great broad desk, and putting his arm around my shoulders walked with me slowly to the door. "You know things are getting very difficult for me," he said. "Many of our old comrades are dying, many are already dead. Some have lost their seats in election defeats. The result is that I'm now left with a number of people who are new, in the sense that they have not gone through the things we have. They have not been welded together by the fires of the past. I feel, if I have to make a serious decision in some crisis, that I need not consult you, for I know how you think and how you would wish me to act. But the new people don't know the things we know, or feel as we do. With them I have to explain it all again, to argue and give reasons. This becomes very difficult and wearing for me. So, self-ishly perhaps, but really for Ireland's sake, I want to keep men like you with whom I can work in perfect confidence and trust."

The moment I left his office, I knew the Chief had won. Two weeks later I went to see him. He was very busy and said quite brusquely, "You have made your decision?"

"I have."

"What is it?"

"I'm going on."

There was no spark of triumph in his eyes, hardly a change of expression. But his voice was very cheerful as he said, "All right. Good-by."

I think he had known my answer all along.

CHAPTER XXV

. . . And a Jew

THOUGH the rescue operations of the New Zionist Organization had come to an end, we continued to function, looking to the future. Some day the war would be over, and when that time came we wanted to be ready for the establishment of a Jewish State in Palestine.

For a year after the death of Jabotinsky we did not appoint a new head of our organization in respect to his memory. The Organization was run by a committee of which I was a member. Throughout the war I spent one week of every month in London, working for the Zionist cause.

How I dreaded those trips to England! Sitting with Lily and the children in the serene little garden of our Irish home the picture of which I was facing in London seemed like a nightmare. This was especially true during the winter of 1940-41 when the saturation bombing and fire raids on London were taking place. I will confess that the bombings, with the screaming sirens, the din of anti-aircraft fire and the hail-sound of falling shrapnel, the ominous, irregular roaring of hundreds of bomber engines and then the terrible crash and concussion of the huge bombs followed by the theatrical red light of great fires, frightened me far more than other possibly more dangerous things I had done.

The British, going normally about their business, laughing and joking during the long uncomfortable nights in the air raid shelters, stoically accepting all the discomfort, danger and personal grief as the people they loved were killed, did indeed have their finest hour. How they stood it day after day, night on night I'll never know. Possibly they became accustomed to it; which I, returning from the green, lighted Irish country, to the pitch black, dismal London streets with their heaps of rubble and great new gaps in the ranks of buildings, could never do. But to be able to get used to such a terrible kind of life was a wonderful example of national stamina. Whatever I may have said or thought of the British in Ireland, the English in England have my profound admiration.

One of the principal diplomatic objectives of our organization was to win the support of the governments in exile in London. There were the Poles, the Czechs, Dutch and Belgians, and later, the Yugoslavs. In meeting the representatives of these nations I was greatly assisted by my good friend Ambassador Anthony D. Biddle of the United States. I had first met Tony Biddle when he was American Ambassador to Poland, where he had been most helpful in getting me the appointment with Colonel Beck. On my trip to America in 1939, he gave me dozens of introductions to people who might be helpful. He was a slim, aristocratic-looking man, always elegantly dressed, the ideal diplomat you would say. But he had two qualities that are not very common in the *corps diplomatique*, a sense of humor and an understanding heart.

In London, Biddle, who was American Ambassador to all the governments in exile, arranged for me to meet such people as General Zirkorsky of Poland and President Eduard Beneš of Czechoslovakia, as well as the Dutch and Belgians. Our attempt was to get statements from these people that they would approve the establishment of a Jewish State after the war. Though they did not commit themselves at the time, they were sympathetic, and I think the missionary work we did had some influence in gaining the approval of the United Nations when Israel was finally founded in 1948.

In addition, of course, we continued to contact and lobby different members of the British Parliament and of the House of Lords, all our old standby friends. This, too, had an eventual value.

Another objective very close to my heart was the organization of a Jewish Army to fight alongside the Allies. In my plan it was not to be a brigade or division of the British Army, but an independent organization manned by Jewish Volunteers recruited from every country in the world. In working for this I sent a telegram to Winston Churchill pleading with him to permit the establishment of such an Army in which I said, "If you agree to do so, I and my son Billy will be the first volunteers."

I was prepared to resign from the Dáil and the Irish Movement for this purpose, because I felt that, while Ireland was justified in her neutrality, none of my old comrades could criticize me as a Jew for taking up arms against the monstrous tyranny which had worked such evil on my race.

The British Government refused to sanction the organization of this Army. However, a Jewish Brigade was formed and proved itself magnificently in the African and Italian campaigns. Though I did not approve of this compromise and would not myself join a brigade of the British Army, I encouraged young Jewish men to enlist. "Let them teach you the techniques of battle as they taught us," I said. "Then you will be able to fight them successfully as we did."

This is actually what happened. The Jewish Brigade was the training ground for the Jewish Army who, after the war, resumed and won the struggle for freedom; and who today are able to maintain the integrity of Israel against the overwhelming numbers of the hostile Arab states by which she is encircled.

Those first years of the war dragged interminably on. At times one almost gave up hope. But when America came in the tempo quickened. Suddenly the London streets came alive again, crowded with husky men in American uniforms. Then came D Day and the wonderful news from France as Patton's Third Army chased the Nazis home. The last winter of the war was again filled with dread and anxiety. Buzz bombs and V-2s were in some ways more nerve-wracking than the bombers because there was hardly any warning of approaching death. Then it all ended in a rush.

. . . *And a Jew*

During the next year I often thought of Dev's prophetic speech before the Dáil. The *entente* of the victorious Allies lasted an even shorter time than he had thought. Looking back you would put it at the three days while English, Americans and Russians toasted their victory in champagne and vodka in Berlin. Then the stresses of chauvinism and ideology tore the fabric of good will and split the world neatly down the middle.

But the flux of nations and the shifting patterns of power, the dislocations of peoples and rearrangements of boundaries gave a splendid opportunity to a single-minded people determined on establishing a national state of their own. Those of us who believed in Zionism went to work, each in different ways, each moving toward the same end.

The transportation of immigrants to Palestine was resumed largely under the auspices of Haganah and the regular Zionist organization. They also formed the regular defense force of Palestine, while Irgun continued the Physical Force Movement to dislodge the British. Naturally I was connected with the latter.

Often I am challenged for my belief in and the necessity for physical force. People think I love fighting for its own sake. I do not. But the whole lesson of history is that you do not achieve freedom without fighting for it, or keep it without a vigorous defense. In connection with this reputation of mine I once had an interesting argument with Mahatma Gandhi. We met some years before the war when I was sent by de Valera to Gandhi's hotel in London to invite him to visit Ireland. Strange to say the great proponent of passive resistance and I got along very well together. So well that upon the occasion of my second visit to him, Gandhi invited me to "share" his meal with him. I found his invitation meant exactly that.

A huge big white-robed Indian brought into the hotel sitting room a wooden bowl of fruit, mostly grapes. There was a pitcher of hot goat's milk and two jugs. Gandhi pointed to the bowl and invited me to help myself; I was the guest. Both of us ate our grapes, dipping them into the same bowl of water. In his customary short white robe Gandhi showed large amounts of emaciated arms, legs and thighs. He was so immaculately clean that his skin seemed to have a sort of sheen.

On this second occasion he told me that he had made up his mind that I was a person worthy of confidence with whom he could talk openly. I asked him how he decided that.

"Since your last visit," he said, "I have had people watching the papers to see if there was any publicity. No paper in Ireland, England or India has mentioned it. Almost everyone else who has met me in England from Charlie Chaplin to Winston Churchill has been photographed with me if possible or at least announced to the press that I have received them. I like a man who does not try to capitalize on meeting me."

Then he showed me a picture of him and Chaplin. He was grinning so that you could see that there was but a single tooth in his mouth, the rest just gums. "That's a friendly smile you have," I observed.

Gandhi laughed and said, "Oh, yes, you see I am showing the one tooth that the British Tommy failed to kick out of my head when I was taken to prison in India. I like to remind them."

After that we had a long discussion. He explained to me his theory of passive resistance. This made me feel a little awkward as we Irish had felt the need to use physical force. However, I challenged him with the statement; "With the great masses of people you have in India and its vast area, surely physical force would be more effective than passive resistance."

He said to me something I have never forgotten: "Whether it would or not, I am determined that so long as I live we will not use force; that the passive way will prevail. By the time my life ends I hope that my people will have attained such a degree of education and self-discipline as will allow them, if necessary, to indulge in physical force without the danger of mass destruction."

I was astonished, for these words were in complete contradiction of what were always thought to be his principles.

To return to Palestine. In 1946, the British announced that they would give up their mandate in 1948. However, during those two years they used violently repressive measures against the Jewish inhabitants. Chaim Weizmann and that magnificent old patriot Ben Gurion countered these by a form of passive resistance, only using the supply of arms which Haganah was slowly building up to defend themselves when attacked by the Arab residents. However, Haganah was organized into a real underground army ready to take over when the British got out. Meanwhile Irgun fought back, as we Irish had fought, with bombs and sudden raids, the techniques of guerrilla war.

In 1947, I decided to go to Palestine to confer with the leaders of Irgun — of the Freedom Fighters. I applied for a visa at the British Consulate in Dublin. They told me I would have to get it in London. In London, they said only the British Consul in Cairo could give me a visa to Palestine. So I went to Cairo. There I got a royal run-around.

The first thing though was a pleasant surprise. When I told the Egyptian official at the airport that I was Irish, he asked, "Which Ireland?"

I said, "Southern Ireland."

That apparently did not seep in until he opened my passport with the green harp on it and saw de Valera's name. "Oh, de Valera's Ireland," he said with a big brightness on his face. "Come this way."

He led me right through the customs barriers behind which the other passengers were waiting. "What about all these customs forms I'm supposed to fill out?" I asked.

"For you it is not necessary," he answered.

It made me very happy to know that the Egyptians had such a friendly regard for Ireland.

Of course, I knew that Shephard's Hotel was the proper place to stay in Cairo. However it was full of English people. This did not suit me. I went to the Continental where anyone could stay, including Egyptians. Then I went to the British Consulate. The official there was a very pleasant Scotsman. He was most courteous but he kept telling me to come back tomorrow. Each tomorrow it was the same story, until he finally broke down and said,

"Palestine is under martial law. The British military authorities won't have you there at any price."

Even the local manager of American Express tried to induce me to get out of Cairo, warning me that the Egyptians were spying on my activities. I did not think it was the Egyptians who were spying. When I saw him later in Dublin, the editor of the *Irish Press* explained the situation to me. He had become very friendly with a Scotland Yard Inspector in London who happened to tell him that in the opinion of the British authorities the most dangerous man in the Palestine situation was one Robert Briscoe. I was highly flattered.

Despite the ominous warnings I remained in Cairo for about a month. I am glad I did, for I accomplished some things both for Palestine and Ireland, and saw some wonderful sights — the Pyramids, the Valley of the Kings, Tutankhamen's relics in the museum — all tourist things, but giving a man a new conception and understanding of this ancient people, who are our enemies today, but I hope will be our friends when their misunderstanding of Israel is cleared away.

The most amazing and amusing thing I saw was in a waxworks exhibition like Madame Tussaud's. It was not very impressive, but there was a particular tableau that intrigued me. It was a scene in about 1890, depicting a Nile steamer landing in Cairo. Coming down her gangway were three English women, and waiting for them on the dock was the Khedive of Egypt, Farouk's grandfather. It was explained to me that the ladies were London prostitutes sent by Queen Victoria as a present to the Khedive.

For this sightseeing I had engaged a guide who approached me the first evening as I was sitting on the terrace of my hotel drinking coffee. He was dressed in the sort of uniform these dragomen wear, a long white coat, red fez and a red sash around his waist. He showed me his credentials and said he would guide me around Cairo for a salary of one pound a day. That did not seem unreasonable and I engaged him.

After a few days rumors must have gotten around that I was a bit of a fool. The head porter of the hotel asked what I was paying my dragoman and I told him. He said, "You're mad. The official fee is two and six. I'll get you one at the regular rate."

The next day he produced this new dragoman. I thought two and six was a beggarly wage and said I'd give him five shillings. That night as I was sitting on the terrace my first guide slithered up to me and said, "Will you take me back? I'll work for a much smaller fee."

"How much?" I asked.

"What are you paying this son of a camel?"

"Five shillings."

"I'll do it for ten."

"Now, why should I be paying you ten shillings when this other chap gives me good service for five?" I asked.

"Oh well," he said, "he's a very lazy man."

"He does not seem so. How is he lazy?"

With a wonderfully sly grin the dragoman answered, "He has only one wife; I have three."

I re-engaged him. His sense of humor was worth the difference.

There was then, in 1947, no tension between Egypt and Palestine. On the contrary they had a common desire to get rid of the British, and there was a good deal of going backward and forward between the two countries. So I was able to make contact with the Freedom Fighters through Egyptian friends and advise with them, without going to Palestine. I was perfectly willing to slip across the border, but they advised me that the British Secret Service was excellent, and I was so conspicuous — again that height of mine and my broken nose — that they'd be sure to pick me up. The Jews preferred to see me in Cairo where we were all safe.

Since I had to stay in Egypt, I busied myself seeing what I could do for Ireland. Arrangements were made for me to meet the Egyptian Minister of Industry and Commerce. I cannot recall his name but I can picture him now — tall man dressed in Arab costume with a very dark skin and a hooked Semitic nose. He was a very gentle man who all through our conversation sat at his desk toying with a string of amber beads.

We discussed the possibility of increasing trade between Egypt and Ireland — we could use citrus fruits, cotton and Egyptian canned goods. They needed Irish meat. I was surprised in my ignorance to learn that pork products were as distasteful to Mohammedans as to us Jews, and also that their methods of slaughter were similar to those required by the Jewish dietary laws. I assured the Minister that these requirements could be met.

Before leaving this man the talk turned on myself. I said, "I am a Jew, but I am sympathetic to Egypt's desire for independence. How do you feel about Palestine?"

"The same as you," he answered, "but the British High Commissioner calls on our Cabinet ministers nearly every day. The relations between our people are bedeviled by his prods and suggestions."

Through the introductions which this sympathetic Egyptian gave me to other officials of the Finance Ministry and the great Mizra Bank, I was able to oil the wheels of trade between Ireland and Egypt.

Now I must give you a little history in which I played no part. In November, 1947, the United Nations approved the setting up of a Jewish State in Palestine and the partition of the country between Jews and Arabs. The first I thought good, the latter bad. On May 14, 1948, as the British mandate for Palestine ended, a new nation was born — Israel. Within two hours President Truman recognized the Jewish State.

But on the third day Israel was attacked by the nations of the Arab League — Syria, Lebanon, Jordan, Iraq, Egypt — thirty-five million against six hundred and fifty thousand. Azzam Pasha, Secretary General of the Arab League announced with ghoulish glee, "This will be a war of extermination and a momentous massacre which will be spoken of like the deeds of the Mongols."

Against the regular Arab armies stood only the secretly trained

Haganah, now joined by Irgun and all other factions. They had only smuggled arms to fight with. But they had that great imponderable of war, an unconquerable spirit. With their light machine guns and rifles they stood off the first Arab rush, though the Egyptian Air Force bombed Tel Aviv unopposed since Israel had not a single plane. But help came from the Jews of the United States, and not only Jews, but millions of Americans who sympathized with the struggle for independence. Bombing planes were secretly flown across the Atlantic. Arms, ammunition, even cannon, bought by money raised in America, were smuggled in. When the final truce, ordered by the United Nations, came into effect on January 9, 1949, the Israelites had thrown the Arab armies back beyond the lines of partition. And there our borders stand today.

Even before the war for survival was won, Israel began to lay the foundation of a democratic state. A constitution was drawn up providing for a president and a parliamentary form of government with a cabinet responsible to a unicameral legislature of one hundred and twenty members called the *Knesset*. Elections were called for January 29, 1949. It was at this point that I became fearful of a new danger for Israel.

Irgun, with which I had been associated, were dissatisfied with the situation — not without cause. The government organized by Chaim Weizmann and Ben Gurion had given them no voice in its councils, no recognition of their services in ousting Britain. Furthermore, when a ship loaded with arms provided by American sympathizers, among them the famous playwright Ben Hecht, for Irgun arrived at Tel Aviv, Ben Gurion demanded that the munitions be turned over to Haganah. When Irgun refused, Jewish guns fired on the *Altoona* and sank her outside the harbor of Tel Aviv. What I feared was civil war in Israel.

The head of the Irgun organization was Mr. Menachim Beigan. Though I had never met him, we had been in correspondence. Now I asked for an interview. I was told that he would meet with me at Irgun Headquarters in Paris.

When I saw Beigan, I was shocked. He was a small dark man

with a sallow complexion; so emaciated was he that he looked like a miniature skeleton. He was clearly in the final stages of a fatal illness, burning up with the intensity of his attempt to pit effort against time. His dark eyes were incandescent.

To this fanatically devoted man and his colleagues I made a strange speech for one who was labeled, even in my own country, "extremist." "At the touch of a match you could have civil war in Israel," I said. "A war such as we had in Ireland. Though I was ardent on the Republican side of that war, I bitterly regret the sorrow and misery and death it caused; for no good came of it. You are in the same position that we were. For God's sake benefit by my knowledge of the disaster which overtook us.

"There is an election coming up in Israel, and it will be a free election. Abandon Irgun as a physical force movement. Convert it into a constitutional party as we did our Republican organization. Choose as your candidates members of Irgun upon whom you can rely and trust. Frame your policy. Appeal to the electorate. You will succeed in having some of your candidates elected.

"This you will not want to hear, but my hope for you is that you will not succeed in winning the government immediately. For I believe that whatever party is put in power first will have enormous difficulties. In the beginning of a nation it is not easy to please the multitude of people. They expect such great things as are beyond the powers of mere men to bring about.

"If you are in opposition you will have the benefit of learning the art of democratic government, as we of de Valera's party learned it. Then, in time to come when the next election comes around, you will be able to contest it as an experienced political party, and should you win you will have gained the wisdom to govern well."

So I spoke to them in the meeting, and privately with Beigan in this strain; I, the old revolutionary, the uncompromising extremist, the pure Republican. Thus I pleaded with them not to do as I had done.

I think it had some effect, perhaps it was even decisive. Irgun was disbanded and the Herut Party was formed. In the election

which made Chaim Weizmann the first President of Israel and
Ben Gurion its first Prime Minister, Herut won only eleven seats
in the Knesset. It was a disappointingly small beginning but far
better than what might have happened.

CHAPTER XXVI

With de Valera in Israel

In 1948, the wheel of Irish politics came around. Perhaps the people were just tired of voting for de Valera. They had returned us to power in five general elections over a period of fifteen years. Fine Gael got in by a coalition with the Labor Party. Cosgrave had retired some years before, so John Costello became Prime Minister. We were out and had a little time on our hands.

One day in 1950, the Chief said to me, "What about coming with me now to Israel, to the Holy Land?"

It was so sudden, and so delightful a prospect, like being invited to take a trip to paradise, that I was struck dumb. Dev evidently thought he had to argue. "You know how interested I am in your people; and how long I have wanted to make a pilgrimage to the Holy Land. I'll go now if you'll go with me. You can show me the ropes and bring me to the right people. On the spot we can judge for ourselves of many things."

"This is a thing I've dreamed about, Chief," I said. "When do we start?"

De Valera with his two sons, Major Vivion de Valera and Doctor Eamon de Valera, Jr., went first to Rome. A few days later I took off in a T.W.A. plane which stopped at Rome on its way to Israel. De Valera and his sons joined me aboard it in Rome.

Dev settled his long legs awkwardly in the seat beside me. He was wearing his dark glasses which he seldom left off now that his eyesight was failing fast. No sooner were we in the air than the stewardess brought us dinner. On each little tray was a half bottle of Burgundy in a wicker cradle. De Valera took his bottle and poured out a glass of wine. "Surely you're not going to drink that wine, Chief," I said.

"Why not?"

"Because you'll be making a liar out of me. I have always said you were a teetotaler."

The Chief smiled and sipped his wine. "Well, now," he said, "you need not tell that lie any more."

Though it was four in the morning when we arrived at Jerusalem's Lidda Airport, it was pack-jammed with a tremendous big crowd waiting to greet Dev. As he stepped out of the plane he was swamped by pressmen, photographers, and people who just wanted to shake hands. We were separated in the rush and I went alone to the customs shed. In my baggage I had a case of whiskey for my old friend, Chief Rabbi Herzog, who I knew loved a drop of the Irish.

I was getting ready to declare the whiskey and fill out the immigration forms when four rather stocky customs officials rushed me bodily past the barriers. "No need for you to answer any questions; no need for you to have any examination. You're through. You're cleared."

From beyond the customs' barrier I saw poor Dev standing at the counter answering questions and attempting to fill out a long form. A light burst in my brain; they had thought I was Dev. "You've got the wrong man," I said. "There is Mr. de Valera at the counter."

They left me like a smart dog dropping a piece of bad meat. But there I was through the barrier with my whiskey, and I did not feel honest enough to go back and start a campaign to pay the heavy duty on it. So Rabbi Herzog got his whiskey tax free.

The Israeli Government had sent some foreign office officials and two government cars for us. As we left the airport in them it was just beginning to get light. It was a magnificently interesting journey, that ride into Jerusalem. The blue dawn light that got stronger and rosier every moment made it all seem unreal. And dreamlike it was to me anyhow to see at last the land of Israel; the slopes and terraces, the olive groves and orchards; the small tilled fields; and then the city of David and Solomon shining on its hills. Everybody in the car was talking at once; and everybody pointing to something different, to places where battles had been fought two years ago or two thousand years ago; and to the Holy Places; those that were reverenced by Dev or those I venerated; and those which were holy to us both.

The King David Hotel astonished me, I had not expected so modern and luxurious a caravansary in little old Jerusalem. Of course one wing had been blown off by my Irgun friends. However, we took up our abode in the King David Hotel.

The following day, a Thursday it was, Mr. de Valera, his two sons and I were invited to a dinner and reception at the house of Chief Rabbi Herzog. In the official car de Valera, whose courtesy is the most scrupulous and gentle of any man I have known, said to me, "I am relying on you to tell me exactly what I am to do in this house for I wish to conform to all your customs."

"That I will, Chief," I answered.

At the door of the Chief Rabbi's house Mrs. Herzog greeted us. She is a warm and friendly person who was a dear friend of my own mother and of Lily. Mrs. Herzog handed us each a yarmulka, a small black skull cap.

"You should put this on, Chief," I said. "It is the custom of my people to wear them during meals and at our religious services."

Dev promptly put the yarmulka on, which made his long face still longer and more solemn.

Rabbi Herzog had invited illustrious guests to honor Dev. Prime Minister and Mrs. Ben Gurion were there, Minister for Finance and Industry Don Josef and several other members of the Cabinet. We sat down at the dinner table and the Chief Rabbi prepared to say grace. As he looked around the table he could see that every head was covered except only the great fuzzy white locks of Ben Gurion, who prided himself on being most unorthodox. As the Chief Rabbi hesitated for an instant, the Prime Minister sheepishly held out his hand for a yarmulka and clapped it on that ocean of hair. Herzog smiled in his whimsical way and proceeded to say grace.

We had our meal. Then pressmen and photographers were allowed in. The big news in the papers next morning was that Mr. Ben Gurion had worn a yarmulka and it had taken the example of de Valera to bring that revolutionary act about.

After we got rid of the press, a most interesting discussion took place. The three main talkers were the Chief Rabbi, de Valera and Ben Gurion. The conversation was not as you would suppose about religion or politics or trade, but about classic Greece. Ben Gurion is a great classical scholar and so is Herzog. De Valera, a wide-ranging student, had just been to Athens and he had a great deal to contribute. After that they talked mathematics. Neither Ben Gurion nor de Valera discussed anything in the nature of their respective experiences or their expectations for the future of their own countries. It was a very pleasant evening.

The next day de Valera had arranged to go to Jordan. He asked me, "Are you coming with me?"

"No, thank you."

"Well if you want to come you can," de Valera persisted, "and if there is any trouble about you it will be *my* trouble as well."

"No, Chief," I said again. "I'll stay here in Israel. You go along and meet these Arabs. Find out for yourself the things they mean and the things they stand for."

He left me reluctantly, for we were traveling together. However, he enjoyed himself. When he returned he told me that he had met King Abdullah of Jordan and found him a very cultured man, well versed in poetry and with a clear realistic understanding of world affairs. De Valera believed that the King was not himself hostile to Israel and that had he been a free person he would have come to very amicable terms with the Israelis.

On de Valera's return he proceded on what he called a pilgrimage to the Holy Places of his faith. On these days I would go to the places venerated by my people. In the evenings we sat together on the balcony of his room and talked about the things we had seen.

This balcony overlooked the walls of old Jerusalem. As we sat there we could watch the people going in and out of the Mandelbaum gate showing their permits to the guards. Occasionally we heard rifle fire within the old city, for the border ran through it and feeling was high. Outwardly the scene was as peaceful as you could wish, with the afternoon sun touching gently the old stones, and the people moving slowly and apparently calmly about their small affairs. Nevertheless there was a tenseness in the atmosphere — a sort of coiled-to-spring readiness for anything that might happen.

I believe that de Valera was impressed with the speed and energy and hope with which the Jewish people were improving the little bit of territory they possess, which they are trying to make into a real homeland for themselves. They truly want to live in security and peace with their neighbors.

I tried to convince the Chief, as I have always tried to convince everybody I talked with, that if no outside interference were about and if the Jews and Arabs could be persuaded to sit down together they could ultimately hammer out an understanding satisfactory to both. Even the problem of the Arab refugees could be settled. The vast empty spaces of the Arab kingdoms could easily accommodate a few hundred thousand people, especially if they were given assistance to irrigate the land. Now, they keep these poor forlorn people in barbed wire stockades as a trading point and a reproach to Israel. However, if a genuine peace conference met, this would not stand in its way. Israel has held the property these Arabs foolishly abandoned in trust for them and would promptly pay fair compensation. If a little of the money it costs to maintain the refugee camps were allotted to resettling them in Arab countries they could be happy and even prosperous again.

I still believe that the partition of Palestine and the creation of the artificial state of Jordan was an evil thing. The Arabs look on

Israel as the Ulster of Palestine and regard the Jews as foreigners
kept there by outside support. The Jews, again, look upon Jordan
as the Ulster of Palestine. Obviously a kept state. Now, of course,
it has joined with Iraq — another matter altogether, but somewhat frightening.

I repeated to Dev, and do so again here, that I have no animos-
ity to Arabs or Egyptians. I hope and believe that the feudalism
which exists in the Arab world will ultimately disappear, to be
replaced by democracy as we understand it. If that democracy is
set up, the Arabs themselves will begin to understand the need for
a neighbor who will help to bring about the awakening of the
Near and Middle East. They in their agricultural economy will
profit by having close at hand a modern, semi-industrialized
country, which by example and trade will help to raise them
from their medieval way of life.

De Valera was, as I say, impressed by what he saw. He sympa-
thizes with the Arab people in their hope of independence and
prosperity. So do I. I want to see all people this way — a world
where every human being is of equal dignity and of equal im-
portance. So also the units of society, the entities, the nations that
make up the world.

As a result of our trip to Palestine de Valera and I became
closer friends than ever. It was not only the wonderful compan-
ionship that we enjoyed, but also the understanding that came
from our joint experiences. I had always known and valued his
great qualities of courage, idealism and moral fortitude. Now I
appreciated more than ever his less obvious characteristics, his
courtesy, his gentle humor and the warmth of his friendship.

In return, I believe he had gained new understanding of the
problems and aspirations of the Jewish people in Israel. And he
came to see the remarkable likeness between Israel and Ireland.

For their circumstances are astonishingly similar. People have
sometimes wondered how I reconciled my loyalties to Ireland
and to my race. That has not been a problem. The only time they
could possibly have clashed was on the question of Ireland's

neutrality — whether from the point of view of a Jew it would have been better for Ireland to enter the war. As you have seen I had no difficulty in resolving that question — I am an Irishman who happens to be of the Jewish faith.

However, there are far more bonds between Ireland and Israel than differences. We have both fought for and won our freedom. We have both sought to revive an ancient language and an ancient culture. And we both faced the economic difficulties of a poor small nation in a world overshadowed by industrial giants. The things we have accomplished were not done by military power or economic strength. They were accomplished by moral force. In the case of Israel the spiritual inspiration came from the age-old desire of the Jews to find sanctuary in their historic homeland, and the religious fervor of our ancient faith. The Irish were inspired by the love of their dear green island; and their unbreakable desire to be free.

The kinship of interest that I feel between the Irish and the Israelis was wonderfully explained by one of the great ladies of Ireland, the widow of martyred Erskine Childers, who said, "I suppose that two peoples who have suffered so much persecution must have a great deal in common."

CHAPTER XXVII

The Hat and the Chain

For twenty-five years, except for a brief interval, I had been a member of the Dublin Corporation, the City Council. Every year a Lord Mayor is chosen by the forty-five councillors. I had never allowed my name to be put forward. For one thing I did not know if I would be able to handle the office with the dignity I felt was due it. For another I was conscious of the problems which might arise should a Jew, a member of a minute minority, become the First Citizen of a predominantly Catholic city.

Immediately after the war in 1946, de Valera said to me, "Who is going to be Fianna Fail's candidate for Lord Mayor?"

I answered, "We have not decided that, Chief."

"How about yourself?" he asked.

I did not know whether he was joking or not — Dev has a way of coming out with things just for the fun of it. But I answered him seriously. "Look, Chief, there are nineteen Fianna Fail councillors, every one of whom except myself is anxious some day to hold that position and receive the honor. Were I to become a candidate I feel that I might only antagonize some of my own party who consider themselves more entitled to this honor than I am."

There it rested for another nine years. However, in 1955, one man, Alfred Byrne, had been Lord Mayor for nine successive years. Alfie Byrne was a very genial and popular character who was supposedly an Independent, though his independence consisted of always voting with Fine Gael so long as they supported him for Lord Mayor. A considerable number of councillors, myself included, felt that this honorable office should not be monopolized by one person, however popular. We felt it should rotate among the councillors.

For this reason I allowed my name to be put forward in 1955. The other candidates were Byrne and Labor Member Denis Larkin, son of the great revolutionary labor leader James Larkin. I offered to withdraw and throw the nineteen Fianna Fail votes to Larkin, saying to him, "Mark you, our support is only for one year, at the end of which the Council should consider the matter of rotation."

Alfie Byrne was defeated and Denis Larkin became Lord Mayor.

The following year, 1956, Larkin wanted to go again. Our group decided that I should make a contest of it, though I did not believe I had a one to five chance of winning. For one thing Fianna Fail's representation in the Council had been reduced in the city election to sixteen members.

That is one evening I shall never forget. Our City Hall is a rather small building of classical architecture with tall Grecian columns supporting its portico. Inside, there is a handsome rotunda with a marble stairway leading to the second floor where the Council sits. Closing my eyes I can see every detail of the Council Chamber, and should I not, since I have sat there nearly every week for a quarter of a century?

It is a rectangular room with tall windows looking out on Corn Hill and through the crowded, narrow downtown streets with a glimpse of the Liffey at the end of them. At one end of this room, in a carved throne-like chair with a velvet baldachin over it sits the Lord Mayor in his robes and the great gold chain of his office. In front of him is a clear space around which rise the dark wooden benches for the councillors and, behind them, the general public. That particular evening the sun was streaming in the windows glorifying the dingy old walls and touching the bright blue and green robes of the councillors.

The usual impassioned nominating speeches were made; and I am afraid my friends somewhat exaggerated my virtues. Then the first vote was taken. The count came out Briscoe sixteen, Larkin fourteen. James Carroll (Independent) who had been elected to the Council only that year had nine. The six members of the Ratepayers Party refused to vote.

According to the rules of the Council Carroll was eliminated. It was now between Lord Mayor Larkin and me. I had only Fianna Fail's sixteen votes for sure, out of forty-five. It did not look good. In the hot politicking after the first ballot, Fine Gael decided to support Larkin, whom they had opposed the year before, as the only means of keeping a Fianna Fail member out of the office. The two members of Clan na Phoblachta were split between us; and the six members of the Ratepayers Party announced that again they would not vote. To get a majority I had to win twenty votes out of thirty-nine. So the voting began:

Each councillor called his vote, which was repeated by the clerk. Frequently they added typically Irish comments on the fitness of their man, or the obvious inadequacy of his opponent. Sitting there trying to keep a mental tally without the indignity of writing it down, my heart was bursting with excitement, though I'm told my long face was so blank I looked like the twin brother of a wooden Indian. It seemed to me that Larkin was getting a terrible lot of votes. But at the end a kind of buzzing went through the people crowding back of the benches and there were shouts of "The Hat! The Hat!"

Sure enough the clerk announced the tally as Larkin nineteen, Briscoe nineteen; seven members not voting.

Now began the peculiar ceremony by which such tie votes are settled by the rules of the Council. It may appear somewhat flippant to select a Lord Mayor by drawing a piece of paper out of a hat, but it is necessary, because we Irish are so stubborn that once having voted for a man we would keep on voting that way while the centuries passed and the very building moldered in ruins around us.

The clerk asked for a hat and a man in the crowd passed over a very dirty slouch hat which he might have worn in the Troubled Times. I was handed a slip of paper on which I wrote my name in a squiggly nervous hand. Larkin did likewise. The names were put in the hat and a very clean handkerchief of beautiful Irish linen was placed over it. One of the nonvoting councillors was asked to draw.

You could *not* have heard a pin drop as he fumbled under the handkerchief, because everybody was breathing so hard, including myself. The little piece of paper was handed to Lord Mayor Larkin who studied it for a terrible minute. Then he said one word: "Briscoe!"

And lo and behold! I was now Lord Mayor of Dublin.

That was an uproarious evening, beginning with a great crash of cheers, partly, I think, because I was a Jew and it was all so unexpected. Denis Larkin stepped down off the dais and in a very gracious manner hung the great gold chain over my shoulders. The weight of it seemed to make everything real and solid.

Then the whole mob adjourned to the Mansion House, for it is the custom for the new Lord Mayor to take it over immediately. I was somewhat delayed by congratulations and handshakes and people shoving, so by the time I reached the lovely graceful white Mansion House there was a great crowd jamming the driveway between the high wrought-iron gates, and blocking most of Dawson Street. Peter Delaney, the Mansion House steward, was making a gangway through the people. I arrived and I stood gaping with the crowd until Peter came along and said, "You're the Lord Mayor, will you for God's sake come in!"

I had forgotten at this moment that I was what I had just become.

There was a wonderful brannigan inside. Lily and those of our children who were in Dublin were there; of course, my brothers and sister; half the Jewish community; and it seemed like all the I.R.A. Of course the drinks were on me and the amount of good Irish whiskey that went down good Irish throats that night would have filled the lake in St. Stephen's Green.

When Lily and I finally reached our modest home at 12 Herbert Park in the suburb of Ballsbridge I was completely exhausted. We had had nothing to eat, and I was even light-headed from excitement. I lay in bed unable to sleep. Finally I sat bolt upright. "What's wrong with you?" Lily asked.

"Lily," I said, "am I in an asylum, a lunatic certified, or am I really Lord Mayor?"

Lily smiled maternally. "If you're certified in an asylum, I must be there with you," she said, "for I truly believe that you are Lord Mayor of Dublin."

Then we both looked at the gold chain of office hanging over the back of a chair. And laughed out loud.

There are three chains of office; all of them solid gold. One is a light link chain so long that you have to make three or four circles of it around your neck. This is the one we allow deputy Lord Mayors to wear when they are representing us at some function we cannot attend.

Then there is what is called the Clancy Chain. It is quite short but exquisitely worked, the most beautiful of all. Together with its medallion it weighs about three pounds, and you wear it all the time. In fact, I only took it off when I went to bed.

Finally there is the old official chain of the City of Dublin to be worn on state occasions. The original ancient chain of Dublin was lost by a Lord Mayor who died in battle fighting for England. The present chain was presented to the City by William of Orange to replace it. It is very long with a great round medallion that hangs in front of your stomach; and it is a monstrous thing to wear, weighing at least seven pounds. It was only after I wore this chain at an official function which lasted some six hours that I realized what it means to handicap a horse in a two-mile race with an extra seven pounds.

Well, the next morning I got dressed in the formal striped trousers and short black coat which I always wore during my term of office and hung the Clancy Chain around my neck. Then I went to the Mansion House to look it over.

Peter Delaney greeted me. I found him to be a very responsible, sensible Dublin man, an official, of course, of the Dublin Corporation in charge of the Mansion House. He showed me over the premises in which I had a right to live as long as I was Lord Mayor. Beautiful as this house is, with its graceful eighteenth century décor, its lovely crystal chandeliers, paintings by such fine British artists as Sir Joshua Reynolds, and its delicate priceless furniture, I decided it was no place for me to live. Apart from its lack of modern amenities, the old Georgian mansion, with its huge, far-flung bedrooms separated from each other by vast wide stairways and long corridors, would need a host of servants; there was no hope of achieving a homely atmosphere in it. So Lily and I unanimously decided to remain in our little crowded house in Ballsbridge.

That settled, there were other details to attend to. Peter Delaney told me about my right to create my own coat-of-arms, which would hang in the Oak Room with those of all the previous Lord Mayors and which would become the arms of my family thenceforward. He said, "You had better do this quickly, for you are expected to send Christmas cards to all the people who call here and write their names in the visitors' book; and to your friends and supporters at home and abroad. It takes quite a while to have it made."

Well, if this coat-of-arms were to hang in the Oak Room and belong to my family for ever and ever, I thought it should have some meaning, a message if you like, for my descendants. First I considered the motto. I had always been concerned about freedom, freedom of a country, freedom of a people, and freedom of the individual. Therefore I decided that the first word should be Freedom.

But freedom means nothing without justice between nations and between individuals; and without it there can never be permanent peace in the world. So for the second word I chose Justice.

Finally I thought of my present position. Here was I, this Jew, sitting in the Mansion House as Lord Mayor of the capital city of a great Catholic country. So little I had thought of my chances of being elected that I had not considered all its implications. As I realized them I was thrilled and delighted that now one could say, "Here is an example to the world of tolerance in my country.

This is proof that there is no bigotry or any other restraint placed on a person because of his private conscience."

On the other hand I did not like the word tolerance because it implies that you accept a person notwithstanding, you tolerate them in spite of something. I searched the dictionaries and consulted Gaelic scholars for the word in Irish, but found that there is no such word as tolerance — the nearest to it is patience. Then I inquired among Jewish scholars and discovered that in the ancient Hebrew language there is no such word, and again the nearest to it is patience. Therefore I decided on Patience and wrote these three words in Irish at the bottom of the page on which I was drawing my own coat of arms.

Now for the shield. Dublin is my city, the only home and place to love I own. So I drew the Arms of Dublin, the three gates which look like three small castles. Now I recollected that in the time of Hitler my co-religionists had been forced to wear on their left arms the Star of David as a badge of contempt. Because of my pride in my heritage and my devotion to my faith I decided to adopt this badge voluntarily. So I superimposed on the Arms of Dublin a large double triangle — the Star of David.

That is my crest and both Jew and gentile admire and praise it.

Another thing Peter informed me I must do was to have my portrait painted for the Mansion House, a traditional gift from Lord Mayors. I began inquiring for an artist and someone mentioned Mrs. Reeves, the daughter of the late Rupert Hartigan. I asked her to come to see me. Accompanied by her husband she duly arrived, and a magnificent-looking woman she was. She studied me for a while and said, "Yes, I should like to paint you."

We agreed on a fee — one hundred guineas.

After the bargain was struck, Peter heard that this lady had never painted a human being before. She had made a great reputation painting horses and had just finished a painting of the famous Irish stallion Tulyar, which had been sold to America for two hundred fifty thousand pounds — the horse I mean. This raised doubts in my mind, but a bargain is a bargain.

On the appointed morning I was in my office when through the open door I heard Mrs. Reeves arrive, and begin setting up her paraphernalia in the drawing room of the Mansion House. Then I heard Peter say to her, "This Lord Mayor is a very restless individual. He is always being called to the telephone or dashing in and out to meetings or receiving people. You will have trouble getting him to pose. Sorry I am for you."

"That doesn't worry me," said Mrs. Reeves. "You know I'm so used to painting horses that I'm sure I can manage a restless mayor."

Peter likes to have the last word. "All right, Ma'am," he said, "tell me when you're ready and I'll back him in."

I threw my heart and soul into the business of being Lord Mayor. My intention was to bring it to the level of dignity it deserved and to be Lord Mayor of all the citizens of Dublin, irrespective of party or creed. I therefore attended public services in churches of all denominations. Prior to my election the Catholic Lord Mayors were not permitted to attend other churches.

Now this office of Lord Mayor is one of great onerousness and great honor, and very little power. We have a system of city management in Dublin. Certain functions are exercised by the City Manager, and others are reserved powers of the Corporation. There are some functions which are exercised jointly by the Lord Mayor and the City Manager. In addition, the Lord Mayor is ex-officio chairman of any committee of the Corporation with which he sits, though, of course, each committee has a regular chairman. I remained chairman of my regular committee throughout my term of office and I still hold that position.

However, the fact that as Lord Mayor I had very little real power did not prevent people from asking me to wield it on their behalf. Every citizen of Dublin who has a gripe rushes to the telephone and asks the Lord Mayor to do something about it. My answer to these people was, "Write a letter to me about your complaint and I will use what little influence I have to help you." If the complaint was just, I did what I could. This took a great deal of time.

Another arduous aspect of the office is the terrible expense of it. The Lord Mayor has no salary, but he is allowed about seven thousand five hundred dollars for his expenses. I spent three times that during my year in office. Recently a friend who knew the chronically critical condition of my finances asked, "How could you afford it?"

I told the simple truth, "I couldn't."

One of my main duties was, of course, representing the city at public functions. It might surprise you to know how many of these a small city can contrive to hold. During that year I expect I opened nearly as many bazaars, laid as many cornerstones, attended as many funerals and patted as many children on the head as the Queen of England.

The first thing I had to do was to arrange my courtesy calls on the President, the Prime Minister, the Archbishop of Dublin and about thirty ambassadors. My first call was, of course, a pure delight. Sean T. O'Kelly, who was now the President, had broken precedent by sending me a telegram of congratulations. I went to see him in the long beautiful white Residence in Phoenix Park which is considerably larger and rather more handsome than the American White House, though no more beautiful. Sean T. greeted me with genuine enthusiasm, and after the formalities I had a drop of Irish and a good talk with him and Mrs. O'Kelly, who, you remember, was my co-conspirator in raising an election stink.

The Prime Minister was again Costello. That call was as brief and formal as possible. Next came de Valera, leader of the Opposition. When he addressed me formally as "Lord Mayor," I said, "Look here, Chief, you can call me Lord Mayor when I lose your confidence. Until then it's Bob."

"But it is as the Lord Mayor I am receiving you," said Dev.

"That I can never be to you," I answered. "I'm still Bob Briscoe, one of your loyal backbenchers."

Archbishop John Charles McQuaid of Dublin was another question. Some people thought he would be offended by my faith. Wagers were struck. It was even money I would not be received.

However, an appointment was made. No man could have been received with greater courtesy, with more consideration.

But the people who had been betting said, "Oh, but he'll never return the call. We'll give double or nothing that he doesn't."

My friends covered the bets. Within a few days His Grace appeared at the Mansion House to return my courtesy visit.

On this occasion I posed him a difficult question. "Your Grace," I said, "what are your wishes in regard to my attending official Holy Votive and High Masses as a Jew representing the citizens of Dublin?"

"What is your alternative?" he asked.

I answered, "I can give you a list of six names at least of most devout Catholic members of the Dublin Council to whom I could give the authority to act as my deputy at these religious services."

The Archbishop smiled and said, "Well now, I know you; I might not know all or any of these six that you could nominate. But that is not any problem. What I must know is to what extent your present position might coerce you into attending our services against your own wishes."

"As long as I can remember, Your Grace," I said, "I have been attending Catholic Masses without any feeling of constriction or offense to my own faith or my own people."

The result of this conversation was that Archbishop McQuaid sent me a letter in which he left it up to me whether to attend Catholic services or send a deputy. However, when invitations were issued for the next official Holy Mass mine came in the form of a handwritten letter from the Archbishop in which he said, "I will be personally honored if you yourself will attend this celebration of the Mass."

Now I was very happy; for I regarded this particular situation as one of great delicacy which might lead to misunderstanding. The fact is that while I was Lord Mayor no one showed me greater courtesy, greater kindness, greater tenderness than this truly pious man, Archbishop McQuaid.

The Hat and the Chain

My only other difficult call was on the Minister of the new German Republic. He was away, and I was received by the chargé d'affairs. However, when the Minister returned to Dublin he came to the Mansion House to pay his respects. As I came into the drawing room he was standing with his back to me intently studying a large painting an artist had made of my coat of arms. In fact, I had some difficulty in attracting his attention.

When we had exchanged the usual compliments, and were seated, he said, "It is quite obvious from your crest where your feelings lie in regard to the Hitler Government. I hope, however, that the present Germany and future German citizens will be able to show by their acts and their consideration for your people that those dark days of inhumanity are gone forever."

It was to this man that I said, "As far as I am concerned, I forgive. I cannot, however, forget, and I hope my crest will be a reminder to my children of what happened, and what can happen."

Later when I returned the Minister's call we had an intimate discussion of Germany in the past and in the future. I told him what is the truth, that I believe the Germans will never again act as they did under Hitler. Until their defeat in World War II, I know from my close contacts with them that the majority of Germans did have megalomanic dreams of military glory, of conquering the world. I believe that now they have resigned such foolish aspirations forever; and that they will not again abandon democracy and attempt to make themselves the master race.

My call on the British Ambassador, Sir Alexander Clutterbuck, presented no problems. I had met him and Lady Clutterbuck frequently and when I called to see them it was quite normal and natural. Nor did the other embassies produce any difficulties. However, my closest relations have been with the American ambassadors.

Of course, all the diplomatic corps are of equal standing except this; the American representation, as far as I am concerned and I believe to a majority of Irishmen, is the most vital of all to our interests. There are some twenty or thirty million Americans who are either Irish born or of Irish descent. Naturally, we regard the American people as our kith and kin. From my point of view it is also the country which has the largest number of Jewish people in the world. Consequently, as an Irish citizen of the Jewish faith I feel doubly close to them. So, when I was invited to come to New York to review the St. Patrick's Day parade, I accepted with great anticipation.

That trip was beyond any possible expectations of mine. It was the most hectic, exhausting, inspiring, humbling, and the happiest two months of my life.

CHAPTER XXVIII

Aaron Go Bragh

As soon as the American papers published the news that I was going to New York, I was buried under a drift of mail. Over two thousand invitations arrived in the next few weeks from Irish Societies, Jewish Societies, and hundreds of groups which were neither Jewish nor Irish. I was not prepared for it all. Certainly the last time I had been in America I was hard put to it even to hire a hall.

I had also received an invitation from Mayor John B. Hynes of Boston to review the St. Patrick's Day parade there. I wrote him that I could not do this having promised Mayor Wagner to be in New York. Lo and behold, Mayor Hynes offered to put off St. Patrick's Day from Saturday to Monday. I was flabbergasted; but very happy to accept in those circumstances.

Then there came to Dublin some gentlemen representing the United Jewish Appeal. They called on me in the Mansion House and told me they had come all the way from America to ask me to make a tour there to raise money for U.J.A.

"Well, gentlemen," I said, "are you sure you want me? In past times I have had serious disagreements with some of the leaders of Zionism."

"This is not just a Zionist activity," their spokesman answered. "It is a humanitarian effort by the United Jewish Appeal which raises money not only to help the Zionist cause, but for our charities in America. The old disputes will not impair your usefulness. We believe that you can help us and the need is very great."

Then they told me what was happening to our people even now, to Jews in Poland and Hungary; and what was happening in

Egypt and the Arab nations of the Near and Middle East. "We are trying to raise a hundred million dollars to bring one hundred thousand refugees from those places to Israel," they said. "We hope you will feel able to join in this work."

"There is nothing I want to do more," I answered. "For all these years I have been working on the same track; and the fate of these Jewish people has been my constant anxiety. But, gentlemen, I am broke. I could not possibly afford to make a tour of six or eight weeks with the terrible expense it would be."

They laughed at that, and said of course the U.J.A. would pay for my trip over and my expenses in every place I visited on their behalf. "You need not worry about accepting this," they said. "We expect to get our money's worth out of you."

"Well, I'll try to give you that and more with every last drop of my strength," I answered.

It almost came to that, for on the trip I lost thirty pounds of weight and my voice entirely. But I believe they got their money's worth; for the one hundred million dollars was oversubscribed, and I have been told that about thirty million dollars of that was raised by me personally, not counting the publicity from newspapers, radio and television. This was enough to bring thirty thousand Jews from places of misery and indignity to safety and a new life in Israel, which makes me very happy and humble.

Due to this arrangement my trip cost the Dublin Council and the Irish Government not one shilling, and I think I was also able to do some good for Ireland as I shall tell. In addition I made some outside lectures for a fee, so I did myself some good as well.

Now I decided I must engage somebody in America to sort things out and co-ordinate my activities there. I appointed Mr. Irving Rockmore of Irving Rockmore Associates to handle my public relations and arrange my tour, asking him to make sure that the least possible offense be given to those hundreds of good people whose invitations I could not accept. By the time this arrangement was made the number of these invitations had increased to three thousand. I bundled them all off to poor Rockmore and announced in the American press that future inquiries about my tour should be addressed to him. How many more he received I never dared to ask.

Before starting for America I went to say good-by to Dev, who had given me leave of absence from the Dáil. He told me that his Irish friends in Boston had written to ask him how they should receive me and he had answered, "As you would receive myself." Then he added, "One piece of advice I'll give you. Be sure to have a top hat for the St. Patrick's Day parade. When I was there, I did not have one with me. That was a terrible *faux pas* and some people borrowed one for me; a very uncomfortable hat it was, since it did not fit at all. I put it on the seat beside me in the reviewing stand until a sweet old lady said, 'Mr. de Valera, put on your hat or you'll catch cold.'

"I put it on to oblige her, but soon took it off. All afternoon she kept after me to wear it like a nurse with a naughty child.

"So now you're warned," he added. "May you have a grand trip and may your top hat fit!"

On the trip I took Lily, my son Joe and Peter Delaney, who wanted to keep his eye on those gold chains of office. I was traveling by KLM and they thoughtfully ordered my eldest son, Billy, who is one of their pilots, to be captain of my plane. My departure from Shannon was quiet enough, because the Irish did not think it such an extraordinary thing for me to be Lord Mayor. But Idlewild Airport was a different matter altogether.

Never have I seen such a sight as when the plane rolled to a stop on the Tarmac. It looked to me as though there were more people to meet me than lived in all Dublin. There were also hundreds of reporters and photographers, and, of course, the welcoming party of New York City officials. As I stepped off the plane there was a lane made by two rows of uniformed policemen. One row consisted of members of the Emerald Society, to which Irish policemen belong and in the other row were members of the Jewish Society, Shomrim. I am told that the reporters were watching me to see which I would shake hands with first.

This did not occur to me, but in my deep emotion over what they had done for me, I instinctively crossed my hands and shook hands with the lead man of each line simultaneously.

All those newspaper men were good to me. They accepted and carried out a thing I told them in that first interview. Right at the start I made my position clear. "In Ireland I hold a post of honor, and I want to act in America with the dignity worthy of that honorable position. I am *not* here to enact a revival of Abie's Irish Rose."

From that moment on everything was perfect, including the weather. Back in Ireland I had predicted a fine day for both the New York and Boston parades. People said I was sticking my neck out, but they turned out to be the fairest days either city had had for their parades in a generation. In Los Angeles I never saw the terrible smog they talk about. It rolled back like a curtain and hung behind the mountain for two days while the sun poured down. Just as I got to the airport to leave for San Francisco I saw the smog rolling down. One of the motorcycle escorts said, "Here comes the smog again. This guy must be Moses."

In only one place was the weather bad. As we crossed the Rockies into Denver we ran into a terrible fierce blizzard. Though Denver was not on my schedule, the Mayor and the Governor of Colorado were at the airport to greet me, standing knee deep in snow. "I must apologize for the awful mean weather I've brought you," I said to the Governor.

With a great big smile he answered, "We've been having a devastating drought. The blizzard has broken it. This snow is worth millions of dollars to our state."

And he gave me a ten-gallon hat.

Well, I was up by 6:30 on that lovely St. Patrick's Day morning in New York. At 8 A.M. I paid a call on Cardinal Spellman, who was most kind to me. Then I went to service in the Synagogue with the President of the New York City Council, Abe Starke. After that we walked together to the reviewing stand on Fifth Avenue. I had a grand time that day and stayed until the last little

Irish girl with green ribbons and the shamrocks in her hair had tripped by.

In Boston, on the other hand, I marched in the parade. Four miles it was, and by the end of it I was shuffling my feet like an elephant with corns. Incidentally, I clean wore out my best shoes and had to buy a new pair next day, which news being cabled back to Dublin made people there say, "A fine salesman for Ireland this Briscoe fellow! The first thing he does is to buy American shoes."

One of the newspapers in Boston greeted me with a great green headline saying "AARON GO BRAGH" in both English and Yiddish characters. The supposedly proper Bostonians gave me such a welcome as almost made me weep. There I made thirty-six speeches in thirty-six hours, and lost my voice. Between speeches they had to keep rushing me to the hospital to have my throat sprayed.

And in Boston Mayor Hynes gave a wonderfully simple and touching introduction of me. He said, "We have here with us two fine fellows — an Irishman and a Jew. I give him to you now, Lord Mayor Robert Briscoe."

People were wonderful to me wherever I went and I can only touch on the high spots. I visited forty-eight cities in twenty states, and each one seemed like a new peak. I also went to Toronto where Mayor Nathan Phillips, also a Jew, was, of course, most friendly. One reason Lily and I enjoyed Toronto was a new granddaughter who arrived there after I arrived in New York. My daughter Joanie, who carried the dispatches in her diapers long ago, had married a Wexford man named Doctor Hugh O'Reilly. She is an M.D. and surgeon — Doctor Joan Brisco O'Reilly, no less! When the hospital nurse showed me my little granddaughter, Rachel O'Reilly, she was asleep. "What color are her eyes, then?" I asked. The nurse said, "Sure, for all I know she has shamrocks in her eyes."

New York City was our headquarters from which I raided the country by aircraft, raising those millions for U.J.A. but not forgetting to put in a word for Ireland. I had literally a ton weight of baggage with me, consisting of fine Waterford glassware, hand-loomed Irish tweeds, Urney's wonderful chocolates, and, of course, good potstilled Irish whiskey. These I gave to officials of the cities I visited. To my surprise, since I was not a government official, President Eisenhower invited me to pay a call at the White House. For him I had some Urney chocolates and a special present, a hand-loomed rug with the Arms of the Four Provinces of Ireland woven into it. When I gave it to the President I got in my sly little bit of propaganda. I stood on the rug covering the Red Hand of Ulster and said, "Mr. President, may I call your attention to how it unbalances the design when one of the four provinces is taken away."

Eisenhower gave his broad appreciative grin and said, "When I'm standing on it, I'll reflect on what you say."

At a big meeting in St. Louis there were two hundred Jews on the platform who had gotten there by saying they were relations of mine. I began my speech by saying that I had no idea I had so many relatives and then added, "In truth, though, I feel I must be kin to all the Jews in the United States. More than that, very deeply do I feel that I am related to all those unhappy members of my race in the Arab countries and behind the Iron Curtain."

At one formal dinner, I forget just where, I was seated next to a very high-toned lady. She turned to me and said, "Lord Mayor, are you really a Jew?"

"I am that," I replied.

Then she turned to the gentleman on her left and asked, "Are you Jewish, too?"

"Yes," he said, smiling.

Seeing the slightly dazed expression on the lady's face, I gently remarked, "Now you know how Christ felt between the two thieves."

In San Francisco I never saw their famous cat-footed fog. There I got one of the finest receptions of all and also the one chilling episode of the trip. Mayor Christopher declared a sort of St. Patrick's Day in April. There were at least a hundred cars in the parade that brought me from the airport. The streets were jam-packed with people and from all the windows they were leaning out smiling and shouting and throwing little small pieces of paper at me.

When we arrived at the airport to leave there was a tremendous something going on. Policemen were all over the place, and brigades of firemen with their large shiny red apparatus. "What's this?" I asked a police captain. "Some new wrinkle in send-offs?"

"It's nothing of the sort," he answered. "We've had a tip that somebody's put a bomb on your plane to blow you to hell."

Peter Delaney and Joe who were standing with me reacted according to their natures. Peter dropped the bag with the gold chains at my feet, produced a rosary and began saying his prayers. Joe disappeared. When he came back a few minutes later, I said, "Where have you been, Joe, and what is it you were doing?"

"I went to buy more insurance," he answered.

When the plane had been searched and all our baggage had also been searched we were allowed to proceed. "Have you had any cancellations because of this?" I asked an official of the airline.

"Only one," he answered. "Why?"

"Because," I said, "if word gets around about this sort of thing, I'm thinking people will be afraid to ride in planes with me; and the next thing I know the airlines won't have me at any price."

But it was all a false alarm. As Lily says, "The only explosive thing on that plane was Bob."

In my speeches throughout the country I told people that we were very keen that Americans should come to Ireland in great numbers. I emphasized that I was not looking for Americans of Irish descent or Americans of the Jewish faith, but all Americans of every denomination to come to our beautiful country and learn to know our people.

I also tried to interest American industrialists to consider investments in Ireland. My argument was, "You cannot export much from America to the soft currency countries like the sterling area because they have not the dollars to pay you. But you could in

Ireland build a factory and you could export its products, made in the same way as in America, to these soft currency countries. The Irish Government will give you every assistance. They will let you bring in the raw material free of duty; you will pay no export tax and have freedom from income tax on the profits from such goods. Furthermore you will be given a guarantee by the state that you can repatriate your capital in dollars and take your profits out in dollars. Make Ireland a branch workshop of your factories!"

In the past year I have seen these words beginning to bear fruit.

Well, as I have said, Lily and I had a wonderful time and I was treated far beyond my proper deserts. Everywhere I was welcomed not only by the mayors but by the governors of the states. I was given three honorary degrees, and made an honorary Texas Ranger; and a southern colonel by the States of Alabama and Kentucky. I have the certificates at home, and for a fact it seemed less strange to me to be Lord Mayor of Dublin than to find myself a Kentucky colonel.

Now I do not propose to name all the mayors of cities who were kind to me, though it is the truth that I felt I had made a real genuine friend in each of them. Naturally, since my headquarters were in New York I came to know Mayor Bob Wagner best, and kind he was to Lily and me. Nor shall I ever forget Governor Averell Harriman's courtesy to us. We were his guests at that great Victorian-Gothic Governor's Mansion in Albany during Passover. To make us comfortable he had a Jewish cook and caterers flown up from New York to prepare the food in accordance with the ritual of our faith.

With that exception we spent Passover quietly among our coreligionists at Grossinger's in the Catskill Mountains at the invitation of that lovely lady Jennie Grossinger. That was another time I shall never forget. Also it was the only rest I had.

Of the few old friends I saw one was Judge Josephs in Baltimore and another was my old colleague in crime, Jeremiah

O'Leary. I got a pain in my heart when I came to his house. The fine old fellow had gone blind. There he stood in the doorway calling out to me in that grand resonant voice that used to make entire juries burst into tears, "Welcome, Bob! though I can't see you. The grave is trying to claim me. It's taken my sight, but it can't have me yet!"

At last in May, after nine wonderful weeks our American visit, like all good things, came to an end. Lucky it was for me, because in another week I'd have died of their kindness. Looking back there is one thing about it that makes me proudest of all. It is that according to what I have been told, this was the first time that an Irishman has won the affection and enthusiasm not of the American-Irish alone, but of all kinds of Americans. Nor were the people of my own faith any more friendly than those of the Christian faiths, Catholic and Protestant. For example the Methodists in New York to whom I brought a special message from the Methodists in Dublin treated me not only with courtesy but with real affection.

This heart-warming co-operation of all varieties of people to welcome me was something I greatly hope to see come about through all the world. I hope and believe that the effect of those fair days lingers on in America. I hope that it will bring closer the joining together of all peoples of every race and faith not only for formal co-operation, but in the warmth of good fellowship and friendly gaiety.

CHAPTER XXIX

"That I Will"

Just before I left for America in March, I had fought one of our bitter political campaigns. To explain the position, I'll take leave to bring you up to date on the circumstances of Irish politics.

In passing I have mentioned that we were put out of power in 1948. It happened this way. Sean MacBride had formed an extreme radical Republican Party which he named *Clann na Poblachta*, the party of the Republic, taking the name of Dev's old party. In the general election of 1948, Clann na Poblachta won ten seats in the Dáil. Fianna Fail lost most of these, and Fine Gael made gains.

Now what did this MacBride, who was so ardent a Republican and so bitterly anti-British, do but combine with Fine Gael, who were the successors of the pro-British, pro-Treaty Party, in order to get a seat in the Cabinet. John Costello, thus became Prime Minister, but he had a price to pay for MacBride's support and he paid it in a very queer way.

Shortly after he became Prime Minister Costello went to Canada to take part in a Commonwealth conference of lawyers. One night the conference was entertained by Governor General Lord Alexander of Tunis at Government House in Ottawa. The first thing Costello noticed was that Ireland was not on the list of toasts printed on the menu. Though he was not there in his official capacity as Prime Minister, he took this as a deliberate snub and was considerably irritated. But what really started his still steaming was the fact that during the entire evening Lord Alexander never addressed a single word to him, not even to say, "Good evening, sir."

The moment the dinner was over Costello did a very rash, ill-considered and illegal thing. He called the reporters around him and announced that Eire would hereafter be known as the Irish Republic.

If he expected to shock the British by this remarkable maneuver he was mistaken. Prime Minister Clement Attlee remarked that its only significance was that "Mr. Costello is now running around in an ill-fitting Republican overcoat belonging to Mr. de Valera."

The Dáil ratified Costello's unilateral declaration. We had to. He had made us look foolish enough in the eyes of the world without the stupidity of disavowing our Prime Minister. The reason for Costello's abrupt action has never been completely explained. It probably was the pay-off to MacBride for his support. But the timing of it and the manner of it can only be put down to personal pique. Its tragic consequence was to further postpone the end of Partition as de Valera had foreseen.

Costello's government remained in power from 1948 to 1951. Long before the end there were signs of cracks spreading through his shaky coalition. I remember Dev's wise remark to me when I called attention to these signs of stress. "If you see flaws developing in the walls of your opponents' edifice, don't call attention to them," he said. "It will only cause them to patch them up. Let them widen unnoticed, and presently the whole thing will fall apart."

So it was with Costello's coalition government. However, when we came to power again in 1951, we found the finances of the state in such a mess that we had to push through austerity tax measures to shore up the finances of the state. The result was that the people turned against us purely because of our tax policy.

In 1954, the coalition came into power again, though there was not much left of MacBride's part of it. Clann na Poblachta became a very exclusive party indeed, its representation in the Dáil consisting of Sean MacBride and friend — down from ten seats to two.

Now, as it happened, MacBride is in my constituency. There are five members from this district who are elected by a rather complicated system of proportional representation. In the election of March, 1957, I decided that MacBride should not be one of the five deputies — I wanted to lay that old ghost from the Troubled Times.

We went at it with all the vim, vigor and virulence of the good old days. Instead of behaving like the elder statesmen we were supposed to have become, we fought it out like young McGees metaphorically with shillelaghs in our hands and our coats trailing the ground to be stepped on. As party leader in the constituency I was the most active campaigner, making speech after speech in which I minced no words and made mince-meat of MacBride.

The results were most satisfactory. Previously the representation had been: Fianna Fail two, Fine Gael two, Clann na Poblachta one. When the dust settled on the hustings it was Fianna Fail three, Fine Gael two, Clann na Poblachta nowhere. Over all Fianna Fail came into power again with seventy-eight seats in the Dáil, the largest number we had ever held.

The results were announced just before I left for America, though Fianna Fail had not yet taken over the government. When I returned de Valera was Taoiseach again and all was well with my world.

June came around again and with it the question should I run for re-election as Lord Mayor? This I was unwilling to do; for I had always maintained that the office should be rotated among the councillors. In my speech of acceptance I had said it would be for one year only. However, many people, strangers as well as my friends, pressed me to go again. Their argument was that conditions had changed since last year. The enormous success of my American tour had made me an asset to Ireland. Thousands of American tourists had said they were coming to see me. If I were no longer Lord Mayor they might lose interest and Ireland would lose their good American dollars.

These arguments moved me. But still I held out for consistency and no second term until Dev himself sent for me to come to the Prime Minister's office. There he said to me, "Bob, I want you to go again. We may not reap all the fruits of your great American success if you retire. I ask you to do it for the good of Ireland."

All I could say was, "When you ask it, I have to do it, Chief."

So I announced my candidacy. For a bit there was talk of re-electing me unanimously, but then the politicians got thinking. The Fine Gael Party reckoned that I was bringing too much credit to Dev and Fianna Fail. They began various deals and machinations to beat me.

So we came again to the Council Chamber on July 1, 1957. This time I was sitting in the Lord Mayor's high seat. There were two other candidates, Jack Belton of Fine Gael and James Carroll, Independent. The nominating speeches began. They were positively weird. Both the man who nominated Belton and Carroll's proposer said what a fine job I had done and almost apologized for nominating their man. However, it was politics before patriotism. On the first ballot Belton was eliminated. Knowing that he could not be elected, Fine Gael had agreed to support Carroll in order to beat me. Even Belton's proposer voted against him.

On the second and deciding ballot, Labor, led by Denis Larkin, voted for me. But the six members of the Ratepayers Party, according to their decision not to support a party man voted for Carroll. The count was a tie — 21 to 21 — one man not voting, two absent. "The hat! The hat!" was the shout.

So history repeated itself with a slight difference. I wrote my name and Carroll wrote his on the slips of paper. I asked the neutral councillor to draw. He did so and handed the folded scrap of paper up to me. I opened it and for a moment could not read it — poor Carroll was so nervous he had made a hen's track. But I knew the name was not Briscoe, so after a long pause I said, "Carroll!"

And lo and behold! I was no longer Lord Mayor of Dublin.

Now, how did I feel about my defeat? At first I'll not deny I was disappointed. No man who puts up a good fight likes being beaten. But as soon as I had a little time to think I felt greatly relieved. I'd never had time to rest up after my trip to the United

States. There had been all the welcome home parties. Then the Americans began pouring into Dublin and every one of them wanting to see me; and I equally wanting to entertain them. Add to that the strain of my campaign and of my normal duties and you may imagine the condition I was in. I was, temporarily, broken in health and broke at the bank.

The next time I saw de Valera he said to me, "I can't tell you how sorry I am about this, Bob. They were striking at me through you."

"Don't let it distress you, Chief," I replied. "It only means that I have deprived you of an experience you have never had."

"What can that be?" Dev asked.

"You have never had the opportunity of attending the funeral of a Lord Mayor."

Now coming to the close of this long book — but not I hope of my career — I have taken time for reflection. Of course I have not had very much time for musing as I am still a member of the Dáil, sitting on various very active committees; and of the Dublin Council where I am chairman of one committee and active on several others. In addition, all the Americans who come to Dublin seem to want to see me even though I am no longer Lord Mayor. I was recently elected President of the Ireland-American Society, which was a great honor and pleasure to me, because of my own close ties with America and my firm belief that our two countries should be closely united in friendship, trade and foreign policy. In fact when a reporter on the American television show *Meet the Press* asked me if there was any chance of Ireland rejoining the British Commonwealth I replied truthfully, "I'd rather see her become your forty-ninth state."

Well, writing this book has brought back very vividly things that were so overlaid by more recent events as to be half-forgotten. If I have relived wonderful moments, I have also reopened old wounds.

The saddest and most trying time of my life was, of course, the civil war. It is very hard to think back and come to any final assessment of your own mind at that time. Civil war in any country is a most horrible tragedy and something that should be avoided at almost any cost. I deeply regret that war between Irishmen; I regret it especially for a very personal reason. Because it is true that many of the weapons used by the Republicans were those I had brought into Ireland in that last big shipment of arms through the British blockade. In the past people have accused me of being the cause of the civil war, because without those arms it might never have happened. Certainly that is a dark thought for a man to have on his conscience. As to my own part in it, you will recall that in the days after the Dáil approved the Treaty, I had terrible anxiety that internal war was coming, and I could not accept the thought of taking part in strife between Irishmen. Liam Mellows then promised me that it would not be brought about by any action of the Republicans. I believe he kept his word. That this tragedy befell was not due to any overt act by the I.R.A. They were attacked, and they defended themselves.

So if the thing had to be done again, my decision would be the same. For terrible as the war was I am convinced that if the Republicans had not at that time remained an entity, separate from the Free State, many of the things we have accomplished would have been lost. We would have been entangled in the mechanism of provincial government and Ireland would have remained a dominion of the British Empire.

Certainly we lost the war. But I believe that by keeping faith in our allegiance to the Republic we made possible the survival of the Republican principle with a hard core of supporters. With time and wisdom came the abandonment of physical force as a weapon either against fellow Irishmen or even against Britain in the North. The emergence of the constitutional party of Fianna Fail was a direct result of the maintenance of a large group of citizens dedicated to Republican principles. Our party has achieved many important things — the settlement of the Land Annuities; the freeing of our harbors from British control; the economic strengthening of our country; and finally and greatest of all, the establishment of the free and sovereign nation of Ireland. I doubt if these things would have been brought about unless we had stood firm in the beginning. Therefore, though I look back on the civil war with sorrow and sadness, I cannot regret that we acted as we did.

Looking toward the future of Ireland I believe that partition will eventually disappear. It is an artificial barrier and in any time of flux such things crumble. Once gone they are never re-established. But this may take a long time, because only the passage of years will remove the suspicions in the minds of the Orange element, the Protestants of the North. It is essential to allay their apprehensions as to the position they would occupy in a united Republic of Ireland where the Catholics will naturally be predominant. It will also take a long time to remove what you might call the vested interests of the professional Orangemen — and the professional Irishmen of the South, too — in the continuance of the strife by which they live.

The outrages, the bombings and shootings over the border recently perpetrated by the young men who call themselves the "New I.R.A." have set the happy solution of Partition back many years. There are at least three groups of them entirely independent of each other, sometimes fighting each other. They are led by anonymous people whom we don't know, and even they don't know. Their unnamed leaders for unknown reasons are trying to bring about a situation which can only be disastrous.

Now these young people are not hooligans or criminals. They are for the most part idealists. They have read Wolfe Tone's passionate words and Emmet's noble speech upon the gallows; and they can quote the fighting pronouncements of de Valera, Cathal Brugha and Liam Mellows made in a time that has gone by. Those fiery words react on them like alcohol on unaccustomed drinkers. A misguided patriotism blazes in their brains, and they set forth to die for Ireland when because of the changed situation they would better live and work for her.

Before this new wave of bombings and burnings and shootings began the old antagonisms between the North and the South were dying out. These idealistic young people, not having lived through the past troubles, do not understand the damage they are doing by awakening again the bitternesses which had begun to slumber and would have reached that deep sleep which would have enabled all Irishmen to get together.

The passionate desire of Irishmen, many Protestants among them, to end partition is not due to patriotism alone, though love of our dear land is a powerful factor. It is also based on common sense. The world position of Ireland, both North and South, would be tremendously strengthened by their union. As a united nation we could live on the most friendly terms with Britain. Furthermore, we could then join with England and America in those associations of nations who are bound together for their common defense such as NATO.

Ireland is, of course, already a member of the United Nations, and we are negotiating to join the European Common Market. However, as long as we are divided our people are unwilling to join NATO. There is one particular reason for this reluctance. It is because one of the conditions of our entry into NATO would be to recognize the status quo. Irishmen will never sign a treaty which binds them to accept partition.

If we joined NATO we would strengthen it far more than might seem apparent from our lack of industrial might; for we have a tremendous pool of manpower on which the hard pressed nations of Europe could draw. The Irishman makes one of the finest soldiers in the world. England would be the first to acknowledge that we are first-class fighting men, who not only fought her to a standstill in our country, but as components of the British Army won her highest accolade for valor.

The unity of Ireland is not only a political goal; it is an economic necessity. Only as a whole can Ireland be a really viable state. The industrial North is naturally complimented by the mainly agricultural South. Together they would form an economically sound foundation for the state.

Meanwhile we in the South have made great strides toward laying the foundations of financial stability in the Irish Republic. Though we have not the resources to establish heavy industry, we are almost self-sufficient in light industry. We manufacture all our own cloth and clothing, the best in the world; also all our shoes, boots and leather goods. We are processing an ever larger percentage of our famous beef and mutton instead of exporting it on the hoof. We have developed eighty per cent of our resources of electrical power and have done a great amount of rural electrification. Workingman's housing has made enormous strides. The slums of Dublin are rapidly becoming an unsavory memory.

All these things we have done without handouts from any nation. We are reluctant to accept something for nothing and build our economy on gifts that may suddenly cease. If we come to depend on the generosity of the United States, we would be in a sad fix if the Americans were no longer able or willing to help support us. Indeed, we are loath even to borrow dollars. At this moment I could get a loan in America for the City of Dublin to finance needed public works. I will not take it for this reason. Our currency is irrevocably tied to sterling. We have no control over British currency and if their pound is devalued ours goes down with it. If we borrow dollars we must repay dollars and we might have to pay far more for them. It is the fashionable thing in Europe to borrow now and worry about repaying later. This is a policy I do not approve, nor does the Irish Government.

We would be glad, however, if Americans in particular would recognize that there is a lucrative field for investment in Ireland. We have very low costs and a great surplus of labor. Fifty thousand young men and women emigrate from Ireland every year. They are our best young people. In 1957, one hundred thirty-five engineers were graduated from Trinity University. How many of them do you think left the country? Every last one of them! American investment would provide jobs for these fine young people at home; and the investors would get a great return for their money. This would be a mutually profitable business. We would neither be begging nor borrowing, which we will not do.

Summing up the situation I believe that Ireland has a future — a political future and an economic future. The development of atomic energy for peaceful purposes will deliver us from a possible future power shortage — we have plenty of power right now. And a United Ireland will eventually play its full part in international co-operation to defend freedom and bring about better relations between all the peoples of the world. Finally, because of her heritage and tradition Ireland will still contribute to the world great things of spiritual value.

It would seem that I have written more than enough about myself already. Nevertheless, I must wind up this tale. Seven things I am unreservedly proud of — my seven children. The fact that they have turned out well is mostly due to Lily — I have been so active sticking my long nose into other people's business I have had too little time for my own family. Joanie, our eldest, graduated from medical school in 1947 and went to Newfoundland for a year to practice medicine. She stayed on a second year for a very good reason. She married Doctor Hugh O'Reilly in 1948. They have two small daughters and live now in Toronto.

My oldest son, Abraham William, was married in 1954. He is a pilot with KLM, and the father of my only grandson. Joe, who came next, is a dentist living in Dublin. He was married last year. Bryan is in his final year as a medical student at the College of Surgeons in Dublin. Benjamin, who also was married in 1957, lives in London, where he is making a business career, like his maternal grandfather, in retail merchandise.

My daughter Ida, who has a magnificent voice — and this is not my opinion alone — is studying singing in Rome. And baby Elise, now twenty years old, is in Canada with Joanie working as a secretary, for which she was trained in Dublin.

Now as to my future — for it is not quite all behind me. I should like to be Lord Mayor again for one more term; and I expect to be. Beyond that I shall remain a member of the Dáil until my present term expires in 1962. By that time I will be sixty-seven years old, which is near enough to our traditional three score years and ten to think about giving up active participation in politics. In short I plan to retire then so that Lily and I can live in a serenity we have never known except for our two weeks' honeymoon on Bantry Bay, and travel to the far-flung homes of our children.

That is my plan. However it is subject to change without notice. For well do I know that if Dev should say to me, "This or that is for the good of Ireland. Will you do it, Bob?" My answer would be, "Chief, that I will!"